Belle de Neige

Tales of Catastrophe, Sex and Squalor from the Alpine Underbelly

This novel is entirely a work of fiction.
The names, characters and incidents portrayed in it are fictitious,
and the work of the author's imagination.
Any resemblance to past events or to real persons, living or dead, is
purely coincidental.

ALPINE UNDERBELLY PUBLISHING
An independently published novel
A paperback original 2013

First published in Great Britain by
ALPINE UNDERBELLY PUBLISHING

Printed and bound in Great Britain

For
Laura, Mum & Nanna

"Vulgarity is no substitute for wit"
Julian Fellowes

To my friend

No. There's something I was meaning to tell you.
It would have made you laugh.
We haven't had that conversation we were going to have,
Or gone to that place we said we'd go.
Had that big adventure.
What about that experiment we were going to try?
I haven't laughed at that hare-brained idea
you were going to have,
Or that totally inappropriate comment
you were going to make.
I haven't made you that promise you wanted me to keep.
We never solved that problem
you were going to tell me about,
Or shared that secret of mine.
What a terrible unfinished mess. So much left undone.
Whose right was it to say "it's time"?
My friend.
Have I failed you precious butterfly?
You have slipped from my fingers.
I will never say goodbye.

Prologue

*"You work harder, work harder, you're told that you must
and you must earn a living, must earn a crust
and be like everybody else."*

Reverend and the Makers

Deaths, and therefore funerals, come when you least expect them.

Usually, I've found, deaths happen at a really inconvenient moment and almost always when you're about to do something you've been looking forward to immensely. Like during a party – or, just before a wedding. People pick the most inopportune times to die. When everything is going along swimmingly and you're feeling that you really have landed with your arse in the butter recently and *isn't life peachy?* One minute you're living the dream, the next you're standing in a boggy field full of bewildered people, in the sheeting rain, thinking "oh bollocks" and watching a coffin being lowered into hole. This routine is designed to give you something people call 'closure'.

My best friend died exactly like this. I was woken by the phone and her mother said, "Are you with people?"

I didn't like phone calls that began like that. I knew what they meant.

The next thing I remember is crouching in the shower,

crying silent, scalding tears that seemed to gouge tracks in my cheeks, and trying to inflict pain on the wall with my fingernails. I thought my insides might come up through my gullet. I felt the rack of crushing, bone-twisting sadness would surely crack me. I would be disfigured forever.

You see, no one else remembered my eighteenth birthday, or kept copies of the rude poems I wrote in biology class - no one else cared about them. No one else teased me about Luigi, the toothless Portuguese barman whom I, regrettably, once snogged. Only she knew my deepest self-doubt and motivation. Only she was so gratifyingly unsurprised by the filth that spilt out of my mouth. I don't know anyone else who can recite all the words to 'Honey Bun' from South Pacific or likes to randomly repeat the words 'Squatternut Bosh' and then giggle stupidly to herself. I shared with her something totally unique; the product of time and familiarity.

So. The deceased: in potted summary, she had a dirty Babs-Windsor laugh, and loved tortoises, and ate a lot of cheese with wine, and enjoyed Leonard Cohen and smoked rollies. You do this, when someone dies - you try to weave together the shreds of the memories to create some semblance of them. You scrabble around, gathering scraps of evidence that they even existed; hairs from their hairbrush, bits of jewellery, a shirt that holds their smell. Her mother told me to take something from her room as a keepsake. I spent an hour or two looking for it - the object that would embody her. A necklace? A page from her diary? A photo? A dress? But I left empty handed.

On the day of her funeral, we, the dearly beloved, even managed to ascribe some sort of symbolic significance to the rain. People said that she'd 'got the last laugh' because we all had to wear wellies and stand in a muddy field reciting Led Zeppelin lyrics while the heavens thundered. *We come from the land of the ice and snow...*Actually, she would have enjoyed that – particularly the fact that several of our more townie friends spent a miserable half an hour scarifying the boggy field with their stilettos.

"It was Sloane Square meets the Somme," she would have said.

How do you let go of the person who's dragged you, no, carried you back from the brink of misery? Reminded you who you are? Only months earlier I'd had (in order of relative importance) a house, a cat and a fiancée. A plan. The course I was on was easy and natural to me, and it was everything I could conceive of wanting. I was just carried along with it, like a gentle river's flow. But there was a big fat bluebottle in the ointment, and it took Shazzer to point out that in all the fuss of being 'in love', I'd forgotten to be myself. When it all broke down and I crash landed back in the floral curtained menagerie of my childhood bedroom, suddenly my job, the commute, the clothes I was wearing, the very nature of my existence felt odd, peculiar, as if it belonged to someone else. Her words brought me down to earth.

"He's not and never has been all you are. You lived twenty years of your life without even knowing his name."

She suggested I take myself off on an adventure. This tended to be her solution to most problems.

"I am setting you an objective to find yourself an adventure by the 1st of November," she said, "so this Christmas you are not re-enacting the opening credits from Bridget Jones in some grotty bedsit in Croydon. Secondly it is a humanitarian mission to give the world the fabulousness of you that it has been denied for so long!"

This stirred something in me. I had already had the same foreboding vision of myself glugging back the wine in a rented hovel in Basildon in my Winnie the Pooh pyjamas watching slasher movies and weeping. The thought of it chilled my very bones.

Back in my childhood bedroom, I was thumbing through some old papers that I'd stuffed in a pile under my bed some years before. They were like postcards from another lifetime; old letters from Shazzer dating back to school; notes, lists. One of them was in my own handwriting, though I had no memory of writing it at all.

Stuff to do before I'm 25

Learn to play the bass guitar (Ease rating 5/10)
Increase knowledge of: politics, Buddhism (sic), films and poetry (Ease rating 8/10)
Have carefree sex with wide variety of hot men (Ease rating 10/10)
Be crew on a round the world yacht race (Ease rating 1/10)
Ski for an entire season (Ease rating 7/10)
Voluntary work in India / Africa (Ease rating 2/10)
Travel somewhere obscure by obscure means (Round India by Tuk Tuk?) (Ease rating 2/10)
Get inch deep all-over tan (2/10)
Work on a farm or work with animals in the jungle (Ease rating 3/10)
Grape picking in France (Backbreaking, but 6/10)
Learn to ride a horse (Ease rating 7/10, front end bites, back end kicks)

Here were my teenage dreams, preserved in biro, staring accusingly back at me from the crumpled page. None of them achieved; all of them given a back seat, or even abandoned altogether, in favour of what? A complete stranger. A set of priorities that were not my own. This was an ill-fitting life I had ended up wearing for want of a better cut. It was as if I'd been kidnapped and forgotten myself - the pang of recognition for the face in an old, dog-eared photograph. How I'd used to sneer at the white wedding brigade and their semi-detached lives. God, how the thought of the things that now governed my own life had used to depress me.

The next morning, there I was as usual, standing on the platform of the Northern Line. A woman to the left of me was yapping to her colleague about 'motivating her team', 'speaking to people on the ground' and 'hitting targets for the quarter.' Behind her head there was one of those ski holiday posters with the happy family in bobble hats, smiling up at the mountains and toothpaste-blue sky. You know, they put them there deliberately so when you're standing on the platform with your face pressed into somebody's sweaty armpit and an unidentified cock sticking in your back, at 7.30am on a dark, rainy Tuesday, you can feel *really* suicidal. Not just mildly. Opposite me, they had plastered the entire side of the tunnel with a gigantic poster for a nuclear disaster movie, complete with burning buildings, skeletal corpses dragging themselves across the scorched earth with their intestines trailing behind, and people weeping with apocalyptic despair. Oh joy.

It was then that I had what Shazzer and I would subsequently refer to as my "Ski season brain belch." This was a bizarrely flippant, yet resolute brain belch. It seemed to explode in my head like an atom bomb, destroying everything in its wake. As the hot breeze that heralds the arrival of a new train began to sweep into the suffocating station, I realised it wasn't the first time I'd thought miserably about my job - my so-called 'career path'. I was seized by the thought of all those silly stockbrokers who jump off skyscrapers because they've been fired. How could anyone let themselves become so defined by one aspect of their being, one roadmap of their future, that they could lose all perspective of the world and the myriad of ways we can find to be happy in it?

"You could be a million different people in one lifetime."

Another nugget of truth from Shazzer that still reverberates in my head.

You could be a million different people in one lifetime...

I thought about the number of hours of my life that I would have to spend in an environment I despised, talking hackneyed bollocks about brand identities and social networking to soporific dullards. The number of times I would have to sacrifice my eyes to this ugly platform. I thought about the clinical, polite routine of my life. The number of smelly armpits I would have my nose stuffed into on a crowded tube for the next ten years. How the most inspiring thing I saw on a daily basis was the symmetrically tiled ceiling and beige walls of my office and my white, rectangular IKEA desk. My boss had banned us all from using post-it notes so as to keep the desks looking 'minimal.' Was I really expected to swallow this bullshit? Why was everyone else swallowing it, internalising it and then regurgitating it as if it were totally reasonable? Had they all been lobotomised?

Then I thought about the weather. The drizzle. The impassable lid of stratus. Yes, I have lived in the UK all my life and it still surprises me how repugnant the weather is. I thought about my aches and pains – I felt like a ninety-year-old woman. There were knots in my shoulders, I had sciatica and tension headaches. I'm not exactly an athlete, but how had my life become so sedentary, passive and one-dimensional? The human body is not meant to sit still. It's designed to be carrying logs around, dragging the latest kill into the cave, chasing gnus across the dusky plains, building igloos and battling the elements. Not tapping away on a plastic keyboard and staring at a screen, gradually, oh so softly losing the will to live.

Finally, I thought about the number of times in my life I'd already pushed to the recesses of my mind the lingering truth that I'd sworn I would never do this to myself. The number of times I'd stifled the sense there was something inside me worth more than this. That by hook or by crook I'd do something I enjoyed and that didn't make me feel so deeply apathetic.

That afternoon, my slim, silken haired, fashionable colleague Alicia put on her Facebook update...

'Lunch! :D '

I think that was the clincher. That said it all.

The highlight of her day: Fucking *lunch*. I had to act.

A month later, there it was on the door mat; my job offer from a luxury ski tour operator, along with their brand spanking new holiday brochure. I stared at the picture on the front. A white-toothed, blonde-haired girl in a red ski jacket, laughed back at me from outside a chalet set in an idyllic, six-foot-of-snow Alpine backdrop, clutching two baguettes. She looked groomed, professional and generally delighted with life. She, I thought, is living the dream, and soon so shall I.

"On the plus side, I do always like to go out with a bang," I told Shazzer, the evening after I'd finished my last day at work. My colleagues had thrown me a leaving do at which I had become hideously drunk and descended into a wholesale rant about ex-fiancées, love and loss, and how (in my own words) *"Life fucks you up the arse no matter how much you try to tow the line."*

I was pretty certain this had put paid to any possibility of getting my job back in six month's time. I can still picture the acidic expression on my boss's face. I had only been there a year, and he thought I was a quitter. I could see it. Bridges were burned. There was no turning back. Behaving like an emotional fucktard in front of your boss is never advisable. Or so I thought. But then, at this stage, I had never worked in a ski resort.

"Darling," Shazzer smiled, pouring me another large vodka, "You *are* an emotional fucktard. But I love you. And anyway, this is no time to introspect. You won't give a toss about your boss, or anyone else, when you're being shagged over the chalet coffee table by a hot French ski instructor."

This was true.

"Look babe. To get what you want in life, at some point you have to stop worrying about constantly pleasing others," she said, swirling her drink. I detected a note of resolution in this that suggested the advice wasn't exclusively directed at me. As usual, Shazzer had a good a point. But when she waved me goodbye that evening, got on her dilapidated old bicycle and set off for home, I am not sure I appreciated quite how deep her insights were.

The next time I saw her she was inside a coffin, being lowered into a hole, in a boggy field.

The trappings of death are grim. Empty words and sympathy from old friends with coffee-table books and toddlers and Tupperware-lives that suddenly seem a million miles away from you. Stock phrases rolled out of people:

There is no rhyme or reason.

What doesn't kill you makes you stronger.

That's life.

The brightest flame burns quickest...

Stock phrases are the verbal comfort blanket one hides beneath when one doesn't know what else to say. In the great scheme of things - evolution and all that jazz - there is logic in death. But what does that mean anyway; "everything happens for a reason"? Friends and family looked at me with helpless eyes, like a child watching a toy boat that has floated just out of his reach. The trouble was the big, gaping, aching, ugly hole in normality where Shazzer had been, with nothing to fill it. The fact other people didn't seem to notice this hole struck me as odd. So in the end, I just left.

I hate goodbyes and any kind of fuss, so I disappeared without telling any of my friends. I simply fell off the map and let rumours of my departure drift through the ether.

On the one hand, given my state of mind, grieving, confused, angry - you could look at my foray into the Alpine underbelly as a tremendously bad decision.

...But on the other hand, bad decisions make the best stories.

Shazzer
To: Me
15th November 2009

My darling!
Do my ears deceive me? Or is that the sound of a
new arse hole ripping open somewhere 'round about
France-way?
Thinking of you on the cusp of the great adventure,
chalet girl! Go forth and shag!
Wuhahahaha...
....I mean ski.
But seriously darling, you deserve this. Enjoy it.
Keeping everything crossed for maximum snowage.
;D
Gonna miss you much.
x

Goals for the Season

1. Ski every day. Whatever the weather. Just because I can. Thereby become proficient at doing 360° aerobatic spins before the season is out

2. Post sickening pictures of idyllic seasonnaire lifestyle up on internet to make hamster-wheel-friends back home spit with envy.

3. Locate and shag a number of fit, toned, tanned European ski instructors, pref. with sexy accents, in expensive luxury chalet — (n.b. this will also help with number 1 — free ski lessons).

4. Schmooze wealthy chalet guests with fantastic cooking and hostess-with-mostest witty repartee, resulting in enormous tips and invitations to join them on all-expenses-paid skiing expeditions and other glamorous excursions.

5. Hang out in glittering hotel bars, looking alluring in low-cut LBD in blind hope of bagging possible oligarch sugar-daddy. Return in April with buns of steel (from skiing), exotic foreign lover, and wallet-busting hoard of cash tips.

6. Try heli-skiing (or other similar intrepid ski-type activity)

7. Don't cry

8. Be fabulous in every way possible.

9. Avoid breaking any limbs.

10. Do not (under any circumstances) shag any ne'er-do-well studenty-ski-bum-types with no prospects and personal hygiene issues.

Slumdog Seasonnaire

"My balls are on someone's forehead as we speak. How d'ya feel about that mother?"

Skater Boy is drawling into his phone. He has climbed up the ladder on to the thin, precarious bunk bed occupied by his roommate. We call this 'The Shelf' because, strictly speaking, it would be a more appropriate receptacle for piles of books or twee ornaments than its sleeping occupant. Skater Boy is now squatting, testicles dangling over the subject's peaceful, sleeping face, mobile phone pressed to his ear, cup of scalding hot tea in the other hand. Half-cut, bearded and unkempt. Still wired. Unhinged.

A growling voice, thick with sleep, comes slowly from beneath Skater Boy's faded boxers.

"Dude......get your *fucking* nuts *off* my face."

This is my cue. I duck beneath Skater Boy's duvet in anticipation of the scene that is about to ensue, as he is subjected to a short, sharp heave that launches him, testicles and boiling beverage, backwards off the six foot high shelf and out across the room. He crashes down with a sickening crunch into a pile of detritus by the balcony window. Crusty socks, volcanic eruptions of ash trays, pizza boxes, bowls encrusted with mouldy food and a six foot novelty mono-board embellished with a Toucan explode all over the room in a shower of tea. Skater Boy's roommate is not a morning person. His head of disorganised, sandy-blonde hair appears over the side of The Shelf, framing the bloodshot eyes which always give him away when he's been drinking. He is an unbelievably scruffy, hobbitesque creature - chunkier than the lithe, wiry Skater Boy - but, in exactly the same way, almost perpetually either drunk or hung-over. He has already groped for his rollies and swung his legs over the side of The Shelf. His hoary, snow-boot-savaged feet dangle near Skater Boy's head while he jams a filter between his lips, growling dangerously,

"You complete Judas! What's the matter with you?"

"Eh up…." Skater Boy swerves away from the revolting feet. "Calm down. Ah *fuck*, there's tea everywhere."

"Fuck you. Jackass."

"Fuck *you* - no – sorry mother, not you!" Skater Boy suddenly remembers the phone in his hand. He grabs the nearest duvet and starts using it as a mop to tackle the tea tsunami that has engulfed, and to some extent sterilized, the surrounding area.

Seeing this, Scruffy-but-Handsome, stark naked and now half way down the ladder from The Shelf, throws himself at Skater Boy and wrestles him to the ground, where they scrabble around in the soggy tea and grime mess for a few tense seconds, knocking over everything in the near vicinity.

"I could quite do with punching you both in the face right now," I say calmly, still sheltering in bed, torn between fury at the chaos and slight arousal over two partially naked, wrestling men.

Actually, I'm too scared to get up and go to the filth-encrusted bathroom. Who knows what unidentified, putrid goype will squidge up between my toes on the way. The floor is an uncharted wilderness of horrifying muck. They've had complaints from the lady who owns the building for walking too much dirt *out* of the place and messing up the hall. The apartment of Skater Boy and Scruffy-but-Handsome is famed resort-wide for its unique effluvium. I have never been able to identify what the aroma is. I think it's Eau de Un-washed Ski Bum. Or it might just be 'Fusty Boy'. Whatever, this place is festering.

Mustering the remains of my dignity, I rise from Skater Boy's bed and pick my way to their filthy bathroom; my hair a tangled mess, my headache severe. I'm still not over the cold I caught at Christmas and I haven't had a shower in a week. As predicted, something unpleasant, cold and gooey squelches under foot and I'm seized with a dread of what it might be. There could be anything hiding amongst the debris. Rotting food? Excrement? Semen? A decomposing finger?

Skater Boy is still on the floor, attempting to push the stained, stinking duvet into Scruffy-but-Handsome's face, jabbering into his phone.

"No – it hasn't arrived yet. You have to send credit cards *recorded* post…"

Another crash as a small wooden table, laden with glasses, more ashtrays and some half-empty beer cans containing stubbed out joints is overturned.

"…I'm skint, so I might need you to transfer a few quid…."

I can hear the pitch of his long suffering mother's voice climb a couple of notches.

"…Well – I work in the most expensive village on earth! A grand doesn't go very far."

He winces and jerks the phone suddenly away from his ear. Mother is clearly not impressed.

Covering the mouth piece now, he addresses me.

"Oi Bird - find us a Rizla can you? I think they're in my jeans."

I poke my head around the bathroom door.

"Er…no. Bugger off and find your own bloody Rizlas"

He pulls a sulky face. "A *real* friend would"

"Fine" I dig out his papers and shy them at him across the room, then return to the bathroom where I consider myself in a toothpaste-streaky, goo-splattered mirror. There is no point trying to make what I see presentable. I'm going to sweat like a pig and have my head down a variety of toilets for the next three hours anyway. I splash some water on my face from the scummy basin, then try to scrub away the mascara under my eyes with some a bog roll. I search around for deodorant. There is none.

When I return from the bathroom, Skater Boy and Scruffy-but-Handsome have disentangled themselves and the latter is sitting on the edge of the bed, still unabashedly naked, rubbing his eyes, smoking and eating a raw frankfurter at the same time. "Breakfast?"

"Your balls are on my jeans"

He looks at me, silently unimpressed, flaccid frankfurter in hand, smoke curling up past his squinting eyes and lifts one cheek so I can retrieve them. The jeans and my work shirt are moist from the tea.

"I'm hanging,"

"Yes, I imagine you are after last night's exertions," I examine him. "Your eyes are all swollen like little squirrels' cunts."

He laughs. The laughter turns into a hacking cough that doubles him over and comes right from his guts. I have this same cough. It is the permanent affliction of the seasonnaire.

"Right I'm off". I make for the door, pick my way past Skater Boy still negotiating finances with his mother, and let myself out of the apartment, into the agonisingly bright light of Sunday morning.

Their apartment is in that customary French 'austere-seventies-block' style with concrete stairwells and a broken lift – not at all quaint or picturesque. It's a few hundred yards down the road from the chalets where each of us work, on a peaceful street that the snow plough rarely visits, high above the main resort. As I step outside, the true shapes and colours of the road are unknown to me. Snow has fallen in the night; dense and pristine. Half in shadow, half in light, the road is silent and untouched, my footprints are the first. Steam rises from an open door at the back of the hotel opposite and the air smells faintly of bacon. It is 7am. The backbone of the ski resort, young, hung-over and wheezing, has risen, scratched its arse, coughed its lungs up, possibly vomited and dragged itself through a snow drift to work, frying sausages and making beds for the rich and reckless.

Welcome to the land of the Chalet Bitch.

Chalet Life

The season had begun in early December. One morning during those first few weeks, before the snow arrived in earnest, my chalet guests were gazing doubtfully out of the window at the brownish streaks across the landscape.

"Can you absolutely guarantee it will snow this week?"

Sigh.

I put the coffee pot down on the table. What do you say to this question?

"Well, I don't know for sure Mrs. Blathering-Cretin, but I tell you what – I'll pop upstairs and have a chat with God, see if I can persuade him to rustle some up for you. He's generally quite clued up on these matters."

Later that evening while I was preparing dinner I went outside for a fag under the eaves. Lights were on in the chalets to my left and right and the street high above the village was peaceful; still. The south face of the mountain across the valley blushed in the sunset and cold air tightened the backs of my hands. My mug of tea steamed and stung my palms. I smoked. Shadows crept across the landscape through wisps of cloud; I caught a glimpse of the moon in dramatic detail.

I breathed a deep lungful of mountain air and smiled – one smile for Shazzer. I stayed for five minutes, and then looked at my watch and realised it was 6.30pm. This time last week I was on the tube.

At 10.30pm, after an excessively long dinner service – *roast pumpkin soup, salmon en croute, chocolate fondant* – washing up done, coffees served, I left the guests playing card games loudly around table and went out. Alone and in search of new friends, I went to a hotel bar, adjoining a Michelin star restaurant near the centre of town. Outside, the trees sagged with over-powered Christmas lights. As the automatic doors swished quietly to one side, a lady passed me with an obedient spun-gold hair do in a cream rabbit-fur coat. There was an unmistakably snooty glance at my ill-matched black work trousers, over-worn ski jacket and flat, fur-free snow boots. Ignoring this, and raking fingers through my sweaty barnet, I shuffled uncertainly across the blood-red carpet into the belly of the beast. Music of the French, crooning variety pursued me through the foyer. The hotel was a bustle of dignified murmuring and clinking cutlery after the solid, safe silence of outdoors. It smelled of Eucalyptus, Christmas trees and expensive leather. I ordered a whisky - Bushmills; 15 Euros. I drank it slowly while mentally totting up the cost of each sip. Still, I thought, one must retain little glamour in one's life *somehow*.

I'd secretly been glugging it back from a bottle of red that was definitely past its best, during service, and the addition of the whisky made me quite pissed. Equal parts tired and inebriated, my elbows growing numb from leaning on the marble counter top, I absent-mindedly picked residue from under my broken nails. A tall guy in sharp, Italian tailoring with neat, dark hair broke away from his cross-legged friends who were swirling brandy glasses around the wrought-iron fire. He offered me a few smooth lines and then a cigarette, so we went outside and smoked. Shortly, we fell into a tense silence, punctuated only by awkward comments and me laughing uncomfortably at my own jokes. It merely lit up the void between us.

I left hurriedly, feeling awkward, and then instantly regretted it. Back in my apartment, I scribbled my number down on the corner of a page of my book. But when I ran back to the bar to give it to him, he had gone.

Rules for the Chalet Bitch: A general beginner's guide

You've read books about chalet girls, right? You've seen 'The Season'? Fuzzy depictions where chalet girls have morals and clean hair, hardly ever have to work, and can cook and function in polite society?

Well, let me just say that in essence, all of this bullshit is a pile of tooth-decayingly inaccurate tripe.

The clueless scribes who created these sugary depictions have clearly never done a season. And if I'm wrong and they did, then they must have done one in cuckoo land, where emerald fairies and pixies serve muffins on candy-coated plates, hearts do back flips and chocolates make you thin. Either that, or they were off their tits the entire time. Actually that's the more likely explanation. You are more likely to be whisked off at gun point and conscripted into a prostitution ring than whisked off for chateaubriand, Cristal and a posh shag by a minted Russian.

As a first time seasonnaire, it's much easier than you might think to commit social suicide or be sucked into an abyss of 'what am I doing with my life?' despair. Indeed, there are certain rules any savvy Chalet Bitch would be wise to keep in mind if they want to emerge at the other end, in April, unscathed.

For example:

1. Don't be a martyr.
   Repeat this mantra, daily. *'I am here to ski'.*
   I am here to ski.
   I am *not* here to (as my guests seem to think) take shit from people or (as my boss seems to think) achieve excellence in sanitary management.

I am here....*to ski.*

Remember the mantra when you are changing the same bed for the third time that week because some guest's offspring keeps pissing itself. Repeat it to yourself. Throw the bed sheets to the floor in disgust and flounce out of the chalet. Don't come back before 6pm. You are paid fuck all – and that's not enough to be a perfectionist. The key to happiness is skiing.

2. Cut corners wherever possible.

   Regarding this – a tip: Windowlene is your friend. Buy a truckload of it at the start of the season, along with that Chalet Bitch favourite E.B.R (elephant bog roll – the big industrial stuff they use in public toilets). It is a little known fact, kept on the down-low by the likes of Unilever and cleaning staff the world over, that window cleaner and paper tissues clean absolutely everything. Soap and water just creates unnecessary work and mess. It's all about the corner cutting, people, and that shit shines everything up lovely.

3. Have, and be proud of, 'chalet hands.'

   These are essentially completely fucked, with cracks, chapped skin, scabs and perpetually dirty nails due to exposure to too much toilet bleach, scalding ovens, cooking oil and freezing temperatures. They should, ideally, always smell of onions. If you can repeatedly cut the same finger with a bread knife in exactly the same location, that's a nice touch too.

4. Accept that you must gaze out of the window and look upon a beautiful bluebird powder day whenever you have to work.

A bluebird day in the skiing world is a flawless, sunny day after an overnight snowfall. It's a perfect skiing day, with a clear blue sky, bright sun, and fresh snow. Whenever you have to work, there will be one of these. Whenever you don't it will be a miserable damp white-out. This is the gospel according to St Bastard. Sorry.

I would actually put money on that last one. It's a fucking guarantee. While other bastards swish down the slopes in style, I have spent the morning liberating congealed black gunge from the crevices under the cooker top with a toothpick, intermittently gawping out of the window in despair at the endless sky, as skiers to and fro on the nearby piste. And swearing a lot. While the great and gorgeous holiday makers of the Alps were sunning themselves on the terrace at Chalet de L'Ange and quaffing vin chaud at lunch, I was scraping some particularly sticky skid marks off the downstairs u-bend with a scouring pad and doing laundry. Oh the glamour.

It's at times like this, when you have spent the entire day scrubbing other people's bodily matter off shower tiles and regurgitating last night's Seasonnaire Nightmare* into the bog you cleaned only minutes ago, that you wonder what possibly possessed you to leave the quiet, sanitary safety of your London office block in the first place.

* that is, a pint containing a combination of anything the barkeeper deigns to include, from tequila and brandy to beer and port

A Day in the Life of a Chalet Bitch

Agonisingly hung over, in the dark, I get up and pull on a hoodie, ear muffs and a hat to keep warm. I make myself an enormous cup of tea, sit at the lopsided table by the window, and stare vacantly out at the dark, snowy, deserted road. There is a roundabout with a tree in the centre that is comprised exclusively from pink neon fairy lights. My tea finished, I step out into the street. Daylight is showing pink behind the jagged molars of the mountains - the sun rising of a set of huge jaws.

I have come to realise that a ski season is full of ups and downs. One moment I'm elated, in this surreal alternate universe full of new faces and sensations. Then I'm lost, homesick, wrong-footed, because my time belongs to other people now – at least 85% of my time. Life can be unbearably claustrophobic.

The rest of my day looks something like this:
Clean toilet
Vomit into toilet
Re-clean toilet
Sit on bathroom floor and contemplate wall
Eat stale croissant
Clear breakfast things
Cobble together a cake from rotting contents of broken fridge
Make a bed
Have fag after exhaustion of clearing breakfast things and making bed
Contemplate mountains and the infinite mysteries of the peaks beyond
Hoover

Ten minute snooze in an unmade bed
Peruse items in guests' suitcases and bathroom cabinets
Try on guests' shoes
Steal pack of fags from guest's carton
Hoover
Check watch and wonder whether 9.45am is too early to leave chalet and go skiing
Hoover some more.
Contemplate making sandwich from left over beef bourguignon and stale baguette while hoovering
Decide can't be bothered
Eat stale croissant
Spray a bit of Windowlene on bathroom tiles and wipe
Fuck it that'll do
Fist about a bit. Bored
Fag
Steal magazine from guest's room and have very long poo while catching up on latest celeb goss from back home
Attempt to assuage nausea with hair of dog - drink vodka from mug (feel smug about sneaky trick as guests think you're sipping tea)
Vomit into toilet again
Re-clean toilet
Lock self in store cupboard
Have a wank
Check watch. 10.50am
Wonder absently what burning smell is
Leave chalet
Go skiing
Have sudden moment of clarity and remember cake
Stop dead, mid-piste and yell "Oh bollocks...*fuck!*"
Pelt to nearest lift at full speed
Get on lift, but swear again loudly as it grinds to halt
Hang in purgatory for 5 long minutes, cursing the idiots

who can't get on and off the chairlift without getting their legs tangled and falling over.
Leg it up road to chalet in ski boots, praying whole place isn't burnt to a cinder
Retrieve charred remains of cake from oven
Slope off to bakery in shame

It occurred to me very swiftly that Chalet Bitching is no more a career, a vocation, a profession or even an occupation, than stacking shelves in Sainsbury's. I am, in essence, a very elaborate toilet cleaner. The irony of this is not lost on me. It dates back to the time my parents threw me a graduation party at the end of Uni.

It was appalling.

"So, what are you going to do now? Are you going to go into teaching?" I remember my mother's tennis friend Deborah slurring at me, clutching a glass of now-tepid Moet and wafting a Mary-Rose-soaked prawn under my nose. Everyone assumes you'll go into teaching if you've done an English degree.

The honest answer to this question was, a) I didn't have a fucking clue and b) I was too busy shagging my new, exciting, first-ever boyfriend to really be clear headed about anything. It was the culmination of three years of people incessantly asking me this exact question and not really concentrating on my answer. Now my parents had assembled their entire social set to mill round our garden drunk and ask it again.

I smoothed a hand over my hip to flatten the white broderie anglaise frock my mother had insisted I wear, trying to formulate an appropriate answer. When nothing came to mind I just decided to be flippant.

"Ummmm..." I said, "I'll probably just end up being a toilet cleaner or something!"

From the other end of the lawn, my Mum audibly sucked air through her teeth.

Deborah, however, was unmoved. Like many of my mother's friends, she appeared to exist inside a pastel-hazy utopian bubble of serenity at all times. Probably safer that way.

"Mmmmmmmm," she said. "Mmmmmm. Fantaaaaaastic."

To be fair, it was a miracle I had managed to navigate my way to passing my degree after three years of skiving off down in Exeter. I spent every available second nipping onto the train to Paddington to see my boyfriend, who, being eight years my senior and having a BMW, I thought was terribly grown up. I liked to show off to all my friends by walking straight off the train into lectures on a Monday morning, still shit-faced and in clubbing gear. I dropped several dress sizes that year.

Now I was planning (terribly sensibly) to move in with him. We had rented a high-ceilinged flat in Brighton, where we would spend the next three years bonking, arguing about being skint and dancing in darkened rooms to cheer ourselves up. At some point the shine started to come off it and then the comedowns started to get really very nasty indeed...

Anyway, I digress. Despite having this 'hallowed' degree, I console myself over the drudgery of chalet toil with the thought that if you believe in working to live, rather than living to work, any job is as much a means to an end as the next one. Every industry is as much a pointless hamster wheel of 'busyness' and 'importance' as the next one. And these days anyone with a hole in his arse can get a degree anyway. You can get degrees in darning, Klingon and eating fruit-corner yoghurts if you want to.

At least I can take some pride in chalet work. Our 'luxury' company, you see, operates under the pretention of providing that 'little bit extra' to guests. We are "the John Lewis of travel" according to my boss, the vile *La Vache Qui Ski* (of whom more later.) It's all about turning the bed clothes back at night, leaving chocolates on the pillow, folding towels into the shape of something that, nine times out of ten, accidentally resembles a vagina, and spending hours fumbling around with the toiletry arrangements in the bathroom. The antidote to this, I have found, is to amuse oneself by adding the odd 'special' touch of one's own. For example, the boss hasn't spotted that the cute little snowman I built outside the front door yesterday complete with a hat, carrot nose and hand-written sign to welcome the kiddies on their ski holiday, is also surreptitiously holding his erect cock in his hand. But when she does, I shall deny any involvement.

Now *that's* something I can take pride in.

Things that Occur to You on Chairlifts

Somewhere around mid-December the snow began to fall almost constantly, in thick clumps. I hadn't made many friends by that stage, so on my day off I went out on the mountain alone and found the forbidden cappuccino foam, untracked, deep, and silky. There were crowds of many descending clouds, rolling in from somewhere far away, sinking under their own weight. Still, and half in sunlight, the day seemed almost steamy. Weightless ice crystals were floating and dancing in half-light, drifting in suspended silence, whispering a diamond prayer. For some reason, my mind drifted to a summer holiday; a dip in the sea and my hand trailing in the scattered green light of phosphorescent plankton.

I lit a cigarette on the chairlift and laid back. Hanging in vast space; surveying the interlacing tracks of other skiers. Ears popping, I let the syncopated sunlight flicker behind my closed eyelids, drifting swiftly upwards through the tree tops. Icy wind on my face, I thought about the unfathomable forces that fold and buckle layers and layers of matter and time into such immense towers of terrible beauty, stretching on, day upon night, into millennia. The mountains, like crouching lizards with great, ridged backs, or breaking waves, white horses and spume crashing in terrible slow motion.

I puffed a white cloud and wondered which of it was my breath and which of it was cigarette smoke. The fast expanding fog around me seemed to enter my head and displace everything else. The wind banished thoughts of home; dried my tears onto my skin. The clouds settled duvet-like down into the valley. A gap in the mist showed empty and blue, and a private jet banked overhead, carrying someone expensive to somewhere exotic.

At the top, I sneaked under a barrier and, with no transceiver, and not a clue in the world, I slid and tumbled down through smooth, flawless plumes as if in a dream about surfing across clouds. I spread my arms out like wings.

The Princess and the Pea

Exquisitely beautiful and completely intolerable - that's the mother of the family staying in my chalet this week. She has a horrible Chelsea accent tinted with a Los Angeles affectation. She can't be more than 28, with waist-length auburn hair and features carved out of alabaster. She rises at 10.30 every day and glides around the chalet trailing her dressing gown belt, with her nose stuck high in the air. She doesn't ski. She's fussy, haughty, self-important and rich, which basically translates as 'a Chalet Bitch's worst nightmare…'

"Bring in the bags, would you?" she said with a great sense of entitlement, sweeping out of the transfer car and into the living room on the day they arrived.

"…It's lovely to meet you," I said as her children bounded past, knocking me into the coat rack and treading on my toes. I followed them into the living room and extended my hand in greeting. Slackly, she gave me the ends of her cold, thin fingers to hold, gazing over my shoulder into the kitchen.

"The poor soul's an insomniac," fawned her husband, at dinner; an immense full stop of a human being, swathed in Breitling and Ralph Lauren, and reeking of Bulgari. They were stinkingly rich. "She rarely gets to sleep before 2am," he said, "so please don't go hoovering until she's awake in the morning."

"Ummm…" I began, "Breakfast is actually only served between 7.30 and…"

"…Also, could you make sure there's plenty of hazelnut milk in the chalet?" she drawled over her shoulder as she stalked off to inspect the master bedroom. Any kind of response from me was clearly unnecessary. She was more of a talker than a listener.

Within minutes of arriving she had handed their warring brats over to a brow-beaten private ski instructor who'd "been with the family for years" and each parent promptly disappeared off in separate directions. She demanded I drive her to the mall where she went shopping for overpriced clothing. He, in turn, sped off down the piste in the top-to-toe black banker-wanker ski garb that is usual for his type.

At 11.00am the next morning, just as I was mopping the kitchen floor and preparing to leave and go skiing myself, she emerged from the dark recesses of their bedroom, leaving greasy footprints in her wake. "Could I grab two poached *uggs*," she murmured, without making eye contact or any attempt at a pleasantry. "And *could you make sure* they're runny in the middle?"

...Could I make sure?

This seemed to be a catch phrase of hers. *Could you make sure...?*

Presumably I could, but since 'please' was clearly beyond her vocabulary, it was unlikely that I would. And *Uggs?* I wondered, bitterly, rummaging in the fridge. What the fuck are *uuuugggs?* I looked pointedly at the furry monstrosities she was slopping around in and considered ripping them from her feet, boiling them up and serving them to her with a slice of toast.

For a moment I chewed over the idea of explaining to her that breakfast service had ended an hour and a half ago. I looked over at her, sitting bolt upright at the head of the dining table, expectantly, fiddling with her phone.

Sigh. It just wasn't worth the aggro.

"Two poached *Uggs*, coming up," I said.

The next day, a Sunday, she convinced herself there was a dead rat (*'raaaat'*) in the laundry room. There wasn't. It was just a slightly smelly drain, and it was barely perceptible.

Nevertheless she kept asking me whether I'd called Rentokil every four minutes.

"I have a raaally raaally well-developed sense of smaaall," she droned, standing in the doorway of the laundry room as I shuffled around on my hands and knees, trying to see if there was a deceased rodent under the washing machine "It's sooooo strong. It's going to keep me up at night. Have you called Rentokil? We've got to get rid of that *raaaat...*"

"Well, unfortunately it's Sunday and they're not responding."

She simply stared at me in icy silence.

"That's France for you!" I shrugged, nervously.

"Can't you ring their emergency line?" she persisted, eyeballing me as I tried to stand back up.

"I don't think there is one."

"There *must* be an emergency line. Just call them up and say it's aaargent."

"Er... I'll see what I can do."

An *emergency* Rentokil hotline?

What the holy hell in fuck was she talking about? Mad bitch! Even if there was one, this wasn't an emergency. An emergency would be a swarm of *raaaats*. A *plague* of *raaaats*. A sea of *raaaats* scurrying all over the house, ransacking the cupboards, biting people and spreading the Black Death. This was not an emergency. *This* was an imagined dead *raaaat*. A non-existent dead *raaaat*. One not-actually-dead-rat in the basement of a chalet, creating a barely-perceptible whiff, an infestation crisis does not make!

Then she started complaining that her mattress was far too lumpy (for *God's sake*, the thing has a goose down protector on it). She commanded me into her room and declared,

31

"This mattress is *super* lumpy. Can you flip it and check underneath?" She then proceeded to demonstrate how I should do this by flimsily trying to lift a corner of the mattress herself. It's most ineffectual trying to do such things with tiny, wasted arms that have only ever experienced heavy lifting in the form of an Hermes Birkin overloaded with Givenchy lip liners.

"Don't worry, I'll do it," I said, cheerfully, encouraging her out of the room before she hurt herself so that I could placate her by pretending to flip the wretched thing.

"...And *could you make sure* there are some extra duvets on top of the mattress or I won't sleep a wink," she called, haughtily, over her shoulder.

Then there was the news that she was coeliac (or as I prefer to call it 'glu-tarded'), that eggs 'made her grumpy' and that she didn't really like meat. This along with being allergic to milk meant that she was, in her own words, "a semi-vegan." This was a detail that both she and her husband had seen fit to omit from the pre-holiday questionnaire and dietary requirements sheet they'd been sent. So, amongst many other things, no cream, no milk, no bread or pasta, no pastry and, of course, no meat. Bang went almost the entire chalet menu and all the supplies I had bought on shopping day. Hazelnut milk is not the easiest thing to find at lunch time on a Sunday in a French ski resort. It particularly stuck in my craw at the end of the week when I saw her merrily drenching the poached pears I'd prepared in cream. Lactose-intolerant my arse.

Despite all her tragic conditions she had a very great liking for cake and reeled off a list of bizarre ingredients with which I could make her a 'healthy' afternoon tea. These were obscure and impossible to buy in provincial France. Things like agave nectar, xantham gum, Olm blood and the powdered feathers of the Marvellous Spatuletail Hummingbird brined in unicorn tears.

Forgive me, but isn't the whole philosophy behind cake the fact that it's naughty? Indulgent? Sinful and wrong? Isn't that the whole reason we eat cake? Making it healthy takes all the fun out of it and the idea that alchemising 'cakes' out of fairy fat and Dodo droppings makes them good for us is simply a fallacy. No wonder her ADHD children pissed the bed and fought constantly. She inflicted her own pernickety dietary requirements on the whole family, feeding them revolting wholefood sugar-free snacks and samphire smoothies.

"They're not allowed chocolate" she informed me, "and only the white marshmallows from the packet. The pink ones make them act up."

That evening, by way of proof, I was treated to a live session of 'acting up.' A full-on apocalyptic tantrum from the younger of the sons when I asked him to stop scribbling in red felt tip on one of the walls. He hurled himself at the floor, shrieking and swearing and banging his head.

"Don't do that, Titus," said his mother, indifferently, stepping over him on the way to the bathroom.

"There's a diagnosis for this," I thought, watching him in silence. "He's suffering from cake-deficit-rage (CDR)."

It could have been the pink marshmallows. It could also have been that their mother was so remote she practically shrank from physical contact with them. I once saw her flinch when her eldest son tried to kiss her cheek. She was all too ready to palm them off on a nanny or a ski instructor 24/7, so she could swan off shopping or sit glued to her laptop in her dressing gown all day. She had the maternal instincts of a cuckoo.

In the end, I took simply to lying about the cake. On Wednesday, I baked a chocolate almond confection and said it was 'wheat free' (true) and therefore 'healthy' (untrue, it contained half a pound of butter and two chocolate bars). I told her that, and then took great glee in watching her plough through all that lard, knowing it would shortly thereafter be residing mostly on her arse.

This afternoon they are leaving, so it was time to strip the bed after breakfast. When I did so I found that one of the kids had somehow managed to get a piece of Lego wedged under the mattress protector. Despite myself, I can't diss the woman for being genuinely regal. I guess that explains the insomnia. Mind you I couldn't sleep at night either, if I was that much of an arsehole.

Strange Mountain Creatures

In my humble opinion, the single most important thing a girl can do in a ski resort, is get to know the bar staff. The reasons for this are threefold:

1. Bar staff are in charge of the booze, and therefore everyone wants to be their friend. Ergo they are your six degrees of separation from everyone else in the resort.

2. If you're Billy-no-mates, you can sit at the bar chatting to them and look popular / in the know.

3. You are far more likely to get free shots on busy nights.

Luckily for yours truly, the main seasonnaire watering hole happens to be bang opposite my front door. Since my guests are usually bastards and my chalet-co-bitch can procrastinate for England, the place is almost always heaving with an assortment of wrongguns and holiday-makers dancing around still in their ski boots in varying states of inebriation and undress by the time I arrive.

The Drop Inn, for that (with characteristic originality) is its name, is overseen by Old Man Swiss, a sinewy, bony fingered bar man with a steely glint and a penchant for philandering with 18-year-olds. Weed-smoker, loan-ranging snowboarder and summertime chicken farmer. Beer-swiller and part-time alcoholic, with an unhealthy obsession with expensive watches, fast cars and a fear of flying belied by his ability to be airborne on skis. Big hearted, deviously clever and slightly tufty on top, he has, apparently, a sixty grand debt hanging over his head from living the high-life in the Alps seven seasons too long. Ask him why he keeps coming back and he'll say rather mournfully: "I have more friends in places I visit than where I live."

Of the rest of the patrons of The Bar, what can I say?

Pick two:
  -Drunk
  -Attractive
  -Deranged

On a Wednesday evening the Drop Inn teems with French Ski Instructors, which sounds rather appealing and sexy but, on closer inspection (believe me), is not. After years of learning to ski in Italy, where the ski instructors are charismatic, lithe, toned, tanned, called Roberto or Fabritzio, and incredibly adept at getting in your knickers, I have come to expect big things from ski instructors. In fact, one's ski holiday was never complete if one hadn't fallen in love with Philippo and his café crème tan by the end. Unfortunately, L'Ecole de Ski in this place looks like a geriatric circus troupe. The younger ones, of which there are about two and a half, are perpetually drunk and potentially dangerous, not to mention ridiculously minted thanks to a glut of big-spending Russian clientele. There is one in particular - Petit Pierre - who prowls the resort using his cock as a divining rod and is currently sporting a piece of limited edition ankle jewelry courtesy of the local gendarmerie. He's quirkily handsome, in a goofy, French kind of way, with long floppy limbs and a slightly lopsided gait. Actually he's rather adorable, until he gets some Jaeger in him. Then he spends the rest of the evening dribbling on your shoulder and trying to grope your boobs, before being thrown out for causing a fracas.

Speaking of the aforementioned, this morning I passed Petit Pierre stumbling out of The Drop Inn, where he had apparently been downing Chartreuse for breakfast.

"*Oi*!"

He was hotly pursued by Old Man Swiss, who was brandishing a snowboard that had been cracked clean down the middle.

"Oui?"

"...are you going to replace this or what, you froggy bastard?"

He shied the two pieces across the road at Petit Pierre, who just stuck his middle finger up and yelled, "*Plonkerrrh whonkerrrh!*"

Not long after this, I spotted Petit Pierre snaking Pied-Piper-style down a red run, followed by a long line of tiny, helmeted toddlers. So there's something to consider next time you book your precious sproglets into French ski school.

The other ski instructor of note is The Man of Leisure who I met because his disapproving and rather dour multisquillionaire Dad was staying in our chalet early in the season so, entertainingly, he kept popping in to visit. Tonight he's drunker than a skunk, swaying and yelling over the din; looking, with his guy liner and glossy black hair scraped back in a pony tail and headband, remarkably like a gypsy pirate captain. He has, I grudgingly admit, the Adonis good-looks of a broad-shouldered, nip-waisted Davidoff model. Tonight, he and The Foxy Chef, our local cougar, are placing bets on which of the uninitiated Chalet Bitches littering the bar will throw up first.

"That girl, with the boobs," he slurs, pointing at one with long, shaggy blonde hair, full lips and rather puffy eyes. The Foxy Chef and I inspect her, as she leans on the bar unsteadily, chatting up Old Man Swiss with slightly too much enthusiasm.

"I recognise her from our staff-training week," I recall. "She works for the same company as I do."

"Apparently she has some 50 Euro bet with a mate that she won't sleep with anyone this season," says The Man of Leisure disdainfully.

"She looks like an accident waiting to happen," I reply, but he is already setting his drink down and making off in her direction.

By all accounts the Man of Leisure should be totally unbearable. At 20 he has his 'own' apartment in the resort and has somehow, between benders, managed to pass all his BASI exams. Much to the chagrin of his local peers he has penetrated the ranks of the French ski school and spends his days lunching care of the credit cards of private clients. His evenings and his summers are then spent shagging their daughters. Most peculiar of all is his confused Lloyd Grossman accent – the jumbled, ambiguous upshot of an international education sent from pillar to post and boarding school to boarding school. Heaven knows how he gets away with it.

Also, due to some 'special arrangement', he works a maximum of eight hours a week. The rest of the time he is either hammered, throwing parties in his retro penthouse opposite the main piste or skiing powder. He is a great teller of tall tales, most of which involve bat-shit crazy bunny boilers who want to kill him, for whom I can't decide whether he is a magnet or a catalyst. But, as I was reminded last night when he came bouncing into the pub dressed as a frog, he's sort of irresistible.

A case in point, the Foxy Chef and I watch in quiet amazement as he sidles over to the aforementioned bushy-haired girl, whom we shall call 'Calamity', says something into her ear and then starts fondling her breasts without a by-or-leave. By some miracle, she seems to find it hilariously funny.

"I think he just offered her 50 Euros for a shag," says the Foxy Chef, looking mildly impressed.

Then, like an oil-slicked eel, the girl suddenly slides off her bar stool, keels forward and throws up on his ski pants.

The Truth About Tour Operators

The next thing you should know is that Tour Operators are a bunch of bastards. If you hadn't already spotted this of your own accord, then let me take this opportunity to enlighten you.

Imagine the worst organised place you have ever worked. Now, times that by a thousand and then insert the phrase 'piss-up in brewery'. This description, in my opinion, barely even comes close to the reality of how these skin-flints (with laughable management skills) will bum-fuck their staff for blood, sweat and tears and con Punters into a budget holiday tarted up as luxury.

I came to the mountains seeking a cushy number for a schmoozer corporate ski dolly bird type. Glamour, excitement, and possibly a rich sugar daddy were on my 'to find' list. I had a friend who had done a similar job a couple of seasons before. According to her reports, when she wasn't snorting grotesquely long lines of cocaine off pearl-encrusted toilet seats in Michelin star restaurants, she was heli-skiing or towing a braying conga line of rich, fit bankers (or D-list celebrities whom she'd been charged with 'showing a good time') into the most expensive and exclusive bars, restaurants and hotels in town. In real terms, actually, this roughly translates as playing Nanny to a bunch of alcoholic perverts with more money than sense, but I didn't realise that at the time. No, it seemed very glamorous.

Being strong in the banter department, I thought I would be excellent at this type of job. I've always seen myself as much more of an executive sort and, after all, one thing I know how to do is hoover up charlie - so how hard could it be? I never actually wanted to be a chalet girl. I thought I was getting a bit long in the tooth for it, and pondered going for something rather more sophisticated and befitting my executive skills.

Fuck knows why, because there aren't many other desirable options out here.

Possible bearable jobs available in a ski resort:

Ski Rep: Commission-crazed sales whore, 27-hour days, public speaking and need for congenital hyper-enthusiasm disorder – yeuch!

Driver: On mountain roads? Take your life and those of your guests in your hands.

Nanny: Sprogs….need I say more? I'm not against children per se. Let's just say I don't have any of my own and can't bear to be around those that belong to other humans. Then there's the fact that Alpine nannies are reputed to be, *en général*, fat, thick, lazy, gossipy and promiscuous/ desperate to get knocked up themselves. Nannies look after the sprogs so the parents can ski. You do the maths. Besides, I threw my friend Fiona a baby shower last year which involved a bucket of lube and a bowl of ketamine. I am clueless with children.

Hotel Staff: Have heard reports of them working in chain gangs, which may explain why they never socialise or ski outside their immediate circle of colleagues. They are connected at the ankle by an iron chain and sleep in an industrial fridge at night. Surely the most overworked and underpaid of any season staff. Never seen or heard. Fed on gruel and left over plain pasta and fustigated with an iron bar when disobedient.

Night Porter: This is a vampire's job.

Plongeur: Skivvy, human dishrag

Bar Staff: Sociopath

Maintenance: Need to be able to fix stuff, operate a screwdriver, be a drug dealer and ideally have a thick regional accent.

...If one does opt for the increased pay, responsibility and therefore legitimacy of a job like Hotel or Resort Manager, (which sounds a lot better when you tell Daddy-dear), it's important to know with that luxury comes the inevitable 'them and us' situation. Managers, after all, are the ones that have to chastise the eighteen-year-old Chalet Bitches that don't turn up to serve breakfast because they're still off their tits on mephedrone from the night before. Your staff will inevitably come to work every day banjaxed, or simply skive shamelessly because they are being paid peanuts (see reference to bum-fucking earlier) and thought they were here to ski, and not to clean toilets for nine straight hours a day. Would you want to be the person in charge of telling that lot to scrub the floors? It could be fine, of course. Or it could be a disaster...

Tour Operators can get away with all this because there's a whole queue of eighteen year olds round the block, willing to work for nothing but free shots, fudge and a shag - hopping up and down, shouting "pick me! ooooh oooh pick meeee!" Resort wages haven't risen in the last ten years. Apparently, sixty five Euros a week, a ski pass, a grimy flat the size of a garden shed, shared with six other people, a highly suspect and probably unlawful contract, and a pat on the head are supposed to command your unwavering devotion. But this is the trade-off, so they tell us. If one wants to spend six months getting wrecked and skiing for free, one must expect to be treated like a twat. Punters want holidays and Tour Operators need gullible slaves. All this basically means is that the average ski holiday is nothing more than a massive turd, gift-wrapped and garnished with a ribbon by a ragamuffin teenager harbouring more venereal diseases than Henry VIII.

Now, obviously, T O bosses don't behave like bastards for no good reason. Once carefree seasonnaires themselves, they are now the harbingers of tattered dreams. You try keeping positive after seven seasons without profits because you're being squeezed by French property owners and taken advantage of by petulant chalet staff and then, to add insult to injury, it doesn't snow. It's only a hop, skip and a jump to becoming totally cynical about all your staff and embittered by life. I can imagine it's hard to swallow the fact you're not living the dream, as you had planned, but stuck in an office fielding calls from wankers and becoming steadily more and more mercenary because you cannot actually afford one of your own chalet holidays.

The Old Man of the Hills

Skiing today, in thick fog, with the Foxy Chef, Old Man Swiss and the shaggy-headed blonde who threw up on the Man of Leisure. Great snow but skiing is rather alarming when you can't tell where the ground ends and the sky starts. By three o'clock, we were getting tired. The Foxy Chef fell off the side of an unexpected mogul and I hit a patch of ice and bruised my hip. I have no idea how Calamity didn't fall over, she snowboards like a maniac Daddy Longlegs, all flailing and erratic. Can't ride for toffee but by Christ, the girl can drink. The self-proclaimed 'Best Après-Skier on the Mountain', she never leaves the chalet without a spare pair of comfy shoes, a hairbrush and make up bag stuffed into her pockets, so she can party comfortably come five 'o clock.

Around lunchtime, as the Foxy Chef and I came snaking down a red run, we spotted Calamity and Old Man Swiss sitting partially hidden in the trees with their skis clipped off, smoking.

"Darlings!" said Old Man Swiss theatrically jumping up to plant kisses on our cheeks. He was wearing a pair of white-framed wayfarers with red reflective lenses so you couldn't tell where he was looking. I suspected this was strategic. When he took off the shades his blue eyes flashed a steely glint.

"Excuse me ladies," he said, storing half a smoked joint in the pocket of his ski pants, "I must go and drizzle my efflu-ent," and made off in the direction of a bushy fir tree a few metres away.

"I love watching him go..." said Calamity examining his retreating behind. She gave us both a sheepish sidelong smirk. As she lay back on the snow I noticed her flies were still undone.

"Are you seriously letting *that* rummage in your knickers?" asked the Foxy Chef, unimpressed. Calamity was still smirking.

"I know," she said, clearly enjoying being obtuse. "He's a complete dick. I don't know what I'm thinking."

The thing is, I can see the attraction. Old Man Swiss with his Peter-pan style and baby blues, a hint of the 'Withnail' about him. I remember when, once upon a time, I thought older men were where it's at too.

"You'd say something to one of them, wouldn't you? In ordinary land," said the Foxy Chef as we watched them canoodling on the chairlift in front of us on the way back up to ski home. "At his age and her age…" She wrinkled her nose as the two of them starting laying into each other in earnest. "I reckon he's going a bit bald under that bobble hat."

"It's the mysterious older man thing."

"I wouldn't mind so much, but he used those moves on me three seasons ago," she said with distaste. "It's his wife I feel sorry for…"

"Wait…he's *married?*"

"He's got a kid, mate. They live in Lyon. Where do you think he goes on the weekends?"

There was silence while I absorbed this information.

"God," said the Foxy Chef, her nose still screwed up in disgust. "Imagine what his wrinkly old ball bags look like…"

"Imagine them banging against your chin."

I'm glad I didn't do a season at Calamity's age, I thought, as we got off the lift. I wouldn't have survived it.

"Hi, I'm a ski instructor.
Shall I put my balls in your mouth now or later?"

In the last 24 hours I have:

1. Driven to Lyon and back… Oh the horrors of the airport transfer. The grumpy passengers wanted the heat on so high it would have sent Lindsay Lohan to sleep in the middle of a particularly aggressive cocaine binge. No matter how much rest I manage to get beforehand, as soon as I hit that motorway the eyes start to go. The soporific effect of the glare from the road and the lights coming at you in thick fog turn everything dreamlike, as if you're in a computer game. Then there's that horrible knowledge that you have at least two more hours of battling to keep yourself conscious before you're even at the foot of the mountain. I did actually pass out a little bit at the wheel at one point. Hit the curb and bounced (which, fortuitously, woke me up), swerved and lost the wing mirror to a passing van. Luckily the passengers were all asleep. Next time, I'm going to stock the minibus with Red Bull and whatever uppers I can get my hands on. So far, I've nicked the central reservation, backed into a chalet roof and skidded almost into a parked car during a blizzard. All with passengers. The boss is not happy. Still, I wanted more excitement in my job than sitting at a desk, didn't I? And stress and excitement go hand in hand.

2. Cleaned about 4000 toilets… I really am quite bored of toilet cleaning now.

3. Shagged a ski instructor.

I had, last week, fallen into the 'day 20-25 hormonal fuck off trap'. This, I have observed, is when you are nearing the mid-to-late cycle and as you haven't achieved conception your body starts to ramp up the pressure by causing you to compare yourself to every woman within a five mile radius and come up feeling inferior and depressed. The bonus of being in the mountains, however, is that one is liberated from that horrible feeling by living in a small village chock full of randy people who aren't too picky. Shagging a ski instructor, as mentioned, is a lifelong ambition of mine. I have, over the years, developed quite a taste for the tanned, toned perfection of that oh so stylish and sexual of specimens, the Italian *maestro di sci*. It only takes a wink, a smile, and five minutes watching one of these guys cha cha cha his way down a mountain with a series of perfectly executed turns to get your juices flowing. Or at least it does when you're 16 years old and go to a private school in the middle of deepest darkest Sussex, where the only male talent you see is generally spotty and obsessed with watching Star Wars video marathons. Italian ski instructors are luxurious, wholenut chocolate. Oh so creamy, with smooth brown skin, hazelnut eyes and super-mobile hips. Mmmmhmmmm.

About a week ago, I got hammered enough to think it a fabulous idea to let the Man of Leisure tempt me into a notorious den of iniquity of a club named La Boite, in a bunker under the piste.

"Let's go clubbing," he said, and promptly I found myself in a club so expensive it actually makes your wallet bleed. For a warm glass (glass! not pint) of Heineken, I paid nine Euros (yes, that's NINE). The fuckers couldn't even be arsed to refrigerate it. And that's with a seasonnaire's discount. If the Punters fancied a warm beer there, you could add another ten Euros onto that figure. Anyway, apparently I met a ski instructor named Roman and gave him my number, because yesterday I got a text from him which started with "Ciao bella". He had me at hello.

We met up for coffee and he offered me an 'off piste lesson', with an invitation to go to a deserted 'refuge' for lunch. This actually translated as a bit of heavy petting in the bubble lift. He caught me a bit off-guard, actually, lunging in for a slightly washing-machine-reminiscent snog. We clattered around awkwardly in ski boots for a bit - let's just say he didn't have the same finesse in the foreplay department as he did in the, er, *giant slalom*. However, all things considered, I let Roman the Italian ski instructor take me off piste... and take me from behind. It's quite novel being rear-ended with your ski boots on and your knickers round your knees while someone whispers "mio angelo" in your ear. It doesn't require as much balance as you'd think, since the rigidity of the ski boots takes care of that. But skiing back with slushy knickers afterwards was less than pleasant and, slightly mortifyingly, my knees seemed to have turned to jelly. I kept falling over in the chopped up snow.

So that's one thing crossed off the 'to do' list, at least.

I returned very pink in the face, with wind burn from being topless in freezing temperatures too long.

"Where've you been?" asked The Foxy Chef, looking at my lobster complexion suspiciously.

Let's just say, I've always wondered what those tiny little wooden mountain huts in the middle of nowhere are for, and now I know.

More Mountain Creatures

Another girl works with me in the chalet. Did I mention that? Perhaps not. In truth, I try not to think about her too much because she's ghastly. For some reason, I appear to have been thrust into playing the role of harassed, short-tempered governess to this giant, crisp eating, southern-comfort wielding child. Not only this, but I have also been unlucky enough to end up sharing a room with her and her cronies, China, India and Asia. They are hags. Moist, just out of school and all podgy with sly little faces, big backcombed seasonnaire hair ('*seasonaah hahh*') and a lot of gunk around the eyes which is applied layer on layer every morning in a slap-dash, trowel like fashion, with smeary bits and patches. I am stuck with these moon-faced horrors, since the only other members of staff in our ski resort who work for the same company, and can string a sentence together, are Calamity, our driver and a couple called Sid and Margery. Sid and Marge are at the other end of the spectrum – pensioner ski bums. Balding and bespectacled, respectively. Sid is one of those men who wear their bobble hats perpendicular to the head like a gnome. He carries his mobile phone in a holster.

On this theme, let me extrapolate and further define the various types of Chalet Bitch that one encounters in your average ski resort:

Private Chalet Bitch: This is as close to the traditional role as it gets. Take the Foxy Chef, for example. She swans about in an enormous car, with designer handbags and watches bought with her gratuitous tips. Private Chalet Bitches have their phones paid for, buy all their ski gear on account and live gratis in the boss's property all winter, eating steak bought with the chalet credit card and drinking the cellar dry. When the boss is in town, they work like dogs. The rest of the time the mountain and the chalet is theirs and everyone wants to be their friend in the hope of a night in a clean comfortable bed and a power shower. This is the golden fleece of chalet work.

Mountain Worshiper Chalet Bitch: These are obsessed with winter sports and work their arses off for meagre wages at the hands of Tour Operators, ski shops and après ski bars. They scrimp through the summer in some dead-end job (or sponging off their parents or on the dole,) dreaming constantly of the mountains. Their raison d'être is to work hard and fast so they can get out onto the slopes as much as possible. No part of the mountain is forbidden to them. The piste is a huge taboo.

Pensioner Chalet Bitch: Robust, early sixties retired-types with a twinkle in their eyes. These have generally sacked off the grow-old-gracefully idea in favour of skiing and toil. Often their own worst enemies, since they actually work hard and therefore get completely taken advantage of. Diligence is the downfall of any successful Chalet Bitch.

Newbie Chalet Bitch Over 29 in Existential Crisis: Newbie mountain workers over the age of about 29 (particularly those who have never skied or snowboarded before) seem to fall into a pattern. The pattern is this: Arrive, thinking you have found the 'thing' you've been searching for all your life. Work way too hard. Exhaust yourself. Have a massive tantrum about how young all the other mountain workers are and how old you are. Complain that you 'haven't made any friends'. Lack any impetus to ski because everyone else is really good and you can't even snow plough and therefore spend too much time sitting in shoe-box bunk room flat. In a half-arsed attempt to get involved, you book a couple of ski lessons but get too drunk the night before and fail to turn up to them. Decide that everyone at home was right, and you ought to grow up, go back to Norwich and get a mortgage. Throw toys out of pram because you're being bent over the cooker and bum-raped by your employer. Quit... Then, immediately, start having more fun than you've ever had in your grey little life, as you now no longer give a shit about the job. Enjoy a surprise bluebird powder day on the mountain and end up dancing until 7am in your ski boots in another ski resort round the corner with your mates. Regret quitting. Realise job was piece of piss and you were just being feeble. Man The Fuck Up. Meekly request job back. Become serial seasonnaire.

Irksome Blonde 19 Year Old Chalet Bitch: These are (not necessarily female) over-privileged, slothful, ditzy, sulky little bastards, fresh out of school on a winter sports jolly gap yah. Often manipulative, arrogant, professionally ignorant, impervious to reason, socially oblivious, unreceptive to advice, encouragement or cajoling, and totally unaware of how ridiculous they look/sound/are to everyone else not in their social category (most other people on the mountain). Goal in life: To consume more alcohol than Shirley Bassey on death row and shag as many other Irksome-Blonde-19-Year-Olds as physically possible. They usually end the season with a two extra arse cheeks and/or a cornucopia of venereal diseases. Mating call: "Lashkagaaaaah, yachts, Daddy, bleeeeeeeeeugh!"

Sadly for yours truly, it is the latter of these that I have had the unfortunate fate of being designated to co-habit and work with. I use the word 'work' in its loosest possible sense, because in essence the Irksome-Blonde-19-Year-Old is little more useful and conversationally adept than a brain damaged pig. Except, to be fair, if you took a retarded swine and taught it to stand upright and bake yoghurt cakes, you would probably end up with a more co-operative and effective employee.

Let me just take this moment to tell you a little about the Irksome-Blonde-19-Year Old with whom I work. A sullen, vacant girl with no more than three quarters of an inch of brain and disproportionately large knockers which are always on show either by way of a see through or low-cut top. She dresses like a Brixton whore, walks like a rugby player, and skis like my Aunty Jean. Her enormous arse receives no favours from being perpetually enfolded into the most ludicrously tight jeans I've ever seen and her hair is always backcombed, piled on top of her head in a cack-handed chignon of *sea-sonnah hah*. Mostly, the Irksome-Blonde-19-Year-Old just slopes about sulking, with her g-string showing above her jeans and taking a fag break every six seconds. She claims she learned silver service at a hotel frequented by the Queen, and certainly she does know how to fold a serviette, but that is about where her talents end. Allegedly, she comes from somewhere remote in Scotland - but she speaks with the cut glass accent of a lady and the adopted intonation of lout. She pronounces chalet wrong – with the emphasis on the second syllable – '*shallaaaaay*'.

"By the way, I was thinking" she said to me once in a rare moment of lucidity, " – d'you raaarrlly think it's on? …all this cleaning we have to do?"

"On?" I was grimacing as I withdrew a long, green, slimy trail of hair and clunge from one of the many plug holes I'd tackled that day. I felt as if I'd spent the afternoon fingering Susan Boyle.

"Yer. Couldn't we, like, look into getting a cleaner or, like, something?"

I laughed. I could see an insane sort of logic to this idea.

"We could split it...it would like, only be a hundred a week or so?" she said hopefully.

We earn seventy five Euros a week. You do the maths.

"I can't be bothered with it all raarrlly. My Dad's matching my income, so it's not like I actually need a job. Just doing it 'cos my Mum's a fucking bitch and said I had to."

"I see"

"Well, I think we should get a cleaner," she repeated, as if that would decide the matter. "I thought I was just going to be a *shallaaay* assistant. You know, with a bit of light cooking. Looking after this *shallaaay* is, like, a full time *job*. It's *ridiculous*. When am I going to ski?"

One has to wonder what the fuck she's doing here, quite frankly. I presume her Mummy wanted to domesticate her to a level where she was able to cater for whichever floppy haired, cross-eyed cousin she's betrothed to marry, although I have my suspicions that she's a raving lesbian.

During our first week in the chalet, after countless hours spent waxing the dining-room floor, shoveling snow, scrubbing and re-scrubbing the oven, buffing toilets, hoovering acres of carpet and sofa, replacing dozens of bulbs, scrubbing mould from the hot-tub and de-greasing all the pots and pans, I was immensely pissed off, but Irksome-Blonde-19-Year-Old was scandalized to the point of threatening to *call her parents*. Gasp!

Not long after that it began to sink in. My fellow Chalet Bitch, the person with whom I had envisaged sharing the burden with all season and having lots of skiing fun, was a complete buffoon. She never skis; she's always too hung over or too lazy. She's a Kevin - a stroppy teenager. I did not sign up to be her nanny, but the creature cannot cope with life. The stuff that comes out of her mouth scores pretty high on my own personal list of "most preposterously stupid questions and statements I have ever heard."

Some particularly choice examples include:

"Are we in France or Switzerland?" (This after a month of living in the resort)

"Do you spell 'chalet' with an 'S'?"

"Why don't the lifts go up both sides? It'd make the queues smaller."

"Are potatoes dairy or vegetable?"

Despite having recently been put through a five grand cooking course by her Mummy, I have personally seen her put raw oats on top of an apple crumble and try to serve it without cooking. Once, she put shallots into a stew, whole and unpeeled, having asked me whether they were prunes only thirty seconds earlier. She also once threw away an entire bag of fresh beef, after thinking the butcher had mistakenly delivered a "bag of guts", and insisted on 'deboning' a beautiful leg of lamb. She requires micromanaging. Yes, as I have said, this is the sort of fuckbucket that Tour Operators employ to cook your food.

A Chance Meeting

As I scale the stairs into the Man of Leisure's apartment one afternoon, Cheese, his best friend, is sitting in his ski gear, as usual, fiddling with something on his computer.

"What are you doing?" I ask collapsing on the ancient little sofa, littered with paisley cushions. He has his feet, still encased in ski boots, up on the coffee table, close to knocking over a priceless-looking hand painted vase and crushing a pair of vintage ski goggles. The place is full of little family knickknacks – badges, slalom medals, technical books and magazines, a pair of wooden snowshoes. On the walls there are myriad colour and black and white photographs of beautiful people with flowing hair from the seventies, doing cross country and slalom, or riding motorcycles on mountain roads. Several cherubic infants in lace-up, antique ski boots and itchy, patterned wool sweaters, squint uncertainly from above the copper fireplace. In one photo, a clutch of skis and a crew of permed girls are hanging, giggling, out of a convertible Sunbeam Talbot. The driver is a slick-headed boy with a cocky expression. Clearly the genetic source of the neatly arranged good-looks of our host.

"I'm nerding," Cheese murmurs, not glancing up.

"Ah, is this a verb now? To nerd. I nerd, you nerd, he she it nerds…" I lean forward and help myself to some congealed bits of cheese stuck to the raclette machine that sits on the table, perpetually unclean.

"Where are the others?"

Cheese points up the stairs. "Haven't surfaced since 2.30 this afternoon,"

Cheese is a mysterious beast that appears to spend his entire life sitting around downloading ski porn and buying second hand kit on eBay. He has over nine pairs of skis, and allegedly he's in race training, but I have never actually seen him ski. His figure is more what you'd expect from a donut eating champion than a giant slalom pro.

"Oh my God," yawns the Man of Leisure, appearing in the doorway in pink, stretchy underpants. He scratches his nuts. "Today was *sooooo* difficult."

He's been instructing a family of Iranians with expensive taste. Their interest in skiing extends only to cursory runs, in between long lunches, with a ski instructor on hand in case of emergencies. They have a penchant for feasting at the flashiest eateries they can find on the mountain, and therefore The Man of Leisure has been mostly living off beef Carpaccio and sushi all week.

"This morning they rang me at 9 and said not to come until 10.30 because it was foggy. Then at 12 they got tired so we went for lunch,"

"I hate you," I mutter, recalling the forty five minute disagreement I had with a bottle of oven cleaner and a scouring pad at around 10.30 this very morning.

"Morning all," says the Foxy Chef, coming downstairs with shagged hair, wearing another pair of the Man of Leisure's underpants and leaning over to pick some lumps of cheese from the raclette machine. Her bedfellow cocks his head to one side as she does so for a better view of her arse.

"Look, are we going out or what?" I say, getting impatient. "I didn't hike all the way here to listen to you whine about beef Carpaccio."

"I'm going for a smoke," the Foxy Chef opens the French window and steps outside barefoot, on tiptoes. On their balcony is the three-legged glittery polar bear covered in snow that the Man of Leisure stole from a shop window last Tuesday. It's draped in a neglected string of fairy lights that boasts only three bulbs.

"Look, I keep telling you, it wasn't beef Carpaccio today, it was Salmon Tartare and a hundred and twenty Euro steak," he rubs his stomach somewhat ruefully, stands up and starts lunging to stretch his legs, his boxers far too tightly defining his balls. "God I'm *sick* of truffle oil. I might put some trousers on,"

"Yes, please, please put some trousers on and let's go out!"

Later, at the Drop Inn, Après ski is in full swing. There's a themed night on – 'travellers' – and accordingly, as we enter, a guy dressed in nothing but a flowery blue suitcase, with a retractable handle, is quivering on the doorstep, clutching a cigarette camply between two fingers. He gives us a blurry grin and wobbles.

Inside, shot after shot of putrid mouth-wash-tasting cough mixture is coursing down the throats of revelers in multi-coloured onesies. A band is playing the usual horrendous covers. *"I aaaaaaaam the one and ohhhhhhnlllaaaaay", "Sweeeet home Aaaaalabama!" "Who the fuck is Alice?"* Swarms of seasonnaires are arriving, hard on each other's heels, filling up every inch of the creaky old place with its tattered, cracked ceiling beams and ski memorabilia, until there is no more standing room and they overflow onto the tables. The boards groan forebodingly under the strain of stamping ski boots. Someone is hanging upside down from the ceiling. Pints of sugary beer and alcopops pass from hand to hand. During the uproar I notice the Man of Leisure and the Foxy Chef exiting the toilet together looking sheepish.

Five wines into the evening, I'm struck by wave of gloom and a pang of loneliness which leads me to seek the solace of a bar stool and a whiskey. The din continues all around me, unabated. It's strange how you can feel so alone in a room packed with over-excited young people. I feel suddenly out of place and long in the tooth compared to these bouncy-boobed, shrieking, jabbering youths.

I haven't really acknowledged that there is a tall, sinewy

stranger sitting on the bar stool just beside me. It takes a few minutes for me to become aware that he's staring, as I nurse my drink. Eventually, I glance to my left and realise I'm being examined intently by this freckle-skinned oik, with tangled hair and curly-lashed eyes that lurk beneath the rim of a bandanna emblazoned with 'Yellow Snow'. His long, straight nose points towards a mocking smile spreading across a broad set of lips. I'm instantly impressed by his exotic appearance. Most girls usually are, I bet. A Hawaiian shirt tucked into a pair of what looks worrying like lederhosen. A profusion of dark facial hair, fingerless gloves unabashedly cupping a half smoked joint and a pint of Guinness.

I don't know it at the time, but I have just met Skater Boy.

"Barman!" he says, waving a hand and pointing at my glass. "She wants some ice in her drink."

Old Man Swiss glares at him.

Clink

I swerve at the glass drunkenly, and then at him.

"Do you mind not defiling my whisky? I like it straight up." His smirk deepens. "Come on Bird. It'll make it last longer. Which means you'll keep sitting here and talking to me."

Smooth. I have to hand it to him. "More ice please barman."

Next morning I wake up in his bed with something that smells suspiciously like puke in my hair and a large, pink piece of chewing gum wedged inside my arse crack.

I have no idea…

Rules for the Chalet Bitch:
A general beginner's guide (cont.)

5. Do – play close attention to fashion. One must wear a (preferably neon, colourful) knitted hat with obligatory huge pompom at ALL times. Whether out riding, hanging out in the bar or cleaning toilets....possibly sometimes while sleeping.

6. Do - wear the most clashing combination of neon colours you can find, preferably baggy ski pants and goggles. Never sunglasses. 'Punterish' gear - anything by Spyder, for example, anything with fur or that is (snow preserve us) shiny is basically social suicide.

7. Do – use words such as 'Sick', 'Badass', 'Rad' and 'Righteous' to describe skiing, skiers and ski gear without any hint of irony or embarrassment.

8. Don't - use blades. Ever. Just not done kiddies. You look like a cunt.

Who's Afraid of My Big Bad Cunt?

As you may or may not have gathered, cunt is one of my favourite words.

I realise, of course, that most people don't think it's very nice for a young lady to go around throwing her see you next Tuesdays about in such a flagrant manner. I realise that, by using it so often (along with all the other profanities I am guilty of), I leave myself open to the criticism of having a limited vocabulary. I also realise that it's pretty much the most offensive word my mother tongue has to proffer. So let me just clarify one point:

I'm not stupid. I'm just vulgar.

When I was a kid, my parents argued; a lot. They would have wild, catastrophic, screaming and slanging matches, where my mother would pursue my father around the house, practically at gunpoint, shrieking and swearing. If my Dad really wanted to upset my mother, that's what he'd call her – cunt - and it worked. It used to really, really offend and destroy her when he used that word. In one utterance, he could take her dignity and erase all respect. Seeing the effect it had on my mother terrified me.

Cunt.

I'll tell you what I find offensive; that there is a word of such power, of which some people – mainly women – are actually frightened. Some people actually physically recoil from it. Why? Why should it be that the most unpleasant thing you can call another person is another word for lady-garden?

Twat's not so bad, is it? But how come there isn't a worse word for penis than cock? If you call someone a penis/cock/wanker, etc, it's mostly just funny. But cunt? That's untouchable. It twists your mouth into a certain shape. You bark it. You cough it out, like a demon. It's been given some kind of bitter, dirty and aggressive connotation that it never used to have.

It wasn't always considered so vile and obscene. It was those patriarchal pussy-haters, the Victorians that did the damage. Once upon a time, (I'm talking millennia ago) a 'cunt' was a powerful, kick-ass lady, to be admired and revered. Where do you think the words 'country' and 'kin' derive from?

The most logical way of counteracting all the negativity would be to start going around calling ladies I like 'Lovely Cunts', and I did try this for a while. Mostly it went down like a sack of turds in a swamp. No. The world, and particularly women kind, as I'm sure Germaine Greer would attest, is not quite ready for this yet. People, I find, (mostly women) have this irrepressible fear of the word and are therefore, in my opinion, essentially afraid of their own bits.

Look at it this way. When a man goes for a pee, he touches his penis without even thinking about it. But women are not supposed to touch their fannies. We have to sit down and hope that the wee doesn't go all over the flaps and that the stream doesn't get misdirected down our legs – which happens sometimes. Even though, what with the pelvic floor muscles etc, most of us could knock spots off any chap in a pissing contest. Why aren't we taught to have a little re-arrange of ourselves down there before we go? It would make more sense, but no. Women are taught it's unhygienic, even indecorous, to do so. You must only touch yourself through the protective barrier of toilet paper.

Well, I decided many years ago, that I refuse to be offended by that word any more. What's to fear? It's a marvelous word. It has such presence...Cunt. What a cunt!

You sir, are a cunt!

I called him a cunt, and now I'm calling you one. CUNT! It has such impact when a woman uses it. No one expects it. If it's going to be an insult, fine. It shall be *my* insult, because I have one. It's the most spectacular of utterances. I'm reclaiming it for womankind. If anyone's going to use our vaginas to insult people, it ought to be us, after all.

Spread Eagle in the Hidden Valley

"Where are you?"

"...I'm here..."

"...where's here?"

"I don't fucking know, where are *you?*"

I can hear him mutter something vehement and unintelligible.

"Can you see me?"

"No, but....I'm above you, I think."

"Can you get up?"

"Yes"

Ooofff.

"No."

"Ah....*bollocks...*"

"Um.... Hold on....it's ok. Just.... give me a minute."

I am indeed trying to get up but the tree I've just had an altercation with has other ideas. It's small, not even my height, and prickly with cones. It seems to have enveloped me into its branches in an embrace of Satan. My skis are either side of it, my arse is in the snow and my ski poles are underneath me. Cold fingers are creeping over the waistband of my ski pants most horribly. My goggles are steamed to blindness and the snow is so deep that every time I try to lever myself upright my arms simply sink in up to the elbow. I don't know where I am, or where he is or the piste for that matter. I would very much like to get out of this. Now please. I'd like to just click my fingers and just be magically out of it and back on the piste. But that is not going to happen. Many people would fall into a panic in this situation. But not I. No... It's true. I am that cartoon ski person who's spread eagled a tree. But don't panic.

I'm only thankful Skater Boy can't actually see me.

"Gonna have to clip out," I inform him. Best to keep him

in the loop. I hear no reply to this, but the puff of smoke I can see snaking up from behind the drop to the south of me tells me that Skater Boy has hit upon this handy break in proceedings as an excellent opportunity for a blaze.

In all absolute honesty, I am way out of my depth. At some point, during a perfectly straight forward afternoon's skiing, he pulled up at the side of a narrow path taking us comfortably down to a bubble lift and peered over the edge of the area between the two pistes at the feathery dunes of fresh powder below. I too squinted down and took in, with mixed emotions, thick, fresh inviting snow decorated liberally with trees, the odd boulder, and the track marks of other idiots who'd thought this was a sensible short cut on a low visibility, high avalanche-risk day. Personally, I was surprised it wasn't littered with frozen corpses but Skater Boy simply shrugged and said:

"Looks alright to me. Dropping in…" before launching himself over the edge into fresh tracks. This was half an hour ago. Since then each of my skis has deserted me at least once, the first time it took twenty minutes of digging to find because it had somehow got buried vertically. You try finding a white ski tip with the visible surface area of a pencil in a blind, white, three dimensional search area, somewhere inside a tree run, where you can't even see your hand in front of your face. It would have been a tall order for a professional search and rescue team, let alone someone suffering from disorientation, paranoia and a severe case of the munchies.

The tree run was a lot steeper after we got past the initial gentle entry point and required extremely fast thinking. It was a seemingly endless series of tight, winding turns through this admittedly breathtaking glade laden with snow, dodging branches and making split second directional decisions. Very technical and quite literally terrifying. It was only a matter of time until I made a serious misjudgment.

"You alright bird?" some moments later I hear his voice again. I'm panting a lot, and swearing, trying to get myself upright, get this fucking tree out of my face and my skis back on. He can probably hear all of this.

"Yes, uh, fine. Coming…"

Actually I'm knackered and not a little bit humiliated. It's my own fault for trying to look like a big, clever girl in front of him. The man is a fine skier. In fact, I think he's possibly sexier on skis than off. He spends most of his time looking for large precipices to fling himself from, usually stoned off his tits. All wrong for me. I am exceedingly earth bound. His inappropriateness for me has been increasingly apparent, thus I have been trying to wean off him, and failing, since the chewing-gum-in-arse-crack incident. Waking up each morning in the tiny apartment of this absurd, stoned, grubby mountain-bum is like coming round and finding you've been handcuffed to a Tasmanian devil, particularly when there is blue sky and powder snow around, when he will dance round chattering and searching for his essential paraphernalia – ski socks, one-piece, t-shirt, 80s headband, goggles, Rizlas, baccie, weed and mobile phone. These are usually either in a crusty heap, underneath something Scruffy-but-Handsome owns, or wedged down the side of the bed, covered in the ash he flicked there the previous evening. He can veer from quiet contemplation to possessed gremlin in a flash. One moment nursing your sore shins with arnica and soothing words, the next prancing round the room holding his nuts in a 'brain' shape, or bursting into the bathroom, leaping on you and pretending to rut you before pulling his pants down, tucking his testicles between his legs and demonstrating what he proudly announces is called 'The No-hander Man-gina Fruit Bowl'. There is no escaping the party. It bounces in the door and comes to you.

Luckily, I was too drunk to notice the state of his apartment the first night we hooked up. That was until after the deed was done (a swift, inebriated struggle in the dark). He leapt up, turned on all the lights and I found myself in the cold glare of reality, perched on the side of his lopsided futon, disheveled and wrapped in a duvet full of cigarette ash, surveying the wreckage of the flat and the horror story of the bed. The place was absolutely tiny, and filled to exploding point with junk. Rubbish, clothes, ski equipment, shoes, mattresses, pots and pans, bags, papers, a broken TV – and bizarre things like a car tyre and an old plastic Christmas tree. The general décor and mood was very reminiscent of a crack den.

Boys are gross at the best of times, but this was incredible. There were rotting raw potatoes, hairs, dirty underwear, shards of glass and several used condoms littering the blackened floor tiles. Rolling tobacco was stuck to everything. His bare mattress bore strange skid marks and was crispy with several months of pizza remnants –it was like lying on gravel. The pillow ....to be honest, I can`t even describe the pillow. Let's just say it was a sort of a greyish colour and for some unknown reason smelt of Tabasco. The duvet smelt rank too – a sort of mixture of rotten milk, feet and sweat and you'd need some chutzpah to call the futon a bed. I was seized by a horrible speculation: How many other people has he had sex with in this bed under this very duvet? A no-doubt loathsome variety of grubby, smelly and no doubt frisky ski bums who have each made their own troubling bodily contributions of hair, skin, cum and sweat.

Anyway, there he was, crawling around on his hands and knees, searching under furniture and rifling through piles of clothes. The crevice of his bony behind was on show over the top of his well-worn underpants. It was becoming clear that this person lived in a permanent state of crisis.

"I know there's a Rizla in this flat", he began flinging belongings all over the place.

"Um… have you checked all your pockets?'

"Yeah yeah there's none in them…come on Bird, give us a hand…"

"I'm not scrabbling around on the floor, mate. It's 4am"

"A real friend would"

"Look, I'm not all that bothered about a spliff really. Have you got any booze?"

"Think there's some vodka in the cupboard" he wafted his arm in the direction of the kitchen – a black hole of doom laden with filthy pots and pans. "I need a spliff."

I sighed. After fifteen minutes of this treasure hunt, I was beginning to get the message. My feminine charms were no match for a good blaze.

"You're going to have to roll with a bit of something else – look how about one of these receipts or something?" I offered, selecting things from the cornucopia of crap on the floor, "this is getting ridiculous".

He had started scratching around under the futon with his fingernails, like a pig snuffling for truffles. I had to give it to him. He had tenacity.

"Fuck that…it hasn't come to that yet…Eh up! Yes! Mega Bon!" he cried, triumphantly holding aloft his trophy - a skanky old cigarette paper.

"Jesus, how long has that been there?"

"Don't care. Main thing is it burns. Now. Where's the baccie?"

How far away from all of this did the nicely turned out house I'd shared with my ex seem now, with its unbroken furniture, art, curtains, cutlery, hoover, bath salts and fruit bowl? One thing was certain though; there was something about this lifestyle - the inherent grime, the fucking around, the grim relentlessness that was starting to seduce me. It was almost as if I was *enjoying* the filth. Skater Boy's world was so far removed from the ordered, corporate life I had left, it felt thoroughly anarchic. I had pulled back the crisp white cover of snow from the Alpine bed and found, underneath it, filth galore. I'd never been with someone so grotty. I liked it.

As I continue to struggle to free myself from my snowy prison I see more smoke drifting up from below the drop and hear his disembodied voice, again:

"Have you sorted yourself out yet, Bird?"

"No…" huffing, wheezing. "I can't get my boot in."

"Well…push!"

"It won't go in!"

"You're not pushing hard enough."

Click

I smile ruefully as the boot slots satisfyingly back into the binding and rest my forehead on my poles for a minute, trying to breathe and not think about how much more of this ordeal I'll have to endure before we reach the safety of the piste. As I slip gingerly around the next corner and coast between the next two trees, I see him sitting down in the snow ahead. My thighs are burning because I'm now nervous and my weight is thrust back. It's a battle to keep both skis in the same direction and at the same speed.

"Eh up…" he says, standing as I come to a stop. "Nice of you to join me,"

I slump into the snow next to him.

"Fuck you clever clogs."

"Sorry," he brushes some snow off my goggles and gives me that gently mocking smile. "I've just never seen someone faff quite so much."

I look dejectedly at him. "I'm tired…"

He stubs out his joint.

"Ah, never mind bird. It's not far now. Just around that

corner, there's nice safe piste."

"Thank fuck."

He offers me a hand up. "C'mon let's go and have a pint, before you hurt yourself. You need chemicals with anaesthetic properties...."

This is My Proper Job

Burning the candle at both ends? Ha! I laugh in the face of it! Try blow torching the fucker from all angles and dipping it into liquid hot magma. I went skiing today having got home at 5am and barely slept. Hauling myself from the vinegary juices of my bed, where I had been poaching for only 1 hour, I then worked a five-hour shift, and I'll be doing it all again tonight. Sleep deprived, jaded. Sick from Jager. My muscles were like jelly on the slopes today and simply standing upright was a challenge but, somehow, roaring down hill strapped to two planks at high speed seemed surprisingly easy. A face full of freezing wind is a failsafe cure for hangovers of any kind.

Life is pain. I am eternally late to finish work and therefore usually still in the pub at 3am, but hideously early to rise. There are hills to walk up, elements to battle with, revolting, sticky cocktails of unmentionable spirits to be poured down my throat, eight-hour airport transfers on treacherous roads, endless cleaning and scraping and polishing, meals to cook, balconies to sweep free of snow...and if you think I'm going to let any of that stop me skiing, or at least sliding with very little control or style, on some of this *neige* stuff, then you've got another think coming.

Not only this, but I am pretty certain I am actually suffering from scurvy. The last time I saw a vegetable was about three months ago. My meals seem to mainly consist of stale croissants, left-over cheese and half-eaten bread, supplemented with left-over yoghurt cake, Jager bombs and scraps from greasy baking trays. I realise now that this is the 'food' included in the contract I signed. The ski company expects me to cater for myself out of the meagre budget they supply, but sadly my guests keep thinking my dinner is their 'seconds'. Bastards.

My Dad has rung me eleven times so far this week. Eventually, I had to answer the phone.

"Poppetto!"

"Hi Dad. How's it going?"

"Oh, fine thanks. Fine!"

"What've you been up to?"

"Oh, not much."

We have this exact, identical conversation every time we speak. And there is always a pause at this point while I wait for him to tell me what the reason for the call is, and he tries to think of one.

"So…is it bloody awful?"

"No, no – it's great, Dad. I'm having a great time."

"I expect they're working you like some sort of slave there are they?" he was speaking in the same conspiratorial tone he used when I was nine years old and ringing him up in tears from this summer camp thing Mum used to send me on, which I hated. "Lots of wankers with big cheque books pinching your arse, I expect?"

"Something like that…"

"If you don't like it, you know you can just say, and I'll be on the next flight out to come and get you."

"Dad don't be stupid. I think I can probably get myself home if it all goes tits up. Anyway it really is fine."

"Do you need any money?"

"Uh… n…no, Dad. No really, I'm absolutely fine."

How do they do it? How do parents do this to you? Turn you into a child in one sentence. He did the same thing when he dropped me off at the coach station in London. Followed me onto the bus, introduced himself to the driver and asked him to look after me as if he was sending me on a school field trip. Dad, I know, thinks this whole ski season malarkey is a terrible idea. He never actually says anything to this effect but, whenever we speak, there's a big elephant in the room with a neon flashing sign above its head screaming:

70

"WHAT ABOUT YOUR CAREER?!"
"WHAT ABOUT YOUR CAREER?!"
"WHAT ABOUT YOUR CAREER?!"

He is not alone. Alongside any seemingly capricious choice of career break, or change, one must always endure the obligatory, totally deflating lecture from various people who think they know what's best for you about life, the universe and everything. There was, in fact, a complete onslaught of disapproving friends and relations to deal with, offering various opinions such as:

"With independence comes responsibility to make adult decisions" (The Big Brother)

And

"Most people hate their jobs. You just have to get on with it" (my perpetually pregnant friend Fiona)

And

"Boredom is a state of mind. Making a change because you're bored won't help. The problems will follow you," (my, in hindsight, very bad shrink)

And

"Are you certain this is the right decision? You really need a five year plan and an exit strategy before you do anything in life." (My boss)

Shazzer's take was slightly different:

"What a load of depressingly conformist, unadventurous bollocks!" she barked. "If we all did that nothing interesting would ever happen, and there would be no gin and tonics, or fireworks, or bubble wrap, or Glastonbury Festival, or butt plugs, or iPhones or Katie Price. Christ on a bike, people are unfathomably boring sometimes. Look, what do you want on your gravestone? 'She paid her mortgage on time every month'? Or 'she had her cake and ate it?' For God's sake. This is chuffing well *it* you know? You only get one life. And all these conventional types who are afraid of taking risks can go *do* one."

Like I said, sometimes I used to think Shazzer was the only sane person in the whole world. Turns out I was wrong about that, too.

I remember lying in bed on the night she died, running her words through my head like a mantra, waiting in vain for sleep to creep over me. Wondering what dreadful, undeniable force had stolen her from me and how words can take on such a different meaning with hindsight and interpretation. How bleak her internal struggle must have been. I blamed myself for not seeing.

Almost as if he'd sensed my sleeplessness, Dad had appeared in the door with two tumblers and a bottle of whiskey. Long-suffering Dad, who'd caught us smoking out of the window so many times when we were fifteen, and collected us, staggering and vomiting, from numerous pubs that we shouldn't have been in. We sank most of that bottle of whiskey, and then Dad put an arm around me and sadly said: "Poor old Shazzer."

And then I cried and finally fell asleep…

"…Well, if you do change your mind, you know it's absolutely no problem. We can get you home," Dad was saying at the other end of the line.

"I know, Dad, I know. It's France, not Ulaanbaatar."

"Never fear, Daddy's here."

"Dad, please."

"Oh go on, say it."

Christ.

"Ok." I whisper it. "Never fear… Daddy's here."

The Evils of the Studio Apartment

Since my demotion into the wonderful world of Chalet Bitching I have also had to undergo a quite shocking demotion in living arrangements. I have gone from living in my own three bedroom home, *avec* super king size bed, memory foam mattress, fluffy carpets and dressing room, huge marble and tile bathroom, and a separate cupboard specifically for my handbags, to living in what is essentially a hovel with three other girls and a shit load of ski equipment. The mentality of putting all one's treasured possessions, glamourous outfits, furniture and high heels into storage in order to share a space the size of a phone box with several stroppy teenagers, two snowboards, five pairs of skis, nine ski boots and four hair dryers has been quite a leap.

The last time I shared a room with someone other than a boyfriend was at boarding school – and I wasn't terribly fond of it then. I hate talking to people in the morning and, most of all, I can't bear to be in a room with someone else who is afraid of mutual silence and feels the need to cluck about bollocks all the time, which all three of my roommates are guilty of. Actually, I hate talking to people in general, now I think of it, and I like to mooch around in my pants and pick my nose unobserved. And while we're on the subject, in a set up such as this, how and where are you meant to have a wank? I like to flick the bean at bed time - so sue me. It helps me sleep. Something I never expected to have to do at this stage in life is to re-awaken the boarding-school-honed art of the imperceptible stealth wank. It requires extreme dexterity and the ability to lie completely still and silent while in the throes of pleasure, thereby almost asphyxiating oneself under the duvet. It often results in an intensely sore wrist and is not particularly satisfactory when not accompanied by porn.

That said, though, it's actually not the mentality of sharing or the sore wrist that's the problem…

Because we spend 90% of our time cleaning other people's shit from toilet pans, dishes and floors, said hovel is never cleaned. And it started out fustily filthy anyway. I mean, in the sense that you have to dust off and wipe your feet before getting into bed if you want to avoid crumbs of unidentified mildewed goype all over your sheets. There is crap everywhere. Ski equipment, knickers hanging off curtain rails to dry, crispy ski socks which have been re-used far, far too many times sitting on radiators, Snickers wrappers, condoms.

Well yes, particularly condoms. And this is the real issue. There's nowhere private to shag. Not that this presented much of an obstacle for the Irksome-Blonde-19-Year-Old last night.

I awoke, bleary eyed from an afternoon and evening of heavy après ski, at about 4am. From of the window opposite my bed, the 'Champois' sign that casts a perpetual seedy orange-blue glow into our gaff burned mercilessly onto my retinas. Every morning, the name of that purveyor of unfathomably expensive diamante decorated ski clothes and accessories for children invades my skull like an axe slicing through an over-ripe melon. I lay there wretchedly for a few minutes, bathed in its glow amid the suffocating blackened stew of our apartment wondering idly why I had been un-timely ripped from the womb of sleep. Then it all came into disturbing focus. Those scraping noises, that squeak-squeak, squeak-squeak, the heavy breathing. The fact that my bed was being shunted rhythmically by the dresser, because some-thing else was rhythmically shunting the dresser. The humpy shapes moving in the orange light cast onto the bed below the window.

Oh. Right. Great. Yeah. The Irksome-Blonde-19-Year-Old is having the back bashed out of her by someone (or something). I can't move or even cough as disturbing them would make this even more excruciating. My head is pounding and I can't even reach for the Nurofen, or my iPod to block out the slapping noises. The fuckers are in my coat.

And I really need a pee.

Resort Meeting

The next day, still bleary and grumpy from my interrupted night's sleep and the unpleasant wake up call, I find myself at our weekly resort meeting. Presumably, one is supposed to be grateful for the kind gesture of being called in off the slopes an hour earlier than usual, fobbed off with a booze-free hot chocolate and made to listen to The Resort Manager wank on about *'really knuckling down'* over the Christmas period. Yawn.

As I enter The Bar pursued by a swirl of snow flakes, Bon Jovi blares from the tinny speakers (why must one be constantly subjected to this hairy, cleft-chinned wailer?). At a corner table, various seasonnaires stare slack-jawed at the TV screen above the bar featuring a bouffy-haired montage called 'Now That's What I Call an 80s Ski Movie'. I note Irksome-Blonde-19-Year-Old and China done up to the nines in laddered black tights, aspirationally tight denim shorts, beehive barnets and a volcanic crust of make-up. Are they planning to go to work looking like Amy Winehouse's ugly sisters? I imagine they have dressed like this in order to fast track straight to drunken oblivion after service without having to go home and get changed. Excellent, this is very entertaining and should go down like a poo in a swimming pool with the Resort Manager, with any luck.

Ah. She is here already. Lovely. Wittering on about some bollocks. Next to her, sits The Geordie Ninja, looking bored and nursing a pint; our chain-smoking, drug-dealing odd-job man and driver, so named for his uncanny ability to disappear under the radar during an emergency (chalet power cut, blocked drain, sewage leaking into hallway, roof on fire) and then pop up somewhere the next day looking hung over and furtive (usually around supper time when he knows there are free leftovers) claiming he's been date raped. It turned out, this morning, in the cold light of day, that it was the Geordie Ninja who'd been rhythmically shunting the Irksome-Blonde-19-Year-Old last night. This fact is quietly terrifying when you think between them they could probably start an Alp-wide plague of venereal disease. Deafeningly terrifying when you realise that I will now be forced to listen to his balls slapping against her arse at 4am on a regular basis.

"Now I just want to reiterate what was said to you at the start of the season, okeydokes?" The Resort Manager is saying to the rest of the group, assembled round the corner table. "Don't think you can pull the wool over my eyes. You *won't* be getting sympathy from me if you can't go to work because you've got *flu*" (mid air quotation marks) "or *mid-season blues*" (haughty toss of hair) 'I want to make one thing *absolutely* clear, okeydokes? As someone who's worked many *many* seasons and is as much your mentor as your boss," (ha! She couldn't mentor a dung beetle onto a cowpat) "I can tell you right now there's only going to be room in your life for either working and skiing, or working and drinking – you can't do all three. And I'm *sure* I don't have to tell you your *main priority* out here is doing a good job. Ok? *Okeydokes?*"

This patronising little speech is highly in the Christmas spirit of her. I like her style. China's eyes have started to roll back in her head. I recall the first time I met the Resort Manager, or as I like to call her, *La Vache Qui Ski...* I thought it was odd that she didn't shake my hand – I assumed this was due to some obsessive compulsive or personal space issues. Swiftly thereafter, I realised it would, in fact, be more accurately compared to the sort of advanced anthrophobia you might associate with, say, Hitler, or Pol Pot. On our arrival day, after a forty five minute wait in the fast descending snow, she arrived in a minibus with chains on the wheels to collect those of us who had been dropped off at the coach depot. She brought with her the same nasty, growling little shit of a Bichon Frise that accompanies her everywhere she goes. It looks like a Toulouse sausage that's been rolled in bum fluff. Broom-handle thin and immaculate, her fashion sense was rather terrifying - leather trousers and a coat that looked like a frighteningly expensive stuffed bin bag trimmed on the hood with the feathers of an endangered species. She is rather ornithological-looking in general, actually, like a bird of prey, with a hook nose, and sharp talons, all topped off with a poker straight coal-black bob. I suppose she's rather attractive, if you like a passive aggressive dominatrix. Couldn't stop a pig in a passage, mind you.

"So sorry I kept you waiting, the hairdresser took an absolute age and then I had to wait for the logistics man to put the chains on. Gosh, the weather is just awful isn't it?" By 'logistics man' we all soon realised she meant the Geordie Ninja.

She looked down at my freezing feet through narrowed eyes. I had ballet flats on, which I'll admit had been a school girl error in terms of arrival footwear. In my head, I could hear Shazzer heckling: "You twat! What sort of dick turns up in a frozen wilderness wearing ballet shoes?" My snow boots were stashed somewhere at the bottom of my suitcase.

"Oh my," she said, "What an odd choice of shoes. You're not going to make a habit of wearing *those* I hope. You won't last long…" This was met with general guffawing and snorting from the likes of Irksome-Blonde-19-Year-Old and China, the former of whom, I might add, was wearing ballet flats as well. I couldn't help thinking La Vache Qui Ski's own choice of vertiginous, fur lined Alpine footwear was pretty useless too, although on the other hand quite versatile if you were surviving on the arctic tundra and fancied braining a small animal for lunch.

From that second onwards, I knew I was going to despise this self-aggrandising, self-serving little twerp. I mean, I was open to respectfully despising her, but that was riding on the idea that there was a possibility of her being good at her job, which she and Head Office appear to think she is, but her entire long-suffering, brow-beaten staff (going back several seasonal generations, if rumours are to be believed) are certain she is not. Later that day, she drove me to my chalet and followed me up the stairs to the entrance way, empty handed, and without offering to help carry anything. She seemed content to watch me sweat and struggle with my many heavy bags. The porch is ornate and tiny, and when we arrived there together, we both tried to cram ourselves into it with all my gear plus her large handbag.

This was the very definition of awkward.

After accidentally elbowing her in the ribs a couple of times, I tried to shuffle into a different position and we found ourselves nose to nose.

"Oooh, this is a bit cosy," she laughed, shrilly. My breath was on her chin. She looked positively stricken at being this close to another mammal. There was a hint of mania in her laugh, which increased, rather than diffused the tension of the scene.

"Okeydokes, I tell you what...could you just stand with your back to me while I find the key? Ok? Right." The request threw me slightly, so I hesitated, but she continued to grin, hysterically, her eyes wide and expectant. So I complied. She started rummaging in her handbag. Then her phone rang and she answered it.

"Christa! Yes, we're here. Yes absolutely, I'll get her to work immediately. Okaaaaay. Okeydokes."

As I stood there facing the wall, waiting for her to finish, I couldn't quite work out whether I should feel humiliated or not. I could tell what she was trying to do. Her prim, sugar-pie demeanour didn't fool me for a second. My bitch-ometer is finally tuned.

As I come round from my reverie, La Vache Qui Ski seems to have finished her lecture. "Okeydokes" she says standing up to leave, "oh yes, and I'll be doing spot checks tomorrow, so make sure your chalets are all looking shipshape for Christmas."

"Won't you stay for another drink?" I ask through clenched teeth. It hasn't gone unnoticed by me that she has said nothing about Irksome-Blonde-19-Year-Old's inappropriate workwear. If I turned up for work in that, I'm pretty sure she'd have a go. However, her main motivation, lest we forget, is to make herself look good to Head Office while doing as little as humanly possible - and needling the daughter of Christa's best friend (you've guessed it – the Irksome one) doesn't fit into that framework.

"Haha! No. I *wish* I had as little to do as you lot," – a note of sourness – "I've got mountains of paper work to deal with, as you know…"

"What do you think she does for fun?" Calamity frowns, as we watch her bowlegged, boney arse disappear out into the snow.

"I imagine she sits alone in a darkened room, gnawing on the bones of last season's Chalet Bitches," I say. "That's how she feeds."

"Either that or masturbating over a picture of Christa," nods Calamity. "Now….thanks to all that bullshit, we've only got twenty minutes to get shit faced before work. Two pints and a Jager bomb chaser?"

"Better make it a Mega Drive. I have a feeling this is going to be a long week."

Pet Hates

Just before I left the chalet today, I received a text from Calamity, who I was due to go skiing with. Calamity, who has asthma and looks so fragile that her arms might fall off if she sneezes too hard, but has the acerbic tongue of a viper.

"Going to be late," it said. "There is a big bag of human faeces on my kitchen work surface."

Hmmm. I'm guessing either fetishists or Russian.

"Put it in the cake." I replied.

"Will do. Fucking babies. The mother will die."

You know, it always fascinates me the way some Punters treat the people who are in charge of preparing and serving them their food and handling their possessions...so naively trusting. So short-sighted.

Later, as I was settling myself onto the chairlift, my phone rang for the fifth time in fifteen minutes

"For fuck's sake..."

"Who's that?" said Calamity, without real interest, sitting next to me in a grubby pink jacket, snowboard dangling. Behind her a vertiginous panorama stretched away into the distance.

"I dunno...Some cunt," I said.

The phone was buried somewhere inaccessible, which would require removal of gloves, and a lot of unzipping, and I knew exactly who it was anyway. Leticia Fucking De Witt. Again. Lesson learned. *Never* give your personal phone number out to your chalet guests.

"Yes, vee are in ze chalet. Vere are you?" she cawed down the phone at me. No need to say 'hello', clearly. "Vee need some extra bread for ze children's lunch and then to be driven to ze shops afterwards."

Madame De Witt is Belgian and whether by pig ignorance, wilful intransigence or simply by virtue of being a mean old bitch, seems not to understand the politely explained concept that I have specific working hours (which she had already eaten well into today just by asking to be driven to the shops at three minutes to eleven). I have tried to explain but it's not getting through. She presumes I am her personal lackey, available round the clock to cater to her every whim.

From the moment she set foot in the chalet, she behaved like an all-round demanding dragon and royal tumour in the tits. It was rather like having The Grand High Witch round for dinner every night, complete with wart-encrusted foot long nose, chin that entered the room three minutes before the rest of her and squawky voice. She had a most unsettling way of saying 'children'

"....*chiiiiildrrrrrren....*" and peering at you out of the corner of her eye, like a vulture examining carrion.

Within twenty four hours her family had performed a number on the chalet, as if a couple of pigs had broken in and had a shag in every room, with possessions and food scattered everywhere. Worst of all, she didn't ski, so had nothing else to do but lurk around waiting to pounce on me, with no qualms about shrieking my name down the stairs and summoning me from the kitchen for some pointless exercise, indicating random objects and dispensing irritating little titbits of advice like:

"A place for *everysing* and *everysing* in its place!"

I fantasised about various sadistic revenge tactics I could use to torture this nightmare, like hammering nine-inch tent pegs into her face. On the evening they arrived, I was detained in the bathroom for half an hour while she explained how her son Phillippe liked his towels folded rather than rolled.

"Love," I thought, *"I really couldn't give a shit."*

One evening at dinner, Phillippe, the pervy old rogue, invited me to crawl around the table with a Mont D'or cheese and a plate of rosemary roast potatoes on my back. I can only assume he thought this was funny. I just thought he was a cunt. He then smacked me on the bottom when I was lighting the fire, which perhaps explained why his wife Paulette spent the week looking as if she was constantly sucking on a lemon. A shrivelled up prune of a woman who seemed physically unable to speak. Mind you, with a mother-in-law like that, I'd probably keep quiet too. One half expected them to leap up from the dinner table, tear off their faces with a triumphant shriek and turn everyone into mice.

"Sorry Mrs. Dewitt. I'm afraid I'm not available now." For the fifth time, I politely explained that I wouldn't be back until after 4pm, at which she tutted disapprovingly and hung up the phone. In conclusion, I must say there are only two things in life I hate. Intolerance. And Belgians.

Rules for the Chalet Bitch (cont.)

So, at this point, I should probably mention the dilemmas of mountain fashion. Packing for the season, after all, was a major crisis for me, I must be honest. How does one plan in a fashion-ological type way for six months in a world populated by Russian snow bunnies and the cream of British gap year society? Which style camp does one fall into? How does one know what one will need, or what image one will want to project amongst the slut-bag leggings and grunge get up of seasonnaires the Alps over? What constitutes cool in this land doesn't necessarily coincide with what's cool on a London high street.

"Hmmmm, wonder if one pair of heels is enough," I had mused, staring blankly into my wardrobe. "Suppose there will be a weekly turnover of guests, therefore no need to worry about the same person seeing me in the same outfit twice. Tough choices though."

It was an entirely flummoxing state of affairs.

In the end, I took the following:

1x vintage Fur Coat (inherited from my Mum – in the hope of finding an excuse to wear without getting lynched by psychotic bunny-hugging protesters)

2 x little Black Dresses, 1 lacy, 1 low cut (for seduction of hot ski instructors)

1 pair black sky-scraper heels (obvo not v. practical, but just in case)

1 pair Ugg boots (for protection of feet against elements)

1 pair Thigh-high boots (sexy, yet warm in the hamstring

area – so actually v practical.)

1 pair black work jeans / 2 black work shirts

3 x thick woolen jumpers (various, to be teamed with leggings and thigh-high boots in nonchalant, sexy-chalet-girl-about-resort type of way.)

Various ski socks, thermal underwear, tights etc

1 pair super-tight black salopettes for showing off toned skier's arse (see earlier ski instructor reference)

1 x fur-trimmed ski jacket (also black)

1 x fox fur hat (channeling Julie Christie circa Dr Zhivago)

1 x warm fleece (not really my style but needs must)

Helmet, Sunglasses, Gloves

1 x Hip flask

1 x camera (for taking pictures of the pretty snow)

…all of which, in hindsight, brings me to Rule 9.

9. If you're a seasonnaire, don't EVER wear fur, not even fake fur or a fur trimmed hood, unless you want to be socially excluded and mocked (because you look like a Russian punter). I made this mistake – just once. Shortly thereafter, I went out and bought myself some steezy, multi coloured gear and consigned all the above civilian clothes, plus the skin tight salopettes and the fur-trimmed black ski jacket to the back of the wardrobe. Steeze, leggings and big jumpers are the order of the day. There. Consider yourself saved from social suicide.

Scruffy-but-Handsome

11.10pm.

A floodlit back-road. The crunch of week-old snow under the thick tread of our boots. A couple passing on the other side of the street with a Dalmatian on a diamante leash.

"If you had a choice between losing a limb and losing your penis, which would you go for?"

Scruffy-but-Handsome has on chef whites and a bulky ski jacket. He scratches his beard.

"If I had a choice? A limb. Clearly! No fucking contest."

He and I like to amuse ourselves with important questions such as this after dinner service, as we make our way down the road that leads back to the centre of town.

Questions like, *how many piano tuners do you reckon there are in London?* And *which member of the animal kingdom would you shag if your life depended on it?* ("Defo a walrus. I mean, if you're gonna do it you may as well do it properly." "Yes, and also tusks give you something to hold on to. Sort of super-charged bugger grips…") It's helpful to have such questions on one's mind during the day to alleviate the boredom of constant toilet cleaning.

"Yes, but…you can *sort* of do without a penis, as long as you've still got balls."

"Fuck that! You can *sort* of do without an arm too. I like my penis just where it is, thanks."

As we round the corner of the third hair-pin bend, a white Maybach with blacked-out windows shimmers up the slick road and comes to a smooth stop outside a three-story, chalet. We can see the oversized flat-screen and kitsch antler chandeliers inside on the first floor. Smoke is rising silently from its chimney.

"Besides, if you lost an arm, you could just get loads of useful attachments for the stump so you're prepped for every occasion."

"That is a good point. Like what?"

"Er…. like a beer-holding attachment for a start, or even better, a beer-holding while page turning attachment."

He is carrying a bin bag full of rubbish from his chalet with one hand like a crap Santa, and makes a page-turning motion with the other to illustrate.

"Wouldn't a hand be preferable?"

"You just asked me a theoretical question, I am responding with a theoretical postulation."

"Ok, sorry. Continue."

At the bottom of the hill, just before we reach the town, we stop and I hold the door of the *poubelle* open for him so he can toss the rubbish bag inside.

"Alright then….how about a hoover arm…."

"Where would the dirt go?"

"Smart arse…Ok fine. A wank attachment."

"What, like one of those plastic vagina things?"

"Yes…or a screw in vibrator… That would be awesome."

"Yep," I nod. "I could get on board with one of those."

"Or… alternatively a foot-hand so I could walk on all threes…"

This, and the way he says it with excited, round goggly eyes makes me laugh out loud.

Scruffy-but-Handsome walks on next to me with a laid back, swaggering gait. He is a remarkably grubby rascal - your typical ne'er-do-well studenty-ski-bum-type, and the only person within a fifty mile radius of this place who seems to have any chat. He has verbal diarrhea and a habit of sticking his foot in his mouth a lot, so we get on well. It's useful what with him being Skater Boy's roommate, too, because it gives me someone nice to have a chat with in the mornings. Skater

Boy isn't always in the best of moods before his 7.30am spliff.

This is how I first met Scruffy-but-Handsome. I was in bed, wavering on the cusp of consciousness, buzzing, uncomfortable and throbbing, clasped in Skater Boy's snoring, sticky embrace becoming vaguely aware of that aforementioned mysterious piece of chewing gum stuck between my buttocks. I opened one eye and was rewarded with the sight of Scruffy-but-Handsome's arse coming towards my face. I made a muffled objection at which he nearly jumped a foot in the air. He toppled to the floor, while hurriedly apologising and explaining this couldn't be avoided because he had to climb over our bed on his way down from his perch on The Shelf to go to the bathroom. Skater Boy, as is his wont, was still asleep, so the two of us bonded over roll-up cigarettes and raw frankfurters for breakfast on the balcony. He had a veritable mental archive of 'Yo Mama' jokes, which he could reel off on demand.

"Yo Mama so fat her BMI is measured in acres. Yo Mama so fat when she went to the movies she sat next to everyone. Yo Mama so fat cos every time I roll off her, I give her a cookie"

It turned out, fortuitously, that our chalets were almost opposite each other on the same road and I was pleased, after many a lonely stroll to work, to have company walking up the hill. It was early in the season, before I had learned the many corner-cutting tricks that were to stand me in good stead, before I had learned not to take everything to heart. The rest of the day was a complete disaster of burnt cakes, broken dishes and time-consuming demands from my guests. By the evening, I was struggling to keep it together. I'd had enough, was seriously considering jacking it all in and going home and I found myself having a bit of a 'moment' on the chalet doorstep, trying and failing to light a much-needed cigarette.

I looked up and, for the second time in 24hrs, saw Scruffy-but-Handsome coming towards me, but this time front first and from across the road, backlit by the fairy lights on a tree by his chalet. I snapped brutally at my failed cigarette lighter and chucked it into the snow near his feet. It had been a long day. I was fighting tears with rage.

"Need a light?" he said, picking it up, wiping the snow off and flicking it deftly so that it sprang into a long, juddering flame. It struck me for the first time what an odd union he was of good diction and ridiculously unkempt hair, how his eyes were lively and sparkling and his smile straight and wide. He reminded me, not for the first or last time, of a scrappy terrier that had just been caught foraging in a bin. We smoked together and chatted for a while and then he suddenly leaped to his feet and said, "I know what'll cheer you up!" He scampered across the road into his chalet and reappeared moments later with two bin liners.

I was skeptical.

"Come on. Let's toboggan down to the pub!"

"On those?"

"On these...."

Moments later I was hurtling down a particularly icy black run, back to front in pitch dark, swearing loudly. He disappeared into depthless murk of beyond, shrieking "Fuuuuuuuuuuuuuuuuuck" and scuffing his boots against the snow. My Ugg boots (which were shortly thereafter consigned to aforementioned *poubelle*) were no help. I was plummeting down now. The ski slope fell away beneath me with an aggressive camber round to the right. It swept into a sharp bend that took it through a tunnel under the road.

"Bollocks!" I screamed, as I failed to make the turn and continued advancing in a straight line. Out of the darkness, a chalet wall was approaching me much faster than I was comfortable with. I entered a large snowdrift under the balcony praying that there wasn't anything sharp inside. My hip contacted with something hard.

It said "Ooff!" and so I gathered, it was him.

We lay there in a snowy entanglement of limbs, panting and assessing the damage.

"I think….." he cautiously started patting various parts of his body, "I'm ok….yep, one, two…and three. Bollocks are still intact. Winning."

He got up and shook himself, slightly dazed – the terrier climbing out of a pond.

"What the fuck just happened?" I said, breathlessly, crawling out of the ditch and trying to deal with the hundred weight of snow in my knickers.

As we crossed the road and went into The Drop Inn, he said, "Whose stupid idea was that?"

"Yours" I replied, with some disdain.

"Oh yeah. So it was. Never done that before!"

"Are you serious?"

"Yep. Did you think I had?"

"You're such an idiot."

Chalet Bitch

Chalet girls, I have observed, are an interestingly British phenomenon. No other nationality seems to have the foggiest clue what they are for. Half our foreign guests, who have bought their holiday online and not understood the English correctly, arrive in their chalet and wonder what on earth this strange, (often spotty, teenaged) oik is doing there and have to have it explained to them that the chalet host is here to cook their breakfast and bake cakes. The other half think you're some sort of personal assistant.

Having recently done some mooching around on the internet, and scoffed my way through a hideously badly written 1980s Mills and Boon style chalet girl's memoire which resembles my life about as much as Paris Hilton's does, I have learned a bit about our sort from back in the olden days. In days of yore, as you may or may not know, people went skiing on very long planks of wood, tied to their feet with bits of string. All the toffs who owned snowy retreats employed chalet maids to keep things ticking over, should they fancy a jaunt Alpside. It appears your average chalet 'ho' was a well-spoken young lady, fresh out of finishing school, but too ugly to marry off quickly. She was tasked with overseeing the chalet, ironing the boss's ski socks and making him a packed lunch. A sort of finishing school for fat-arsed no-hoper debutantes. They'd turn up looking shell-shocked on a bus with six or seven other clueless girls, get shagged by every randy ski instructor in a three hundred mile radius, and run their chalets on a shoe-string budget, despite having never boiled an egg before in their lives - think left-over beef bourguignon sandwiches and fish paste for lunch.

In some ways, this is far removed from the corporate (*ha*!- that's a laugh) co-educational world of strict contracts and work hours in which I exist, where chalet girls are not chalet girls, but chalet *hosts* - boys as well as girls. (If you're really in denial, it's 'chalet managers', although most couldn't manage a fuck in a whorehouse). It's the same in that we still have a shoe-string budget, and most have never boiled an egg. It's the same in that we still make your breakfast, clean your bathroom, make your bed, bake you a cake, and cook your dinner. It's the same in that we still serve you wine and canapés. But we no longer do it with pride. We do it because we have sold our arses for a ski pass. We come in uniformed tribes, 90% comprised of vacant *gap-yah* students and 10% comprised of shrewish, disillusioned drop-outs, like yours-truly.

I blame the internet.

No seriously. You see it's the internet that's made it possible (via email and Skype, for example) to completely centralise everything that goes down in a ski resort. The British Tour Operators can control it all remotely from the UK in an evil-super-villain-seeing-all-from-headquarters sort of way, so staff no longer even need any talent in the kitchen, let alone initiative, professionalism or, indeed, brain cells. I half expect my boss to materialize as a hologram in the kitchen most mornings, to make sure I'm frying the bacon right. They can micromanage to atomic levels, which explains how so many of my peers get away with being inordinately stupid and not knowing either their arse from their elbow or a roast potato from an apple. (By the way, I've always thought that arse/elbow mix up could form the plot of a pretty hair-raising scatological porno, but that's another discussion for another time).

Yes, I'd like to introduce you to the people, or should I say buffoons, making your beds, cooking your food, rifling through your personal belongings, playing your iPods and stealing the packs of Silk Cut and sweeties left lying around in your bedrooms. These are the fucktards trying on your fur coats, giggling at your grey, soiled knickers and reading your magazines on your toilet while you're out skiing. These are the wingnuts finding that used condom in your bin, helping themselves to the pharmacy of drugs in your bathroom cabinet and sniggering about your toilet habits down the pub. You didn't think we did that did you? Well we do. I know, because I do it.

From the moment these characters are shipped out en masse and disembark the Tour Operator's coach in early December for the obligatory 'training week', bleary eyed and clueless, they will stun you. Nowhere else will you encounter such utter incompetence and inability to deal with life, let alone the concept of doing a job properly. You literally would not believe the array of vacant, lazy, limp, socially and mentally inept public school fuckups that they employ year on year to deliver your ski holiday and represent their brand. ...spoons....Youngsters for whom the word 'initiative' has absolutely no meaning whatsoever and who think a hard day's work includes a fag break and a tantrum every ten minutes. I mean, where are the repercussions to losing your job when you know Daddy will just rent you an apartment and a buy you a season pass anyway, to soothe your tortured soul after the trauma of being sacked? No wonder the whole thing is just one giant, God-almighty cluster fuck.

Of course, it doesn't help matters that in charge of micromanaging this rabble is a woman with the tact, grace and managerial style of a rhinoceros - *La Vache Qui Ski*. It's very difficult to ascertain exactly what it is that the woman does. Since my first interaction with her, and weeks of speculation, I'm still at a loss. She certainly seems to spend vast amounts of time locked in her apartment 'doing paperwork', but when the shit hits the fan she usually manages, by some nifty excuse or other, to shift both blame and responsibility on to someone else.

On day one of staff training, and our deep clean week, a

mere twenty four hours after I had arrived in the ski resort and at 6.20am I was woken by a text from her.

"Morning! Have to do list for you.
Urgent! Please come to my flat for 7.30 meeting.
Need to hit ground running."

Fucking hell, I thought.

The 'meeting' consisted of me hovering on the doorstep of her little one-bedroom apartment, being snowed on, while she stood there with a cup of coffee dispensing orders.

"Sorry I can't ask you in, but I've just had the place cleaned," she said. "Now, yesterday lunch time I had a chance to have a little look around Chalet Christina and I *really* think you've got your work cut out to get it shipshape, okeydokes? It's in a teensy weensy bit of a state isn't it?"

"Erm, I suppose so yes," I conceded, trying to ignore how horrifically patronising she was and not quite clear on why, despite the fact I'd only just arrived, she appeared to be insinuating that the dirt was my fault. Personally, after having a quick scan around the place the day before, I'd thought it was pretty clean and just in need of a spruce, but then I'm not a neurotic, sexually repressed megalomaniac with OCD.

She replied with what I would come to know as her obligatory withering expression and then…

"I think you'll find there's quite a bit to get through, okeydokes? I suggest you get started immediately," her eyes flicked here and there with excitement. "I was going to write you a list but I haven't had time - I'm disappearing under an absolute mound of paperwork, you see. Sooooo, if you could just jot this lot down…"

She looked at me expectantly.

"Oh…" I said. "Oh, sorry I didn't bring a note pad. Do you have something I can scribble on?"

She rolled her eyes, sighed and furrowed her brow in disappointment. "Come *along* now. I really need you to get your head screwed on and be organised, okeydokes? Just because you're no longer a – what was it you did in London?"

"Marketing…"

"Well, there's no need to leave your professionalism at home is there? This is a job, you know, not a joy ride." She eyeballed me with the condescension of someone who thinks you're a total idiot but wants to make you feel listened to and gave a Cheshire Cat grin.

I felt my blood boil, ever so slightly.

"Didn't you take a note pad to meetings when you worked in London?"

"Er… yes…"

"Well, why should this be any different?"

"I…uh…"

She cocked her head to one side.

"I …just….didn't realise I'd need one. I'm terribly sorry."

"Hmmmm. Well that just *baffles* me. It really does," she shook her head and looked down at her fingernails. "As a more mature, experienced member of staff, I had hoped you'd be on the ball and help me set an example to the other staff. Okeydokes?"

Christ, it's only a note pad, I thought, rummaging in my pocket for my phone and saying brightly, "I'll type it all on here." *Just get to the point and give me your sodding list, fuck-face.*

And so it was that I settled on the idea that this woman was a psychotic whore-hound from hell almost immediately - some sort of frustrated fascist dictator.

Okeydokes?

The Big Deep Clean consisted of the following:

Walls – washed and bleached of dirty marks – scrubbed with a toothbrush

Cooker – removal of ancient greasy gunk containing what appears to be mysterious cat hairs (and possibly pubes) with toothpick from around dials and all crevices

Grill trays – scoured to remove ten years' worth of carbon deposits until silver and shiny again

Cupboards throughout chalet – emptied of rotten food and mice turds. Scrubbed. Traps laid.

Crockery – every piece cleaned and polished.

Fireplace – swept of ash and scrubbed

Skirting boards – scrubbed and rescrubbed

6 Bathrooms – tiles bleached, plugholes emptied of hair and slime, chrome polished

Appliances – blender, kettle, toaster, hoover, juicer, coffee machine, fridge and freezer disassembled, washed and reassembled.

Light bulbs – 51 all checked and if necessary replaced

Stone floor – waxed and polished

Porch and boot room – washed from floor to ceiling

Store cupboard – emptied, cleaned and restacked

42 windows – polished on both sides

Hot tub – De-slimed of green algae–type stuff (took three goes using a spatula to scrape off) and serviced

Logs stacked - 173

Cleaning products used:

Windowlene – 3 bottles
Bleach – 3 bottles
Lime scale buster -2 bottles
Floor wax – 3 pots

Chamois – 16
Toothpicks – 4 million
Toothbrushes - 4
Scourers – 22
Mops – 2

Later that afternoon, armed with my enormous box of cleaning products (the Box of Doom), La Vache Qui Ski frogmarched me from room to room, getting great pleasure from running her bony finger along the top of every bit of furniture, with a pained expression creasing up her impeccably groomed eyebrows.

"Are you taking notes?" she asked at one point.

Luckily for me, the uninitiated lackey, she is always full of useful cleaning tips and tricks to aid my progress, which she bestows with great condescension and pride.

Did you know newspaper is best for getting grease marks off windows, and a toothbrush dipped in bleach can clean any black mark off any wall *(with a good lot of elbow grease)*? Did you know if one wraps chrome bathroom taps in cling film after spraying them with Viacal one gets a really tip top shine?

No, I didn't. And quite frankly, I don't give a crap.

I couldn't be less interested in learning my bed sheets by weight, or that cream cleaner is best for getting poo off toilet seats. I used to co-ordinate board-room discussions and create business strategies. This is nothing but a nightmare fusion of *Trinny and Tranny* meets *How Clean is Your House?* After all of the bleach fumes and almost three hours of listening her various verbal ticks, it was a miracle I didn't go clinically insane.

"Okeydokes"

That's the one that really gets on my tits.

"Ok. *Okeydokes.* You'll need to get some bleach on the

grouting between *those* tiles," (points with a manicured finger that's never done a day's hard graft in its life).

I can't help musing over whether she used this same pert, managerial tone and catchphrase in the sack:

"Okeydokes. Now I'm just going to pop down here and suck your left ball. If you could flick my cli-*tor*-is that would be super. Okeydokes....yes... that's just the spot...Okeydokes! Ooooh, OKEYDOKES!"

She arrived at the chalet to make the inspection at 3.30pm and it lasted 2 hours.

"I *do* hope you've got really stuck in," she mewed as I opened the door.

But alas, she was disappointed with my work and the rest of the day turned into an epic plughole cleaning extravaganza.

"These plugholes!" she gasped, unscrewing one and wrinkling up her nose with disproportionate disgust. "They just haven't been done properly. I don't understand...." She looked at me expectantly. As if I had some sort of complex justification for my lack of plughole excellence. There are thirty plugholes in the chalet, in total. Not including the hot tub filter. Now think what goes down the plughole when you're in the shower. Skin? Hair? A bit of snot maybe? Wee? Period blood? That bit of poo you didn't quite get off your arse because you were getting in the shower? Yeah. Now imagine scooping an entire year's worth of that out of thirty plug holes.

"If Christa comes up here and sees this she will have absolute kittens."

Christa. Ugh. The second of the ugly sisters. She owns the company and reminds me of the fat, freckled ginger pig at school that got made head girl because her Mummy was on the parent's committee. Yes, that type. La Vache Qui Ski is her nodding dog; desperate for her attention and approval, yet secretly plotting her demise with an evil plan to usurp her as CEO. I swear the bitch has set her sights on world domination through ski holidays – millions of innocents will be enslaved into deep cleaning the entire universe while she spends her time ticking off things on a to-do list and sucking up to rich people. Christa and the Resort Manager spend the entire time blowing smoke up each other's arses. Listening to them converse together makes me physically sick.

"Do you *know* Christa. I happened to be driving through Milton Keynes the other day to visit my mother – gosh! I never realised how *attractive* the place you live is…"

"Mmmm yaaah, yaaaah….it's juuuuust incredible. It's soooo underrated. People just dismiss it, but there are some looovely places to take the horses." (Christa's arse and chins wobble in synchronicity when she speaks).

"My *goodness.*"

"Well next time you're driving throoooough, you should pop in and have a coooffeee."

"Oh I *will*. Do you know, Sainsbury's do *the* most fabulous tarts? They're just so cheap. My *goodness*. And *just* delicious."

"Mmm yaaaaah. *Juuuust delicious.*"

Tarts. Huh. If you ask me the last thing Christa (or her poor, long suffering horse) needs is refined sugars. That arse could replace the Thames Barrier.

Anyway….back to the plugholes.

"Sorry…." I said, poking my nose down one seemingly spotless exhibit. "What do you mean? They were absolutely chocca with filth this morning. I spent a good couple of hours bleaching them and degunking. It was rank. Trust me. That's a vast improvement."

She pointed to some small, residual specks of goo that remained and could quite obviously just simply be rinsed away in about four milliseconds.

"Well, that just *baffles* me it really does. If this is the standard you think is acceptable, I'm going to have to keep quite a close watch on you aren't I? Hahahaaa. Now really, you've just got to have a better eye for detail. Okeydokes?"

"Okeydokes" I nodded, smiling beatifically, while imagining garroting her with her own shoelaces.

Pet Hates

Evening time on changeover day. The chalet is ready, spotless, creaseless, candlelit, fire crackling. We are waiting for the new arrivals. A supper of soup, cheeses and meats with fresh bread and coffee cake has been laid out in case the guests are peckish after their journey. The lucky bastards. Sometimes I really hate the guests. Ok fine, I know. Without them, I wouldn't have a job. But really, they are so aggravating.

Take *la semaine dernière*. Not a happy experience *dans le chalet....* basically if we'd had a bunch of farmyard animals living with us, it would have been a less chaotic experience. They were the hairiest, messiest and loudest Brazilian family on earth for sure. Charming enough socially, I concede, however I refuse to believe you can shed that much hair without being an entire family of werewolves. I also refuse to believe that you can accidentally stick dental floss to the wall, tread an entire packet of cream crackers into four metres of carpet, and somehow leave poo on the floor of the shower, without noticing. I refuse to believe that you can create skid marks of that magnitude without suffering one iota of shame or self-loathing. I refuse to believe that you can do any of the above, and unapologetically leave it to someone else to clean up, without being some sort of cunt.

There are many things of the same ilk as the above, which conspire, on a daily basis, to irk the chalet girl. Here are a few more:

The Cupboard Of DESPAIR

Our store cupboard. Essentially a mélange of shite. A dumping ground for everything we don't know what to do with. I'm talking bottles, bags, hoovers, mops, cans of drink, dirty laundry, general goype. You can't find anyfuckingthing in it. It's an under-stair cupboard, so you can't walk into it - only lean, precariously and painfully whilst clinging to the door frame, while you rifle through all the crap and become more and more enraged and emotionally scarred by the experience. There's only one place on earth that's ever been more depressing than this cupboard, and that's Auschwitz. I have lain in it, completely flat on my stomach to try to reach some coke cans at the back, flailing around with the hoover head sticking into my groin and my face in a plastic bag - it was at this point I had a moment of 'what the fuck am I doing? I have an English degree!!' clarity.

Door-way lingerers

Chalet girls do a lot of shopping and are often to be found dragging enormous bags of either laundry or food in or out of the building. Why, therefore, do both men and women (and children are the worst) have an unbelievable habit of ambling in front of you when you are clearly staggering under a heavy load? They then grind to an oblivious, gormless halt. Because, obviously, them standing with their fat arse in the doorway is much more important than you not breaking your back with your shopping bag full of meat, vegetables and cheese. Items which, no doubt, they will later stuff their faces with at dinner, rendering their arses even fatter and more difficult to get past next time. Move! I'm not standing here like a bloody mannequin.

Vomit

Two days ago, I found what can only be described as black goo, on the carpet by the bed in one of the rooms inhabited by a particularly snotty teenager. Innocently, and perhaps naively, I dipped my finger in it and had a whiff, thinking it was chocolate milk spilt by some charming, yet clumsy child. Alas. It was chunder. Teenage-boy-I've-drunk-too-much-Jager-or-some-other-disgusting-shit chunder. It was the consistency of tar. I wouldn't mind but said teenager lay on the bed and watched me scrubbing it out of the carpet without so much as an embarrassed flinch. His mother didn't apologize either.

Toilet brushes.

Slimy, choc full of poo and just generally pretty unacceptable.

Piss under the toilet

How they manage to achieve it is beyond me. I can't figure it out.

Non-tippers

I spend my week picking your hairs out of the plughole, wiping up after you, making your bed, tidying your clothes and belongings away, cooking you delicious food and ferrying you around the resort like the sodding Queen of Sheba. You're worth four hundred and twenty eight million. Yes! Four hundred and twenty eight million! Count them! And you leave me no tip? A pox on you! May you tread in dog poo all the remaining days of your life.

Tinkerers

Punters who come into the kitchen and fidget around when you're cooking. The worst offenders sample your ingredients, rake their grubby paws through your lardons and put the kettle on repeatedly. How many cups of fucking tea do you need? Piss off out of my kitchen!

Brats

They never say thank you and the ones that do invariably have such exactingly anal parents that you know you will probably get a complaint about something at the end of the week. Most people assume everyone loves their kids. A woman complained one week that she was disappointed I hadn't played with her sprogs because apparently the year before the Chalet Bitch had made pancakes with them and stayed in the chalet all day entertaining them when they didn't want to ski. That, my friends, is what you call a Chalet Bitch brown-noser. If you want a Nanny then book one.

Cliché conversations : Snowboarders vs Skiers – Don't Mention the War

For God's sake, don't bring it up. Everyone out here is so bored of it. We all now live at peace. Yes. It's true. Without skiers to tow them on the flat, the slopes would be littered with the frozen over, skeletal corpses of boarders with one foot clipped out, who got stranded and didn't have enough energy to punt home. Someone needs to invent some kind of snowboarder's extendable pole thing that pings out from the sleeve or glove like a Wolverine Claw. But until they do, just shut the fuck up and give the poor bastards a tow.

Je Suis un Skieur

Today, from the safety of the bubble lift, soaring a hundred feet above the piste below, I saw a guy without a helmet wipe the entire length of a run. From top to bottom, at bone-cracking speed on sheet ice, unable to stop. About half way down, his limp body hit an obstacle and began to tomahawk. After completing a course of two or three complete rotations he had pretty much yard-saled his entire outfit, skis, goggles, gloves, poles. His body bounced like a child's toy thrown down stairs. He eventually came to a stop in a pitiful, unmoving heap, in the crevice under a steel chair-lift support. Whatever he was, he certainly wasn't conscious.

Scenes like this remind me why skiing isn't everyone's cup of tea.

That said, I do firmly believe that people who won't even try it are weedy pigeons.

I do appreciate that, to the uninitiated, it looks like the occupation of a bunch of rich snobs with too much time and money on their hands. Ridiculous to nail oneself to a sharp plank covered in wax and then cry when one falls to one's death off the side of an icy precipice. Having to spend weeks being cold, wet, terrified and having a bruised arse in order to 'get the hang of it'. Hmmmm. No thanks. I hear you say. I'd rather coil one out on my own chest and then fester in soiled undergarments for a week.

Well, fair enough. But there's a reason people love it so much. Singing, laughing, shouting your way down any accommodating hill you can find with a bunch of elated ski bum friends. Speed junkies that turn every run into a race, flat lining everything or venturing off into an unknown, untracked land of mystery and snowy fortune. Caution to the wind. Mountain worship. *Je suis un skieur!* That feeling of the sweeping turn, covering huge, epic expanses in only a few seconds. Freedom to explore places unreachable by others. Soaring on clouds. You can't beat it. It's the best feeling invented by humans since we discovered our genitals.

Yes, there are a few hurdles to overcome before you can get to that point. It's cold, there's the humiliation of seeing three-year-olds whizzing past you at fifty while you wobble down the nursery slope, knock-kneed and caterwauling for blood. White outs, injuries, fashion faux pas. The beginner snowboarder is afflicted with a purple arse from falling on the same spot thirty times a day. The skier, legs akimbo in a gusset-ripping snow plough with their forehead scraping the snow, simply looks like a dickhead. Yet, in the same way that people leap out of aeroplanes and attend Glastonbury when it's under eight feet of mud, people persist. Because it's the best fun you can have that doesn't involve some form of coitus.

Nowadays though, I must concede that times have changed. When I was a nipper it was all about Schuss, langlauf, vagling and snoods, Italian ski instructors with absurdly small posteriors, and those rubbish plasticky ski pass contraptions that you clipped onto your jacket so the pass pinged back and smacked you in the eye when you went through the barrier. Also, ski resorts may still look all twee and be full of ginger-bread houses and frosted pines, but they are also now full of wronguns. The European piste is a land populated by a bizarre conglomeration of conflicting cultures; old sticks-in-the-mud, rubbing shoulders with the rich and famous, being tripped over by park rats and downright weirdoes.

A park rat, if you are unfamiliar with the term, is a little fucker, usually about twelve years old (or wearing a t-shirt ten sizes too big) that has learnt to do a three-sixty on the flat before they could hold a lucid conversation or wipe their bum. They come from every direction, on twin tips or snowboards. They fly past you backwards, gazing lazily over one shoulder with irritating nonchalance, their trousers round their knees and their mittened knuckles scraping the piste. They don't even need snow. They use half pipes, or banister rails and park benches. It's most irregular. One wonders why they even bother coming up a mountain. Much cheaper to hang out at the local car park.

"Pull your pants up!" I keep wanting to shout at them. I mean, it can't be much fun landing in a metre of powder and getting snow in every imaginable orifice can it? That, after all, is what the much maligned onesie was invented to prevent. Is that level of discomfort worth it to look trendy? I wouldn't know. I am not one to sacrifice comfort for fashion. See, there was no such thing as a 'Snow Park' when I learnt to ski. There was just ski school, noodle soup, traverse, bendzeeknees and plantzeepole. These days, no ski resort can call itself a destination without a man-made playground full of kickers and rails upon which to mutilate yourself in bright orange ski pants that would swamp Barry White, and Snoop Doggy Dog's night shirt. Everyone's jabbering on about jibbing, big air, rails, fiveforty corks, gnarl and steeze. You are not skiing or snowboarding but *riding*…What the fuck is any of this? Where did it come from? Where is the nice, polite, middle class ski holiday of the 1990s? What happened to schnapps and langlauf? Mind you, saying that, what the fuck is vagling, anyway?

Suffice to say, all of this perturbs me somewhat. I used to be with it, but then they changed what it was. Now, what it is scares me…it happens to us all. I thought I was a pretty capable skier, until I realised that most other seasonnaires could ski backwards down most things faster than I could ski forwards, and spent most of their time airborne. Personally, I am entirely suspicious about these kicker thingamabobs. I don't, and never have liked the feeling of being detached from mother earth under my own pilotage. It's the knowledge that what goes up must come down and therefore the landing is in *my hands*. And I haven't got a fuck's clue how to execute a landing. I'm not a sodding aviator and I don't have wings. We don't belong up there with all the feathery things. In my book, unless you've been launching yourself off a thirty foot wall, strapped to a four foot plank, since before you could walk, I think you're on a trajectory headed straight for not being able to walk, forthwith. It would be massively daft to start trying this at the age of 25, when you're already a bit creaky and have 24 years of randomly tripping over in the street as concrete proof that you are an inept clutz.

You want me to *what?* Ski towards that wall as fast as I can, leaning forward with my legs apart and then suddenly lean back as I'm launched twenty metres into the air, where I should ideally do a backflip in time to come back down and land on my feet? Except since I'll have skis on, I will still be travelling forwards at speed? Right. How am I supposed to know how fast to go, and whenst I'm going to land? Should I not do some sort of mathematical calculation before I attempt this? Is there not some sort of equation? (Kinetic energy x gravity) ÷ ineptitude squared, perhaps? Will I not end up buried headfirst in mother earth and spend the rest of my days sucking pureed porridge through a straw, watching Ski Sunday and imagining crying because even my tear ducts are paralyzed? What's that you say? That does happen, does it? Right. Ok, I think I'll give it a miss then.

Irksome Blonde Shopping Fail

When I said the Irksome one cannot cook, I made the understatement of the century. Not only can she not cook, but she has no concept either of the value of things, or what constitutes food.

It was her turn to do our weekly shop today. She spent three times our allotted budget, and came back with frozen pizzas, tins of soup, Dolmio pasta sauce and pre-packaged Betty Crocker cake mix. Now, I'm no trained chef, but I know you can't serve jars of carbonara to people who are forking out several grand a week for a gourmet catered chalet experience.

"What the fuck is this?" I asked in disbelief, withdrawing several cans of corned beef from one of the shopping bags. "Where's the meat?"

"I thought we could give ourselves an easy week," she said looking pleased with herself and brandishing a can of baked beans happily. "I've got some friends coming out to visit me today and I don't want to be stuck in the shallaay all the time. I'm going to need to leave at 9.30am most mornings and not come back before six, or I'll hardly see them."

"How is that relevant to this can of *corned beef*?"

"Well I thought we could reheat some pizzas in the microwave one night, order in a take-away...stick the corned beef in a curry."

"Sorry? Corned beef curry?"

"Yer"

"My God. Right." I examined the tin and then looked at her. She was expressionless. "I know you're stupid so I'm going to keep this simple......*FUCK!*"

She gawped at me listlessly as I brandished the can.

"Where did you even *find* corned beef?"

"In the deli section."

"You can't serve corned beef curry to people who've paid for lamb shank!"

"Oh......" she huffed, "Who *cares*, anyway?"

She has a point there. The problem is, it's me that will take the heat when the complaint letter comes through because, lest we forget, the Irksome one is Christa's friend's daughter. Only I could pull a straw that short. In addition, though her own product choices were somewhat off the wall at best, it was also clear that the Irksome one had been a victim of some pretty aggressive 'Pineappling' during her time at the supermarket. Probably at the hands of Skater Boy and Scruffy but Handsome, who clearly think she's even stupider than I do.

'Pineappling' is a fine art, handed down like folk lore through generations of Chalet Bitches. It is the practice of sneaking unwanted objects, vegetable, mineral or animal, into your fellow chalet crew's shopping trolleys without them noticing until they are back up the mountain, in their chalet, everything nicely beeped through the till – and it's too late to take them back. Things that they have absolutely no need for and are incredibly difficult to explain away to their manager.

"I have no idea where that bumper pack of ribbed-for-your-pleasure condoms came from," I found myself saying this afternoon, as the La Vache Qui Ski stood over me and the accounts sheet, a ball point pen dangerously pincered between her fingers. "If you remember it wasn't me that did the shopping this week."

"Well regardless, the fifteen Euros ninety nine is coming out of both your wages - really I think finger pointing is a little unnecessary, we're all a team here," she said, self-righteously. "And perhaps you could explain why you needed, sheep's brains, cat food and a family pack of incontinence pants, too?"

Unsurprisingly, Scruffy-but-Handsome found it utterly hilarious when I relayed my meeting to him in The Drop Inn.

"I am never letting that brain dead pig do our shopping again," I said. "And don't laugh. Because of you my boss thinks I enjoy being 'ribbed for your pleasure'."

"Awesome!" he spluttered into his Mutzig. "I cannot believe she didn't notice the pack of Tena Lady, it was massive!"

"That doesn't surprise me at all. Her head is so far up her own arse, she can't see. We're talking feet deep here."

The fact I will have to do all the shopping from now on, to prevent further embarrassment and idiotic purchases, pains me because in truth, I've always loathed supermarkets. It's some kind of mental scar going back to days of excruciating boredom, being pushed round by my mother in a metal torture seat and being tantalised with shelf upon shelf of exciting colourful things. If my pudgy little fingers got within three metres of any of the merchandise she would shriek "DON'T TOUCH!" as if it was made of depleted uranium.

I associate supermarkets with discomfort, self-denial and abject boredom. So pretty much the last place on earth I want to be is in some kind of alternative episode of Supermarket-Sweep-Goes-Alp-Side, where the aim of the game is to make sure you filch the last non-mouldy iceberg lettuce for your chalet before Arianna from Ski Total gets there. Hell is battling down the aisles of a French superstore against a current of erratic, over-excited teenagers on a spending spree with a pocketful of their employer's cash, trolleys overflowing with bumper packs of toilet roll, industrial sized olive oil vats and stinky cheeses. Not only this, but all the staff clearly want to kill you 'rosbif plonkeurs!' and every other British person in the near vicinity.

Supermarkets are bastards.

The only way to make it bearable, arriving by minibus, still half cut from the previous night's excursions, groggy eyed and resentful that you're not skiing, is to run-a-complete-mock.

Riding around in the trolleys like bumper cars, vandalising the shelves, hurling abuse at the staff and generally helping ourselves to the produce as if it's some sort of buffet-theme-park. I once saw Skater Boy munch his way through an entire packet of raw frankfurters and a whole roast chicken during a particularly hungover shopping trip, before slipping it through on account along with a soft porn DVD, without batting an eyelid. It's only a matter of time before a full-on war breaks out between the chalet crew and the supermarket staff. Actually, I might start one next time. An afternoon spent hurling frozen pizza death-Frisbees and mayonnaise grenades at French people's heads would really lift my spirits.

Rules for the Chalet Bitch:
A general beginner's guide (cont.)

Some additional regulations, according to Skater Boy...

10. Do – have your arse and boxers hanging out of your jeans, dirty nails, cigarette-stained fingers and greasy long hair under a mouldy bobble hat that hasn't been washed since 1992, at all times.

11. Do – just enough work to avoid (by a hair's breadth) getting complaints about the cleanliness of your chalet, and therefore somehow always manage to start work last and finish first.

12. Do – arrive to work most mornings pissed as a fart, still in your ski gear from last night, but somehow manage to 'pull it off' riding solely on your ability to charm and flirt, despite putting salt on your guests' cornflakes and getting caught wanking in the toilet on changeover day.

13. Do – ski back to your chalet to do service, pissed to the eyeballs, in the dark. Hoon into a steel tow wire attached to a piste basher coming up the mountain and almost behead yourself.

14. Do – puke in the street at least once a week.

15. Do - be in a constant state of crisis due to either smoking too much weed or not having enough weed or Rizlas.

16. Do – always somehow seem to end up with a gaggle of fit young rich birds for guests. Woo said clients into letting you off dinner with your on-ski and après-ski performances.

17. Do – decide you can't be bothered to cook dinner one night, as there's a very good dubstep DJ playing at The Drop Inn, and leave your guests 30 Euros on the kitchen table along with a note that says, 'By yourseves *[sic]* a pizza on me'.

18. Don't – ever get caught doing something you shouldn't...

....actually, that last one should be the singlemost sacred commandment for any newbie Chalet Bitch. You can miss as many services as you like, nick enough chalet wine to drown Bridget Jones, serve dinner cold, shag any number of dirty stop outs in the chalet hot-tub, and use the company vehicle to give your mate Simon a lift to the airport while stoned. Just don't get caught.

The Screaming of the Orphans

In the shopping mall that forms a diamante-kitsch centre of the ski resort, the Sherpa supermarket rubs shoulders with Louis Vuitton. Walking through, I stopped to buy a baguette for lunch in a boulangerie-cum-café. A white out had rendered the day unskiable and I hadn't anywhere particularly to be for an hour, so I had a coffee. Black. No sugar. The woman behind the till was austere – shriveled - not at all the kind of jolly, fat person you expect to be served cinnamon swirls by. I sat for a minute in the lunchtime throng of punters gorging on sandwiches, chocolate éclairs and leather handbags, and mused that the advantage of living somewhere this small is that you're guaranteed to bump into someone you know at least twice a day. It's never lonely. But that can also be a curse. You can never disappear or blend into the background. People can be incredibly fatiguing, sometimes watching them from a distance is safest.

There were two local girls at a table next to me, discussing something about a wedding in fluid French…something about the dress… *robe de mariée* and then something about a grandmother – *grand-mère* – and blue flowers. My thoughts drifted idly in an unwelcome direction; to the dress I'd earmarked for my own wedding. First, there had been the distraction of searching for it online at work, when I should have been writing reports. It was a pale, empire line gown; plunging neckline, dusted with gemstones, a waterfall of silk and chiffon puddling behind on the floor, something a nymph might don to frolic in the woods. The fantasy of it had been intoxicating, but on the day I saw it in the flesh, in a shop window near our new home, I stared at it, imagining the intimidating, oily fabric against my legs, not daring to go inside and try it on. What if it didn't suit me? The illusion would be destroyed. In a way, the whole wedding idea felt the same. I tried to imagine how I would feel if there was no expensive dress, no guests, no elaborate reception, but just he and me and a ring and a droning repetition of empty vows uttered by a billion lips before us. The impression was one of banality. I went home, to the new house - to all the commitment and reality it represented, and tried very hard to ignore myself.

He had to work that weekend, and it was left to me to manage the large and laborious task of unpacking our things. The outgoing family had left it dirty, dusty and stuffy. I felt so ill at ease there on my own that when Shazzer arrived to lend a hand, staggering under the weight of a 'welcome to your new home' cake box, my relief was palpable.

"Give me something to clean!" she demanded, seeing how harassed I was. She burst in the front door in customarily ripped jeans and a baggy off-the-shoulder number. "I love a good deep clean."

In the evening, we sat on the rough wooden floor amid a city of box towers and upturned furniture, drinking a bottle of red wine and eating large hunks of the cake.

"You're not going to go on one of those crazy-ass diets are you?" she scoffed, through cakey teeth. "And turn up looking like a starved sparrow instead of your beautiful boobed and butted self?"

"Have you ever known me to diet successfully?"

"No. But still. My sister in law dropped to a size 12 for the big day only to leap straight back to a size 16 within months. Bizarre to get married with someone else's body, I think"

"Agreed"

"Mind you, we all complained about your brother's bouffy hair do at his wedding, and now it's become a permanent fixture."

"That's true. Well, I'm not planning a crash diet. However, it would obviously be of enormous help if my Maid of Honour is obese and dressed in a pig costume. You don't mind do you? I've found one online that has a curly tail and hooves and everything…"

"Oh. Don't you worry. I'm already on the case with the morbid obesity project," she said, reaching for another slice of cake and stuffing the whole thing in her mouth sideways so the cream squooshed out of the corners. "Nexsht to me your gonna look fushing unbelievable shexshy gorge!"

The local girls have ceased their chatter and are glancing uncomfortably at me because before I can gulp it back, two unexpectedly huge, hot tears are dripping heavily off my chin into my coffee. I sweep the tears away with the backs of both hands, and glance around, in the hope that no other ghastly stranger or random acquaintance has seen.

… As I've often observed, if you ever need a good cry, a busy public space is unquestionably the best place to do it without fear of interruption.

I gather myself together and head to Skater Boy's apartment where I know I'll find him smoking weed and watching pirate copies of films from his bed. He spends many afternoons like this, in half-wakefulness, hung-over, waiting for the conditions to improve, like a bear biding its time. Watching snow drift down outside the window.

"Ah never mind love" he says, enveloping me into the duvet beside him. It must be patently clear I've been crying, but he doesn't ask why. We don't invest in details, we skim the surface of each other. A mutual self-preservation. It's a relief, as I have no desire to go into any of my skeleton closets with him. Instead, I lie in his embrace, listen to him babble languidly about his hopes and dreams, and realise that I'm not the only one who's been guilty of living in a fantasy world my whole life.

"One day I'm gonna get a chalet of my own and do away

with all this bullshit," he murmurs. "All I need is some capital."

"When?" I ask

"I dunno. One day. It'll happen."

I smile quietly at his passive certainty and wonder where exactly he thinks this capital is going to come from. The guy is so skint he's been living off raw potatoes for three weeks. I have realised by now, however, that Skater Boy's self image is a fragile thing. He has convinced himself, and many other people, that he's a pretty terrific guy. But if one wanted to dismantle his fantasy, one could do so quite brutally and with relative ease. It's safer, and a lot more fun, to simply play along.

It's undeniable though, that an unshakably chemically unbalanced feeling has started to permeate through me today. It has begun, inevitably, to leak in and attack the lovely synthetic layer of happiness with which I have carefully coated myself. In life, I figure that most problems, if ignored stoically enough, usually either go away or sort themselves out on their own. Apart from maybe Syphilis, or piles. I believe they call it 'the Ostrich approach'. But unfortunately, it seems that some problems, if denied, tend to manifest themselves in devious ways. Some problems don't like to be ignored, they fidget around for attention, and eventually they begin to overflow.

There are strange things a person does to distract themselves from all-intoxicating grief. To deny it's there at all, in fact. Hedonism works wonders, you know. Consumption of all things gratification-shaped, in huge amounts. With one half of my brain full of the lack of Shazzer in my life, I have done my best to fill the other half of my brain with pleasure-seeking:

Skiing. That helps.

Shopping for ridiculous clothes that I would never wear at home.

Fucking the extremely skinny, wildly inappropriate and

wrong-for-me Skater-Boy type - a welcome distraction.

Drinking.

More drinking.

Skater Boy is a major part of this process. I am perplexed by my own obsession and also the ease with which I have broken my own rule of never shagging anyone whose arse is smaller than mine. In fact, let's be honest, he has no arse whatsoever.

The truth is I haven't cried, not really properly at all, and that can't be good. Things are bubbling away inside with no release valve and it has started to seep out through the pores. Dappy is not the word. In the last three weeks, I lost my work phone, arrived late to take someone to the airport, forgot to do countless chores, broke about a thousand glasses and have just generally been distracted, useless and dippy. Oh and also I had a (small) crash involving a minibus and a chalet. This was an issue that the Resort Manager particularly relished. I had reversed into the eaves of the chalet opposite ours, dented the top of the chassis and blown out one of the brake lights.

"It's going to cost an *awful* lot to repair. Christa is not going to be happy," she quacked, as we stood outside her flat on that sleety morning, investigating the damage. "I'll require you to get several competitive quotes. And then you'll have to work the cost of the repairs off, okeydokes? Ok? There's a rather large insurance excess I'm afraid."

She insisted that we go inside her obsessively immaculate flat and discuss my problems in depth, presumably to fulfill the 'pastoral' element of her role.

"Don't sit on the sofa, please, it's just been hoovered," she snapped, indicating a small kitchen stool by the window. The only evidence of her habitation was neat pile of papers on her desk, her laptop and a tidy row of pens, arranged in size order. Everything else about the room was creepily box fresh.

"Thanks" I sat down.

"I really have no idea what's wrong with you," she said looking at me side on, rather in the way a Magpie looks at a baby bird it's about to devour. "Whatever it is that's going on in your social life – you've really got to show some tenacity and put it to the back of your mind when you're at work. It's so unprofessional, it really is. What is it? Is it a …a boyfriend or something?"

She really had no idea, this bitch. It wouldn't be so hard to swallow if she wasn't the same age as me, or had ever displayed the capability to manage her way out of a paper bag.

"Look, I appreciate this minibus thing has been a massive pain and I certainly didn't expect to be congratulated for it, but, you know, it wasn't like I was doing handbrake turns in the car park. I think I'm just a little tired right now."

"Well, I hate to say I told you so but…perhaps you're just not getting the work-play balance right. I want to start seeing you really make an effort. Everyone gets a bit of mid-season blues. You've got to rise above it. Okeydokes?" she did an expansive, theatrical motion with her arm, presumably to indicate the dignified manner in which I should rise above these trivial issues.

I felt ready to gouge out her black little eyes with a spoon.

The Wankers are in Charge

For three days straight, it has been snowing. Low, opaque clouds. Huge, soft, downy lumps coating the world. This morning, it stopped and the temperature promptly dropped viciously into freeze-your-labia-off territory. Dressing for work in the afternoon is now a nightmare. I always leave it just that little bit too late and underestimate how long it's going to take me to do one more run. Then I only have ten minutes to leg it down the road in ski boots, clatter up three flights of stairs, tear off my sweaty underclothes and make myself look presentable before dragging my sorry arse uphill for twenty minutes to Chalet Christina.

The problem with Tour Operators is they don't think about the logistics of things. Not the really important stuff anyway. For example: How is the thin, red, piece of crap jacket they have issued me with, and demanded I wear to work, supposed to keep me warm when it is minus 22 degrees outside, with three-inch-thick icicles hanging off the roof of the chalet, knee-deep snow on the pavement and Baltic wind-chill? "Layers" was The Resort Manager's response when I questioned her on this. "The jacket's only meant to be a shell." Oh great. Fucking brilliant. Thanks. So this means that in order to avoid turning into a living ice mummy on the way to the chalet every morning and afternoon, I have to supplement my work clothes with tights, three hoodies, a scarf of the orange and green merino wool variety, turquoise crochet bobble hat, sheepskin ear muffs, thick suede gloves with woolen interior, thermal socks and rubber-soled snow boots. Even wearing everything I own, and looking like a huge cotton-wool-stuffed sumo-wrestler in winter safari gear, I start to get so cold at the bottom of the hill that my labia have practically solidified. By the time I get to the top, I am sweating like a paedo in a playground, tearing layers from my back, and inevitably arrive at work wheezing, swearing and looking like some sort of manic, bedraggled Ranulph Fiennes person. And I'm fairly hygienic. Imagine the stench floating off the armpit of your average pustule-ridden, teenager with hyper-active, oozing glands as he serves you potatoes of an evening, after three days of binge drinking, and skiing around in thermals without showering. Either provide me with a decent fucking jacket, or accommodate me somewhere that doesn't require me to make an arctic expedition to get to work!

And then, when I get there, where am I meant to put these extra garments, bearing in mind there is fuck all 'staff room' in the chalet? I have to stuff it all behind the freezer or in the Cupboard of Despair, which makes it even more difficult to find the toilet rolls.

Accommodation on a season, in case you haven't gathered, is a major sore point. The Resort Manager, in her cosy little flat, has the audacity to tell me that our shoebox studio, shared by four people (not including conjugal visits) is a virtual palace compared to what she'd had to put up with in the past. What a joke. She speaks like some sort of geriatric extreme survival veteran.

"Oh yes," she said tossing her head with pride, "On my first season I was in a flat half the size with six other girls. We had to draw up a shower rota. Honestly you girls these days. You don't know you're born!"

Ha! The place is a shit hole full of broken furniture. A grotto that swings between asphyxiating gas chamber, when the heating is on, to miserable ice-box of despair when it's off. The night I moved in I went to sleep wearing everything I owned, including a fur coat, to fend off the incessant cold. The oven and fridge didn't work and there were no working light bulbs. And the thing that irks me most, is that it's the Resort Manager's job to address all these things.

I don't care what she says; more than two people in that

broom cupboard at once and you end up sexually assaulting each other just by breathing out. It should be illegal for anyone who hasn't actually *been* a Chalet Bitch to run a chalet company. Fuck this shit.

A Bastard Behind the Eyes

Day off.

Have woken this morning feeling as if every cell of my being has been industrially plastered in a treacle-thick layer of tar.
Right. Breakfast:

1 x rehydration sachet
2 x Neurofen Plus
Tea: 1 x bucket
Several stale croissants
1 x unidentified pill closely resembling valium found randomly at bottom of a guest's wash bag while cleaning yesterday

Now I feel half way human. Just half.
Right. Skiing.

The Abominable Ski Bum

My conversational skills today were not up to their usual sparkling brilliance, I must admit.

It turns out the Valium was actually Modafinil, which is narcolepsy medication. Who keeps that in their wash bag? It tends to make one rather focused on the little things in life, in a bulging-eyeballed-paranoid-self-scrutinising kind of way. I spent a good hour examining the inside of my own skull. Luckily, I was skiing with Skater Boy, Scruffy-but-Handsome and The Man of Leisure, who behave like they're on the mother of all acid trips all the time anyway, and quite often are, in fact, tripping their tits off.

Life with these three is never dull. The weed smoking is utterly ubiquitous. There is rarely a waking moment when a spliff isn't hanging from Skater Boy's lips and I, by proximity, am therefore almost always stoned too since every bubble lift is turned into a hot box. This makes skiing with the three of them somewhat of a death trap. Every run of the day turns into a flat-line men's downhill, with each of them disappearing off the lip at the side of the piste into heavily wooded areas for several minutes at a time and then emerging back abruptly like a man fired out of a canon, almost taking you out and screaming something unintelligible or profane.

Skater Boy is a chef, but being a tip-top skier, he also enjoys a lucrative side game in ski guiding. This basically involves taking clueless punters on a magical mystery tour of the mountain whilst showing off outrageously, doing three sixties, front flips off wind lips and riding switch to impress them. It's usually quite easy to impress punters in this way. The tips pay for the disturbingly enthusiastic doobie habit too. I must admit, I am at a loss as to how he gets away with it. Imagine turning up to go skiing with your bought and paid for ski guide and being confronted with a bearded beanpole with almost dreadlocked hair (the variety that's dreadlocked because he couldn't be bothered to wash it, rather than for any hippy or fashion reasons). He is wearing an ancient, grimy yellow and blue onesie, with nothing but his baby-pink-bottom underneath. Top this off with a grey Alpine shepherd's hat, tutti frutti goggles and a bandana emblazoned with 'yellow snow'. Your mountain terrain 'expert' is a stoned, Northern degenerate with an Austrian twist, a death wish and a penchant for yelling 'Judas!' at people who displease him. Last week, he went off to take two fourteen year-olds skiing, wearing a t-shirt that proclaimed 'Fat Kids are Harder to Kidnap.'

"You're gonna go down that black run over there and wait round the corner for me," he drawled to the wide eyed pair, pointing down a hairy bit of piste. With that, he started hiking up a rock face in the other direction towards the entrance of a couloir which may or may not have had an exit. One can only speculate as to their astonishment when they saw this heathen Bananaman descending from on high, scarring a massive 'S' in the powder and screaming "Mehaaaaaaaah!!" at the top of his lungs. And what, pray, was the story they relayed back to their parents later that day?

Feeling, as I did this morning, like a pig had shat in my head, I'd had no intention of going skiing. Instead I was lying, naked in a pool of my own filth, groaning and sweating when, at 11.15am, someone leant purposefully against the doorbell.

"FUCK ORRRFFFF!" I growled at the door.

"It's *me*" Scruffy-but-Handsome's slightly wounded, muffled voice came from the other side of it. "Shit" I grabbed the nearest clothing – a hoody – but could only source one shoe to avoid contact with the floor, so had to hop one-legged to the door, doing my best to stretch the jumper down over my fanny.

"Yes?"

"Terribly sorry old girl," said The Scruffy One, as I opened the door. He looked down at my exposed undercarriage with amusement. "...but I believe I left the old twin-tips here yesterday....fancy a ski?"

He, I and The Man of Leisure squeezed on to the chairlift and went to the top of the hill to meet Skater Boy. The latter, in one of his flamboyant moods, turned up in full onesie regalia and had brought with him the famous Toucan embellished monoski. Without doubt the most ridiculous piece of sports equipment ever invented.

"Where did you get that piece of shit anyway?" I enquired, sitting down on the snow to mitigate my nausea.

"I found it in a skip," he said proudly, stubbing his fag out between two asbestos fingers and throwing it over his shoulder. It bounced off the helmet of a passing punter. He and Scruffy-but-Handsome, more than any people I have ever met, live true to the statement 'one man's rubbish is another man's treasure' and are adept at finding random and wonderful things in skips. Other gems this season have included a pair of Head racing skis, a pair of Hestra gloves and a dog named Bruce. Well, the dog wasn't in the skip, but you get the idea. It slept on the end of Skater Boy's bed for two weeks until the owners showed up and demanded it back. I don't understand how they do it. The best things I've ever found in a skip were some disused insulation and an old sock.

For the rest of the day, Skater Boy proceeded to show off, to everyone's slight irritation, whipping down each hill with the lithe flexibility and confidence of a cat, often with a spliff still hanging out of his mouth. Despite my cynicism about the monoski, after an hour of watching his incredibly pert little bottom and elegant left-to-right swiveling movements I was feeling pretty keen on the idea of shagging him sometime in the very near future.

"Hey…" I said, pulling him to one side as we clipped out of our skis and trotted down an icy incline to an après ski bar. "Let's have a shag in the toilets!"

For a moment, he looked rather put on the spot, then he shook his head dismissively and gave me a look tinged slightly with pity. "This is drinky time, not sexy time," he explained. I tried not to feel totally mortified, and decided to scratch this response up to the effects of being perennially baked. Although there seemed to me to be something intrinsically awry with a state of affairs where *I* was pestering *him* for sex… But then hey, what do I expect from someone who goes out at night wearing a teabag on a piece of string around his neck? Someone whose party trick is dangling his nuts in people's mouths while they're asleep (The 'Arabian Goggles').

The bar was crowded with dancing loons passing around jugs of Mutzig. Ski boots stamping, sweat stinking, feet tingling in their plastic prisons, merry with fresh air, ultraviolet overdose and beer. My hair was soon sticky from all the toffee vodka that was being poured all over me by a fat perspiring bloke in a bobble hat. There were two guys playing guitars vigorously and kicking a wooden box for a bass drum. We drawled along to 'Hotel California' – *you can check out any time you like, but you can never leave…* The place was full of people we knew and so I didn't see Skater Boy for much of the evening, until later, when he excitedly ran over to tell me he had 'accidentally borrowed' someone's skis. They were an extremely long, thin pair of eighties classics which he spied propped up against a post outside. He had tinkered around with the bindings, he said, when no one was looking and then had hiked up the now dusky piste for a sneaky try.

Unfortunately, the owner, unaware in the bar, had come to look for them moments later and concluded they'd been thieved. By the time Skater Boy arrived back down from the mountain and good-naturedly stacked them back against the wall, the gendarmes were sniffing around. He grabbed my hand and we made a swift exit.

Why You Should Never Lose Your Key

7am. I am woken by enraged hammering on Skater Boy's door. I elbow him in the ribs.

"Door"

No response.

"Door"

I have no idea how long this hammering has been going on but it's really pissing me off.

"Fucksake"

Resentfully I get up and go to tell who ever it is to go and get stuffed so I can get some sleep, tripping over a half-empty pizza box and some dirty laundry on the way.

As I open the door, Scruffy-but-Handsome barges past me in a rage, yelling.

"You could have *sodding* well woken me up!"

Seven seconds later the apartment is filled with the sound of a random cockney thug bellowing *"Wake the fuck up!"* over a cacophony vaguely reminiscent of a Bugatti Veyron having sex with a flatulent Sherman tank inside an iron mine.

Dubstep. The Scruffy One has put his iPod on.

He kicks Skater Boy, just slightly too hard in the hip. "Get up you Judas. You're late for work."

"Whassafuckinproblem?" croaks Skater Boy, angrily rolling over in bed.

I am struggling to piece together some kind of coherent picture from these various clues, that would explain the Scruffy One's ire, but for some strange reason I don't seem to have a brain. There is just a void where it should be.

"You're very huffy,"

"What do you expect?" the Scruffy-One storms, his voice getting entertainingly higher and higher in pitch. "I've been awake all night on the fucking door mat thinking no one was in!"

Oh. Yep. It's starting to come back to me. The 3am drunken ski back in the dark. The hobbity figure asleep on the doormat in the foetal position. Skater Boy poking him lazily with his foot.

"Whysee sleepinthere?" I frowned, quite smashed. "Probably lost his key again,"

Then Skater Boy (capable of militant levels of organisation and efficiency in the field of self-preservation, if nowhere else) produced his own key from deep in one of his baggy pockets, unlocked the door and stepped over the Scruffy One's slumbering, helpless form.

I hung back for a moment.

"How do we make it move?"

"Ahh, just leave him there...Timmy. Shouldn't 've forgotten his key should he? Come on..." he beckoned me inside.

Ooops.

The Cockney Thug seems to have had the desired effect, cajoling Skater Boy into the land of the living. He is sitting upright and grimacing through hair that looks like a menagerie of woodland creatures could be nesting in it.

"You shouldn't 've got so drunk and lost your key.... *again,* you Timmy," he yawns, getting up and scratching his arse. "You were unconscious, mate, you weren't moving..."

"I would have at least dragged you inside."

"Ha!"

"Why didn't *you* wake me up?" This is directed pointedly at me.

"Uh....I'm sorry. You were un-wake-able."

"*Un-wake-able?* Do you realise the lights outside work on a motion sensor? Every time I *blinked* they came on! I've had no sleep, now I've got to work a seven hour shift."

Wow, he really *is* cross.

"You know what?" he points at Skater Boy and fixes me with red-rimmed eyes. "You're turning into as much of a wanker as *he* is"

Hmm.

I do find Skater Boy's general apathy towards other people's feelings amusing, and, to a certain extent, liberating, but I'm not certain it's the modus operandi I'm ready to adopt and become known for myself. Particularly in relation to a good sort, like the Scruffy One, (well, good apart from the verbal diarrhoea, the bloodshot eyes and the habit of eating raw frankfurters while standing naked on the balcony.) I examine my grubby feet and try to look compunctious, but all I can think of is how terribly funny he looks when he's cross; crashing around the flat in a tirade of expletives, getting dressed wrong.

"You have your work shirt on back to front"

"Fuck off!"

"I am calling in an emergency capacity. I need you to talk me down."

"This is the third time this week. What's the problem this time?"

"The number of minutes I've spent today musing on various different methods of murdering my boss…"

"Yes?"

"It's starting to worry me."

"What have you come up with?"

"Umm, trapping tie in paper shredder, various poisons, faked fatal auto-erotic asphyxiation…"

"Inventive."

"This whole thing is bullshit. I don't even know why I'm doing it any more. I need a job with some sort of justification for its own existence. Like…I dunno…humanitarian fundraising or some shit."

"Mate, Don't get any big ideas. I don't think that even exists…I spend my day phoning up grannies and extorting money out of them."

"It's philanthropy."

"That's just branding. Six months and I'm fucking off to Mongolia. No. China. Haven't decided yet…Oooh. I know what'll cheer you up."

"I'll take anything."

"This morning I had to phone a man whose surname was spelt K, U, N, T."

"…Mr. Kunt?"

"Yep!"

"Um, Shazzer. Are you sure it's not pronounced 'Koont'?"

"Aahhm…."

"I think it's German"

"Oh…. shizer."

"My boss is a koont…"

"Well, do something different then. Stop being so fucking mopey. Have you actually applied for that chalet job you found?"

"No…thinking about it…"

"Just do it! You know, you don't actually need a brain to clean toilets. It's like Lord of the Flies out there. You'll get a job in about 4 minutes, considering you're so despicably diligent and good at everything you do. It's disgusting really. Actually we must clone you. Hey, if I prove to be infertile could I have a loan of an egg please?"

"You can, just don't give it one of your stupid hippy names like Sky or Sunshine."

"What's wrong with Sky? It's a lovely name…"

"…Ugh. God. I feel like just walking back in there and quitting on the spot."

"Mate, do it! Why stop at that? If one is burning bridges it might as well be an insurgent's rocket propelled missile up your boss's arse as an indoor firework. Throw down your pen, leap up and shout 'How dare you? Fuck you!' then climb up on the table, pull down your pants, squat over the keyboard, coil out a perfect Mr. Whippy over the keys followed with a little patter of farts, then whip up your pants, jump down and say: "Ooh! good to get that out of me system! See ya!" and sashay out-to the soundtrack of R.E.S.P.E.C.T à la Bridget Jones."

"Is this deranged, sordid fantasy some kind of vicarious catharsis for you?"

"Probably. Now look, I want to tell you something. You are undoubtedly the finest example of woman I have ever chanced to meet. And I know I am biased, but I'm also fussy and as such, you should take me seriously."

"Aww, thanks mate."

"From now on you have to say 'yes' to everything. Ok?"

"Right."

"Ok. I've got to go and extort more grannies. Don't phone me again unless you've quit your job."

"Right."

Christmas Day

Oh…

that feeling…

when you know only a bottle of vodka…

is going to get you through breakfast…

"Bad times isn't it? When you're sitting on a dustbin eating leftovers out of a baking tray?"

Christmas Eve is a bit of a blur.

The fact that I woke up still in my Chalet Bitch uniform substantiated the idea that I had, in fact, made it to work that evening. The rest I had to glean from Facebook photos, which told the story of a gurning woman with eyes like saucepan lids, draped stupidly over a burly random with foppish hair, in a graffiti-scarred den with sweat dripping down the walls.

Whoever this chap was, I woke up in his bed on Christmas Day morning.

A peek under the duvet at his cock confirmed it had potential. Shame I never saw it in full plumage. At least I don't think I did.

Christmas sucked balls.

My guests didn't even wish me well, or offer me a glass of wine. The Irksome one went AWOL and never showed up at work and I had to spend Christmas all alone locked in a grimy kitchen. The last time I had seen the little cow, the night before, she was being rutted up against a wall next to the toilet by an unidentified individual wearing a crocodile costume.

Actually, I was vaguely concerned about her. Very vaguely.

What I was more concerned about was how to cook a Christmas lunch whilst still off my face and unable to taste. There were four of everything. Four turkeys. Four Christmas Puddings. Four of me in the bathroom mirror.

At some point, Skater Boy came over from his chalet across the road and knocked on the window.

"Eh up... you look like crap..." he said. "Have a brandy" He passed me a bottle through the window. "Merry fucking Christmas...Did you shag some random punter last night?"

There was a pause while I drank.

"No. Just spooned..." I gave him a half apologetic, half triumphant smile.

"Spooning leads to forking!" his relieved expression cheered me up a little.

"Well, not this time. Anyway, how come you look so normal?" I asked, remembering that the last time I'd seen him, he'd been teabagging some hapless individual who had fallen asleep on a bench in the Drop Inn.

"I'm drunk"

"Ah"

In a way, I was secretly quite proud of myself for my stoic ability to carry on in adversity, with time and fate against me. Shame it's not the sort of story that one can use in an interview situation, as an example of showing tenacity against all odds. Oh well. I console myself that I tried my best under extremely difficult circumstances, not (entirely) of my own making.

Merry Fucking Christmas

C is for Children – Because that's what Christmas is about right? An endurance test to see how long you can put up with a bunch of aggressive, spoilt, precocious ADHD brats bed wetting and running screaming from room to room, hurling food at each other, ripping open presents and discarding them, without having a complete mental breakdown, flipping out and attacking the entire family with a sharp blender attachment.

H is for Hospitalisation – The likely result of making merry on one too many vin chauds then skiing home in the dark after service.

R is for Rain – We don't want any more, thanks. Watching a ski resort get rained on is like watching a child's sandcastle get pissed on by a drunk old man.

I is for Irksome Blonde 19 Year Olds – And another mind-blowing clanger as she turns up to breakfast service on boxing day wearing a butt-asphyxiating Juicy Couture-style pink tracksuit, stinking of booze and looking as if she hasn't washed in a fortnight.

"But the guests eat dinner in their pyjamas," was her excuse.

"I suspect they can eat dinner in full leather gimp suits if they want," I retorted "go and put your fucking uniform on."

S is for sick – May none of your guests chunder on or in anything in your chalet over the festive season. Picking chunks out of the carpet is not my idea of a *Noel joyeux.*

T is for Turkey – Foisted on chalet guests by tour operators Alp-wide. Who even likes that uninspiring mound of dry, tasteless flesh anyway? Foul to begin with, then further destroyed by the incompetent teenager cooking it, who thinks stuffing is something you do after twenty Jager bombs. Serve charred on the outside, pink and ripe with bacteria on the inside, to a family of confused and alarmed Greek people who don't celebrate Christmas until March anyway.

M is for despicable management – La Vache Qui Ski is doing 'spot checks' today. This will mainly involve her turning up and letting that bastard little dog cover the place in muddy footprints and hair before helping herself to canapés, buggering up my plate arrangement, and deflecting any issues the guests might have onto my shoulders.

A is for Arse – Specifically Calamity's. She got blind drunk last night, and decided to toboggan home on it wearing only leggings, resulting in severe freeze burn. Her buttocks now look and feel as if they've been dipped in boiling oil and then sandblasted.

S is for Scruffy-but-Handsome – Who showed up on my doorstep with a homemade Christmas card, featuring a scrawled drawing of us tobogganing, and a bottle of champers he filched from his chalet supplies. He has thereby restored a modicum of my long-lost Christmas spirit.

Punters

I met the Foxy Chef for an off-piste picnic today. The rain has at last turned back to snow and it was my favourite kind of afternoon. Dusty clouds hung low and stratified, so that gaps of brilliant blue sky and sunshine suddenly appeared between thin veils of drifting snow and mist. We brought sandwiches and beer in our backpacks and picked our way along a ridge on an outcrop, to sit between two trees, surveying the grandeur of the scenery between the clouds. The Alps rolling off interminably into the distance with a river of fog sitting in the valley. We set our poles in the snow with our gloves sticking upright on top of them and sat on The Foxy Chef's snowboard to eat. People we knew, and didn't know, waved and called to us from the chairlift.

"My boss's wife keeps leaving her period pants in the middle of the bedroom floor for me to pick up and launder," said the Foxy Chef, examining her iPhone distractedly, as if she'd never seen an object like it before in her life.

"I hope you *don't* pick them up,"

"I did the first time. Now I've taken to just hoovering around them,"

"That is really fucking disgusting. Why would someone do that?"

"I think it's some kind of alpha female signifier to keep me in my place."

"Yuck,"

"If it continues, it may merit some kind of silent but deadly revenge attack. I'm biding my time,"

Punters are just people. I know that. Ordinary, hard-working people, like you and me. People who, in the most part, have spent the last two years locked in an office with other ordinary, hard working people they hate, and travelling with their noses pressed into sweaty armpits on the tube and a mystery cock sticking into their back. They do this just so they can afford five minutes with their family and friends on this meagre holiday they've booked with whichever hateful Tour Operator they've fallen into the clutches of. They've saved, nay, scrimped for that precious week on the (hopefully) glistening slopes of a trendy French ski resort. For that freshly made bed, roaring fire and home-baked cake to come back to after an afternoon spent whizzing around, giggling their socks off in fresh, clean air, with the sun on their face. They might only get to do this a handful of times in their lifetime. Of course they want it to be perfect. Of course they want to get what they paid for. They deserve to. Hell, I'd be furious if I paid all that money and arrived to brown grass and muddy fields and found myself greeted by a fusty red-eyed teenager in an ice cold, dirty chalet that smelt strongly of sewage.

With this in mind, it is an unfortunate truth that some seasonal workers do the minimum amount of work to get by. The fact is, the least a Punter deserves is an unforgettably lovely holiday. It's a fair exchange – after all, someone's got to do all the 'proper' jobs, or there'd be no roads or websites or Toblerone or soap. But some, (particularly newbie), seasonnaires see the whole thing as a gigantic game where the only rule is "see how much you can get away with not doing." I'm not singling anyone out here. Every seasonnaire is guilty of doing this at one point or another during the season, for various reasons. But for some it's a permanent modus operandi.

That said, another unfortunate truth I cannot defend is that some Punters seem to believe that being on holiday from work also means they can be on holiday from not being a fucktard. And it is a further sad fact that where mutual understanding breaks down under these circumstances, you have a recipe for tears, tantrums, passive-aggressive retribution and law suits. I speak from bitter experience – but it must be said - often the worst people in a chalet are the Punters, not the Chalet Bitches.

The Punters I have little sympathy for are those who swan in expecting an on-call butler and anal smoke-blowing service, when they've paid discount prices. To be fair, this isn't always the Punter's fault either. Tour Operators make their money out of elevating their expectations about what a fantastic deal they're getting. They print mouth-watering brochures and launch websites full of stock photography of sparkling champagne, sipped by Victoria's Secret models. Smiling VIPs scoffing haute cuisine around enormous open fires in plush, candlelit, silk-upholstered rooms. They don't show the truth: a bunch of chronically unfit, middle-aged IT consultants sitting around on a sunken couch in their thermals, slurping cheap red plonk, scoffing yoghurt cake and yelling at their children next to a pile of smoking embers in a darkened room. They will then sit down to a meal of burnt lasagne, stale bread and undressed salad.

However, the Punters I have no sympathy with whatsoever, absolutely none - those who get the royal, insidious, Chinese water torture treatment over the course of the week - are the ones who decide it's acceptable to treat you like an idiot because they misguidedly think that you are only capable of cooking and cleaning. These punters show no interest in you as a human being, just because they've paid for your services. That's just rude. That's just dire. That's just not cricket. People like this are supposed to be on holiday – but you wouldn't know it. They are congenitally miserable and bent on making everyone else in their group feel the same. "Listen" you feel like saying, "I am not some sort of 'house boy' who masturbates with excitement every night about cleaning your bathroom."

Take heed - when exposed to these sorts of attitudes and behaviours, it doesn't take long for even the most well-meaning and diligent Chalet Bitch, with a couple of brain cells to rub together, to realise she's being treated like a dickhead and sink into apathy, followed by rage at the effrontery, before a swift descent into pondering the very depths of moral depravity. It doesn't take much, when you're sleep deprived – and particularly if, as in my case, you've got problems of your own on your mind. Patience and fortitude are the keystones of a successful Chalet Bitch's personality which didn't bode well for yours truly anyway. I quickly succumb to people fatigue and certainly don't suffer fools and petty behaviour at the best of times, which is a bit of an affliction to have in a job where you are constantly surrounded with humans demanding things of you (mostly bastards).

As a coping mechanism, I have developed the following revenge tactics, which I pass on to you as a cautionary tale, for next time you're on holiday or working in a chalet of your own:

Optrex in the morning tea

Let's just say it loosens the bowels. Best administered first thing on Sunday morning, in time for flight embarkation. Don't shoot yourself in the foot by administering it midweek. You're the one cleaning the toilets.

Fanny batter

Go to the loo and wipe yourself cack-handedly, using not quite enough loo roll. Don't wash your hands, then handle their food / personal possessions and watch in glee as they ingest your fanny batter and wee.

Pubes

Snip off and sprinkle inside ski gloves of victim. Unbelievably satisfying.

Toothbrush sabotage

Wholly fulfilling and ingeniously sinister. Also a surprisingly efficient way of getting rid of skid marks.

I have millions of these little tricks up my sleeve. Inventing them is a fun way of passing the dull hours of an evening. However, a word of warning on the last one: the subject of your own toothbrush. Don't forget it works both ways. In my experience, this is your most vulnerable spot. Protect it. All I'm saying is this: if your room mate Camilla can take quiet, cold revenge on her savage, rude, smelly, unpleasant guests by removing their toothbrushes from that little sink-side-cup and scrubbing brown encrusted skid marks off the bog pan - then what's to stop her doing the same to you? Perhaps you have an irritating habit that's wearing thin on Camilla - like using her hair dryer without asking, or slopping snow into the flat so her socks get wet when she's walking around. Perhaps you've drunkenly shagged a hot kitchen porter with his arse hanging out of his jeans that she's been mooning over all season. Therefore, do not leave your toothbrush, trustingly, oh so naively, in that scummy, toothpaste encrusted empty yoghurt pot that Camilla has placed to the left of the sink. You have got to live and work with this cow, arse-to-armpit, for the next six months and you are going to get pissed off with each other. I guarantee it.

As for me – I don't care if I am the only person in a thirty mile radius; my toothbrush is kept suspended in a laser-protected force-field in a sealed reinforced steel, air-tight unit, accessed only by a seven-digit pin number and retinal scan. I'm not taking any chances.

The Fireworks

"Did you know there was a blue moon over New Year?"

The Scruffy One and I are sitting on a ridge of snow overlooking the Hotel Mathilde further down the hill, the village spilling out in dotted lights below.

"Did you see it?"

"Yep. I showed it to my guests, but they didn't seem particularly interested."

"I thought it was amazing."

"Wankers. Some people are made of stone."

I remembered that when I was skiing on New Year's Day, I had spotted this unusual sight, stopped and stared at it, a moment, vast and wraithlike, suspended above the bone-white shard of a high peak. It was strange to see the sight of the moon in the day time, not the night. And the previous evening, in all the chaotic revelry of a New Year's party on the piste, I had glanced up and seen it while everyone else seemed to rage on obliviously. One could have counted the enamel etchings on its face.

Scruffy-but-Handsome and I have paused to sit for a moment, midway down the piste, with only the light from the moon reflecting off the snow to guide us home. I sip wine from a stolen bottle, pass it to him and look at the sky. To our left, the dark lace of fir trees trims up the hill into dark fathoms which are up-lit supernaturally by the snow. The sound of a piano drifts out of an open side-door of the hotel.

He sighs appreciatively and lies back on his elbows. "I've figured out one of the reasons I like it here so much," he murmurs, "It's all the light that's about. It's all a bit visual..."

In the distance, I can faintly hear a current of water from a trickling brook that isn't quite frozen, a piste basher rumbling on the other side of the hill, laughter from a gathering crowd somewhere just out of sight.

"Here's an idea," he says after a few minutes' of quiet. "What if you filmed a porno in space?"

We both look at the moon and consider the question.

"It would have to be one of those fetish ones…" I say, in agreement, "You know those people who are into breathing apparatus and stuff…"

"I've always wanted to do a gravity-free cum shot."

"Explain."

"Well, space stations have those long tunnels, right?"

"Yep"

"So, you stick the chick at one end. I whack off at the other end and then she has to jump around with her hands behind her back and catch the globules,"

"That is rank. Is this a regular fantasy of yours?"

"It's called the Space Facial"

"I see."

"Obviously you'd need to take into account Newton's third law…"

"Obviously."

"Equal and opposite reactions…."

"Yes, I know what Newton's third law is, thank you. And cheers for complementing this gorgeous evening with such delicate imagery,"

"Give us the wine."

As he takes the bottle from me, finally, it happens. What we've been waiting here for. A burst of purple and green light from a corner of the village and distant crack that ricochets and appears to come from somewhere behind us. Then another, and another. A spray of gold and a swirl of accompanying music. I let my vision blur. The colours trickle together in front of my eyes and intermingle with the sounds into one indefinable sensory experience. The fireworks continue for ten minutes and then subside, to the cheers of the unseen crowd, but neither of us move. We stay silent for a very long time and throughout it, I have something on the tip of my tongue to say. But I don't know what.

This is Your Luxury Ski Holiday

It was the day La Vache Qui Ski received a really quite long complaints letter about Chalet Christina, and she was almost purple in the face with rage.

"It's just such an audacity.... *Okeydokes?*"

She was strutting backwards and forth across the room, while Irksome-Blonde-19-Year-Old and I sat there in silence looking at our shoes.

"To be quite frank, your overall performance so far has been completely below par!"

La Vache Qui Ski was in her element. To my left, the Toulouse Sausage sat licking its fanny luxuriantly on the cream felt couch I'd just spent an hour hoovering.

"The whole thing just baffles me, okeydokes? I just don't understand this sort of unprofessional behaviour."

For a moment, I imagined how much pleasure it would give me to actually baffle her with something...like a cricket bat.

"I don't want to have to discuss this with Christa, for your sakes, but you leave me with no choice! I expect you to write me a full report with an explanation for each of the points in the letter, by this evening, or I will confiscate both your ski passes for the next three weeks." she stormed.

Ok. Fine. Allow me to annotate the complaints letter as follows:

Dear Sir / Madam

Ref: McGrath Christmas ski holiday Chalet Christina Dec 20 - 27ᵗʰ

How very disappointing to have to write this letter. Whilst I appreciate that in these times of economic difficulty, tour operators and individuals alike are struggling to survive, I feel compelled to write and complain after, to put it mildly, a most disappointing stay in Chalet Christina over the Christmas period. Indeed, I feel you demonstrate quite some chutzpah in offering your guests such a lacklustre package in terms of both accommodation and service.

Chutzpah indeed. Good word.

We have not holidayed with your company before and I'm sad to say, after the horrendous experience we had, we will not be holidaying with you again.

Good. I wouldn't wish that charmless cretin on any other hapless Chalet Bitch in future years. When he arrived, I knew I had living proof that money can buy neither charisma, nor manners, nor cleanliness. He, Alistair, owned a company that manufactured strip lights and was worth about £156 million, had the figure of a heavily pregnant woman, gel-soaked, blondish, American Psycho style hair and acted as if he'd had his arse wiped with £50 notes his entire life. She, his Czech wife Magdaléna, was about as warm and cuddly as a slug and clearly of the age at which a woman has to choose to cultivate either her face or her arse – and had evidently gone for the latter, since her face was as haggard and gaunt as Ronnie Wood's would be if he sucked on a lemon soaked in acid. I observed that this (and her sour expression) was probably as a result of the fact that whenever she appeared to be enjoying her food, her husband would snipe her with a poisonous remark like,

"Oh, we are enjoying our full fat holiday diet, aren't we dear?"

What a bastard. The woman was fully bulimic. I had two wait fifteen minutes between serving courses while she dashed to the bathroom to chunder.

All your staff members, including your Resort Manager are clearly under-trained and inexperienced. The younger of the two was totally under-qualified to run a chalet of this caliber.

Now that I can't argue with. Both these women are about

as useful as a gypsy flavoured cock.

On the first night we arrived, in a taxi, no one was waiting to greet us. We had not been given the full address by head office and the resort manager was nowhere to be seen. It took three phone calls and 45 minutes before we could get hold of her. Finally she sent the chalet staff out to meet us. They turned out to be an extremely slovenly and under-dressed school leaver and a slightly more (we hoped) mature girl, neither of whom looked particularly pleased to see us.

Oh. Apologies if we weren't shitting ourselves with glee at their arrival, but they omit to mention here that they arrived at 2am, instead of the pre-agreed 7pm. We had therefore been waiting in the chalet for seven hours, after spending the entire day cleaning it and were fucking knackered and not a little bit peeved. They also omit to mention the delicious supper we had prepared, but which they declined to eat, because they'd 'had a MacDonald's' on the way.

I would also like to address what, on your website, you call your 'award-winning' cuisine.

In my opinion this would be better described as a culinary festival of torture, featuring, among other things, Carrefour budget cornflakes, burnt lasagna containing no béchamel sauce, crumble made with tinned potatoes (a remarkable, if audacious, take on a traditional British favourite desert) and a gelatinous lemon tart that hadn't set. On the subject of lasagna- how you people have the gall to serve this dish on what you call a 'luxury ski holiday' is beyond me.

On the last point I can't help but agree – but this isn't my fucking fault is it? It's on the company menu. By declaration of the hideous Christa, we have to cook it don't we? And who designed the menu and wrote the recipes? You've got it! Therefore, Christa, is it my fault or yours that the lemon tart didn't set? The recipe is a complete pile of shit! I do recall, also, your arrogant outburst during training week when someone questioned the validity of lasagna as a menu choice:

"Our guests can't believe their luck when they see lasagna's on the menu," I believe you said. Well, yes, everyone loves lasagna, don't they Christa? That's until they realise that the recipe was dreamt up by an obese, lard-swilling egotist and executed by a pissed-up teenager. All that aside, can you really expect me to turn out a decent lasagna when you call me into work at 7pm on my one treasured day off, because the guests have been making a fuss? I was shitfaced by that time Christa! I'd drunk five pints, smoked a joint and had a Jager Bomb chaser. So yes, I turned up drunk, forgot to put the béchamel in and then, if memory serves, sat eating the remains of the lasagna out of the dish at the end of the table because I had the munchies. Should I not have done that? Perhaps if the Resort Manager could cook, she could have stood in for me, considering it wasn't her day off! Oh yes. I can explain the potato crumble too. It seems, after some investigation into the contents of the rubbish bin, that the Irksome one got her Pommes mixed up with her Pommes de Terre. Could happen to any retard or inanimate object.

The younger of your two hosts showed a quite distressing lack of interest in either personal or food hygiene. Her hairs were a regular garnish for our dinner. Once, my son found a false nail in his tiramisu and no cheese or coffee was ever offered after dinner. In addition, we actually found a whole, uncovered raw chicken had been placed on top of a cake in the fridge. At no point during the week was the chalet cleaned to our satisfaction, in particular the toilets, which were, to be quite frank, a complete fright.

Ok. Most of this is complete bollocks. First of all the chicken wasn't *on* the cake, it was *next to* the cake, and that was only because Alastair (the booze soaked halfwit) had demanded we move half the food out of the top of the fridge, so he could fit in extra bottles of plonk. There was never any cheese offered after dinner because on the three separate occasions that the McGraths got arseholed, they were afflicted with the munchies and scoffed all the camembert, including the sacrificial one I keep for just that purpose.

On the subject of cleanliness, I can't help feeling this is a severe case of the pot accusing the kettle of being a bit sooty. Magdaléna's room was, at all times, an unreasonable tip. A thick stew of soiled towels covered in make up – lipstick, mascara and unidentified brown smudges; dirty, streaky underwear; junk; wet tissues and food often trodden into the carpet with wine sploshes on the furniture. Alastair, on the other hand, made a constant habit of flooding the bathroom and leaving the most copious skid marks that I have ever seen in my life all over the inside of the loo It was impossible to stay on top of and still get five minutes of skiing time each day.

The Christmas dinner was the straw that broke the camel's back. The horrendous like of it I have never encountered in my life. Only one of the staff actually deigned to turn up on Christmas Day and she didn't seem to know that Champagne should be served chilled! She was so drunk at work she fell asleep inside the store cupboard and we weren't served our meal until half past nine. The turkey was charred to a crisp on the outside and raw inside!

There may be some truth in this…but come on, I was in a chalet-Christmas-comedown nightmare with very little motor neuron function to help me.

On the whole, your staff showed a complete lack of manners and professionalism…

Ha! That's rich coming from a man who every morning thumped downstairs, banged open the kitchen door and gruffly demanded coffee while treating me to a magnificent silhouette of his low-slung ball-sack, with the light streaming sublimely from the window through the kaftan that he wore to hide his enormous belly. A diabetic, whole-sale collapse waiting to happen.

153

The most disappointing aspect of the whole week was the fact that your Resort Manager completely failed to deal with our complaints. We just couldn't understand her lack of action at all.

Well that's easy. She's always way too busy thumbing her arse, and telling us all how busy she is, to actually be of use to anyone

P.S. Oh yes, Mr. McGrath, I almost forgot to say. I do hope you enjoyed your aggressive bout of in-flight diarrhea on the journey home – I put an extra helping of Optrex in your tea on changeover morning just to make sure you got the hit of the whole fruit.

Yours with all cordiality and respect

Etc...

Irksome-Blonde-19-Year-Old in a Scrape

I couldn't stay angry at the Irksome one for dropping me in the shit at Christmas for long. Not after I found out what had really happened to her on Christmas Eve.

She had told the Resort Manager that she was ill with a sore throat and suffering home sickness. This was utter bollocks. I knew exactly where she'd been. Up to her tonsils in crocodile. Anyone would have a sore throat if they'd had their lips wrapped round such a varied assortment of genitals recently as she had. Shortly after I lost her on Christmas Eve, Calamity had spotted her being bundled, giggling and screaming with delight, into a car by the crocodile– aka Byron – one of the many good looking, licentious bar staff who work in The Drop Inn. She didn't look particularly depressed on Boxing Day, when she finally materialized in our apartment glowing from ear to ear, with cum in her backcombed barnet.

However, it turns out Byron wasn't the only inebriated reptile that got lucky with her. In fact, it appeared she may have been the victim of a prank. Don't get me wrong, she only had her own stupidity to blame, but no girl of 19 deserves to have a video of her with three cocks in her mouth broadcast on a giant, flatscreen telly in a busy club. Well, not unless she's been paid a princely sum for it, anyway. Everyone saw it - all her friends, colleagues and even some of our chalet guests. No matter how much of a silly tart she is, she didn't deserve that.

"Fuck me" said Calamity, as we sat there aghast, staring at the spectacle on the screen. "That's poor. She's not even deep-throating."

By the looks of it, they got her drunk, stoned, possibly mashed and properly went to town on her. This explained why she could remember nothing of it, and actually endorsed her explanation for her absence on Christmas Day (she claimed she woke up naked in the bath, in an empty apartment). They filmed her fellating all three of them, still in their costumes (crocodile, frog and, somewhat appropriately, Bananaman) with the full intention of broadcasting it to the entire resort. They even took a sound bite of her moaning…"Owwwww, they won't all fit" … and got the DJ to mix it into his set. I mean, apart from being fucking hilarious, that's just cruel.

Kind of a sinister edge to the whole thing, though, in my book. The poor thing was mortified. It took a while for her to cotton on to what was happening, but suffice to say, that evening found her sobbing in the toilets in hysterical tears.

"…do you think it's gone round the whole resort?" she wailed, when she eventually let me in.

"No, no….I'm sure it hasn't. And anyway, you're probably not the first girl this has happened to and you won't be the last," I soothed. "I bet they make a habit of this sort of thing."

"Bastards. Those lads are bang out of order," said The Foxy Chef, looking round the door, genuinely enraged. "I'm gonna have words."

"Yeth it'th dithguthting behaviour" agreed Fenella, the Irksome one's best friend. "Perhapth we should tell the Re-thort Manager?"

"Christ no, don't involve her. Look it's not that bad" I lied, rubbing her back. "You're just going to have to brazen it out. Scratch it up to experience."

"Yeth. If you act like you don't care, neither will anyone elth" agreed Fenella.

"I think I might be sick…" grimaced the Irksome one, and promptly leant forward and spewed on my shoes. Due recompense for me for giving her sympathy.

This is prime example of how people completely lose the

plot on ski seasons and do things, almost every day, that in the real world would be considered utterly illogical, completely regrettable, perverse, unfeasible and ridiculous. Things like jumping off roofs into snow drifts and climbing up buildings, or setting off in the dark to remote, frozen locations without a torch or a phone. It seems to me that ski resorts function unabashedly on the slave labour of randy British teenagers, without taking much responsibility for their welfare. It is, after all, very similar to university, with no lectures or exams. Public school daughters and sons scuttle off to do a season in the Alps, with the uninitiated parent under the erroneous impression that it's some kind of finishing school. What returns home? An alcoholic sex-maniac with syphilis and possibly a life-changing injury. Which, in many ways, means it's exactly like a finishing school, come to think of it.

You hear about it in the Daily Mail...

SEX SKIVVYING AND SQUALOR, MY TEEN ROMP AS A CHALET GIRL

....then some gut-churningly pedestrian confess-all article about the loutish behaviour, drug taking, and sexual deviancy exhibited by upper-middle class British teenagers turned loose in the mountains, drinking each other's piss and having bum sex in the middle of the road. Legends abound. According to folk lore, there was once an 18-year-old girl named 'Harriet the Chariot' who slept with a total of two hundred people during her time as a Chalet Bitch. If I've got my maths right, that must mean she was bonking about two a day. Every day.

Personally, I don't think it's a wonder people go slightly nuts under these close-knit, sexually pent-up circumstances. There's something about the mountains that disturbs the mind; deranges you. It has something to do with the enormity of the landscape and piffling smallness of man, and something to do with being in a carefree bubble where it's always the holidays and never Christmas. Endless Winter. Oh, the stress and strain of being a serial seasonnaire. The main focus of one's daily concerns:

1. Has it snowed?

2. Where is the next drink/joint/shag coming from?

3. Is my ski gear outrageous enough?

5. Where the fuck am I?

Pet Hates

This week I have two particularly irritating additions to make to my list of Pet Hates:

Veggies

AKA a fucking pain in the arse. The family we were looking after this week has a vegan mother. She's sweet enough - Vicky is her name – but is like some sort of locust, ploughing her way through the fruit bowl as if it is the only the thing to eat in the chalet, and drinking this revolting bright green health drink that's the colour of the sludge you find in the bottom of a ditch. For this, she needed me to get the blender out every morning and combine it with apples and cucumber to make it taste acceptable - although from her face it clearly still tasted like horse manure.

Hair

Yes, hair. I'd like to talk about it. The amount some people shed is both intolerable and fascinating. Hairs are like toenail clippings and grandparents. You don't mind your own but other people's are revolting and you don't want them anywhere near you. When you're cleaning, there is always one sticking out of the sponge or wrapped round your fingers. Sometimes, it's hard to tell a pube from a chest hair and it's just not worth the risk either way. Wherever it came from, you don't want it anywhere near you and especially not your food. Some marriages are made in heaven. Smoked salmon and avocado, for example. Strawberries and cream. Chas and Dave. Others are not. Rum and raisin. A hellish idea. Charles and Diana. Hair and food. Wong dot com. For the above reasons, clearing up after children in a chalet is a dream come true as the little darlings haven't yet sprouted. They do leave the most appalling skid marks though, or quite often don't flush at all. Adults are another story. They seem to spend their entire time either shedding like a mangey St Bernard or harvesting crops of body hairs from god knows where. If you're not scraping a film of minute, freshly cropped sproutings from the side of the bath, or untangling long slimy hairs interlaced with goo, secretions and excretions from the plughole, you're sweeping heaps of unidentified strands from the bathroom floor. Either the nanny staying in our chalet with that Brazilian family had alopecia, or extremely long pubes. I could have stuffed a mattress with it. Seriously. So next time you're staying in a hotel / chalet / catered accommodation, spare a thought for the poor mite scrabbling around on her hands and knees in your bathroom in the morning, collecting together your deposits. I might create some kind of follicular art installation.

Birthday

For the third time this week, I wake up in Skater Boy's bed and am seized by the horrible idea that I've overslept and missed breakfast.

Then it hits me with a wave of euphoric relief. "It's my day off."

Simultaneously, the Scruffy One, who has been sleeping in an uncomfortable half-sitting position on The Shelf, with a semi-eaten raclette baguette on his chest, sits bolt upright and hits his head on the ceiling.

"*OHGOD-Imlateforwork.....*" his eyes goggle and spin around the room wildly, "Jesuz*fuck*" he clutches his head where he's banged it. "Judas!"

"'s ok" I groan from the bed, raising my hand weakly. "S'day off....."

"Mmmmmm?" he frowns down at me. "Oh.....oh thank fuck." He collapses back on his pillow and moans.

Not long after this my Jager-hangover kicks in. Jager hangovers are a savage breed. Second only in severity to the champagne hangover, which comes with a healthy tinge of self-loathing and depression. Jager gives you a tingling, nervous-all-over feeling, a raging fire in the brain, flashing lights in front of the eyes and a creeping nausea in the belly that never quite subsides all day. I lie on the bed in agony, semi-conscious, with one foot on the floor to stop the room bucking and spinning. To my right, the Man of Leisure is asleep spread-eagled in puddle of beer in the kitchen, still in ski boots and his frog costume.

I know I've chundered somewhere. But where?

Desperate for the loo, but also naked and suffering from a bastard behind the eyes, I wave one arm around the near vicinity and blindly come across Skater Boy's pyjama bottoms. Wrapping them round my boobs, I wobble into the bathroom, still drunk.

"I can see your fanny you know." The Man of Leisure is prostrate, but not, as I had assumed, unconscious.

"Yep. Thanks buddy. Brilliant."

I pee, and then it comes -the chunder. It comes fast. I have to turn around and do it into my own wee. As I heave, I feel a towel being placed over my naked shoulders and a hand holding back my hair. The Scruffy One. His chivalry is slightly mortifying but nausea is usurping embarrassment.

"Hey…don't worry," he says soothingly, rubbing my back as I spew. "I threw up on my own cat once. All over its back and head. It started eating it, which made me be sick even more. It was excellent."

"This isn't helping," I gag between heaves.

"Focus on the chunks. It'll all be over soon."

Purged, I sit down heavily on the toilet and survey the bathroom helplessly. Why are all the dirty plates in the shower? The Scruffy One sees my confusion and explains, "We've been using it as a dishwasher."

I allow him to guide me back to the bed where I sit down, rather crestfallen, next to Skater Boy's unconscious form. I try to focus on what's around me, but I feel as if someone has taken out my eyeballs, dipped them in superglue, then drawing pins, swapped them over, and put them back in the wrong sockets

"Ugh… I keep stepping in squalid, damp things," The Scruffy One is trying to pick his way back to the kitchen. The floor is a sea of discarded clothes and refuse. He bends down, cautiously retrieves an old, dried up tea bag from next to the skirting board and switches on the kettle. "I can't remember a thing…what the fuck happened in here last night?"

"An after party" The Man of Leisure says helpfully, rolling languidly onto his back and making the Scruffy One jump.

"Ooh, fuck me, where did you come from?"

"I dunno buddy. But I'm nursing the most enormous semi," the Man of Leisure wiggles his hips around to illustrate.

The Scruffy One reaches the kitchen and rinses the teabag under the cold tap.

"Ahhhh… you feel wonderful!' he leans back his head and puts the teabag on his eye. "My god. My eyes are on fire. I want to be in a warm fizzy bath of Alka Seltza. I want to be cuddled from inside." His activities are making me feel peculiar. The fear is gaining on me.

"Why are you putting a manky tea bag on your eye?"

"Because they're sore and it feels amazing. It's like someone's scrubbed my eyes with love," he sighs passionately, removing the teabag and dropping it in a mug into which he then pours boiling water.

"My God, this place is a shit hole. I got out of bed just now and nearly put my foot in a puddle of sick."

Oh. That was me.

Skater Boy belches loudly and croaks, "…'ass djin" waving a hand in the air at the Scruffy One.

"What's that? You want gin? Under these circumstances? My God man, that's disgusting. What's wrong with water?"

"No…passsss th' bin" he tries again.

"Oh, you want the bin"

Scruffy-but-Handsome kicks the bin towards Skater Boy, into which the latter vomits copiously and lays back on the bed, pale faced and groaning. For a few minutes, we all lie in silence, sweating and panting under our duvets and contemplating our individual purgatories. Then Skater Boy raises his head and looks pleadingly at his roommate.

"Make me a breakfast, will you buddy?"

"What? Handle food? You must be joking…"

"Tea then? C'mon. A real friend would."

We all voice an objection to this familiar emotional blackmail in unison, and grudgingly the Scruffy One hands over the cup of recycled tea. Watching as Skater Boy sips it makes me retch.

Later, somewhat revived, we sit round in bed eating breakfast consisting of several gulps of 4 Euro red wine from a bottle with the cork pushed in, three raw frankfurters, half a stale croissant, some cold, week-old left over lasagne, and a joint.

"I can't remember anything about last night," I decide. "Was there a man in here with bloody knuckles…?"

"Oh yes," says The Scruffy One, with lasagne hanging from his moustache, "Campbell Campbell."

"What? *That* was Campbell Campbell?"

"Yep"

"Christ, she's scraping the barrel with that one," Skater Boy snorts. Campbell Campbell is another of Calamity's somewhat suspect season squeezes. She has been getting through them at an alarming rate since Old Man Swiss broke the seal. There was YoYo Dan so named, according to the Man of Leisure, "Either because he always carries some stupid yellow yoyo round with him, or because of the mood swings associated with his drug habit. I forget."

For a while, she was mooning after Petit Pierre but now she had her sights set on Campbell Campbell – to all intents and purposes a criminal psychopath chef at the Hotel St George, who had been arrested the previous winter for locking his kitchen porter inside an industrial dishwasher. Allegedly it was a dare, but that was somewhat irrelevant in light of the fact he almost killed the guy - boiling water comes out of those things. The hapless chap was carted off to hospital with the back half of his skin missing. Needless to say we were all petrified of Campbell Campbell.

"Has an enormous cock apparently."

"Oh, well that's alright then," said Scruffy-but-Handsome, scanning the apartment suspiciously, "Where is he by the way? Did somebody chuck him out?'

"She took him home and shagged him," says Skater Boy. "I told her we needed to get rid of him because he was freaking everyone out."

"Jesus, do you think it's ok for her to be going out with that?" I ask.

"She'll be fine. Her vagina has teeth and spits acid thirty feet when threatened. It's him I'd be worried about.""Oh, fuck – Happy Birthday!" The Scruffy One suddenly remembering what day it is.

"Oh gawd, don't remind me"

"Ahaaaaa!" Skater Boy is suddenly upright, eyes gleaming. He scoops me into a chest-crushing embrace, pins me to the mattress and starts dry humping me and trying to lick my face, like a dog, his naked arse on show, inches from the Man of Leisure's face.

"Oh Christ! My eyes!"

"Right. This calls for a celebratory red wine and herbal breakfast" Skater Boy leaps off me in business like fashion. "Where did I put those Rizlas?" Skater Boy has been planning my birthday for weeks. Half of me feels flattered; the other half knows that only in a situation where he is guaranteed to get off his tits, would he show such single-minded determination and purpose. The ketamine he sourced from The Geordie Ninja a month previously and managed not to bosh all of it himself (well apart from a couple of lines, 'just to check it'). The weed he'd had Fedexed to the ski resort tourist office and casually collected yesterday morning, as if it was a perfectly normal package containing socks from his mum. He had also managed to score a gram of Charlie from a dodgy bloke called Dutch Dave (actually from Basildon) who he had 'bumped into' off-piste a week previously. The Valium, I had come by myself one morning while I was cleaning that neurotic Vegan woman Vicky's bathroom (I made sure it actually was Valium this time). Her bathroom cabinet was like a walk-in herbal and prescription pharmacy: Valium, Diazepam, St John's Wort, vitamin supplements. We had uppers, downers and sidewaysers, and now some smoother-outers.

The plan was to meet Calamity, bosh half a Valium each and neck a bottle of vodka on the lift. Then ski over to the other valley go to Gringos, get wrecked to the point of inability to stand, let alone ride, and thumb a lift home.

Good plan.

On the way back from the toilets in Gringos, where we have none-too surreptitiously been shoving coke up our noses, Scruffy-but-Handsome and I are greeted by the sight of Skater Boy sticking his tongue down Irksome-Blonde-19-Year-Old's throat. He is grinding her up against a pole in the middle of the dance floor.

"Huh," I say to Scruffy-but-Handsome, matter of factly. "And on my birthday as well. How nice."

As per usual, it has all turned out peachy keen for The Irksome one since her little cock sucking incident. The Geordie Ninja took umbrage to Byron and co's ill-treatment of his beloved, and heaped justice upon her chief tormentor by treating him to a knuckle sandwich. Byron has been wandering around the resort showing off a very fierce purple shiner, and was laid off work without pay until it went away (black eyes send out the wrong message to customers apparently.) The Irksome One then declared the Geordie Ninja her knight in shining shell suit, and fell into his arms like some sort of damsel in distress. They have since been ensconced in each other's nether regions twenty four seven. Still, even shagging The Geordie Ninja is impressive work for a girl with an arse that has its own gravitational pull. Lord knows what the fallout will be now that she's turned her attentions onto Skater Boy.

"I'm going for a fag," I say crossly, glancing at the snogging pair with disgust.

We sit outside on a bench while Scruffy-but-Handsome makes rollies. It's a night of crystalline clarity. A white night in sharp focus. He points to an arrangement of stars. Three of them, equidistant.

"That's Orion's belt."

He has the filter tip poised, balanced between his lips, and it moves gently up and down as he speaks, one eye slightly squinted with the effort.

"Nice try. You don't know any constellations really do you?"

"I do actually," he removes the filter tip and places it gently into the Rizla, raising his eyebrows slightly. "My Dad taught me when I was a nipper. He said it was a failsafe way of pulling birds."

I look at him mockingly and he laughs, lights both cigarettes at the same time and hands one to me.

We sit quietly, looking up.

"It reminds me a bit of Mongolia," he says. "No light pollution...I've never seen stars like it."

I glance at the silhouette of him next to me. It has started to snow in large, heavy flakes.

"You've done and seen quite a lot for one so young, haven't you?"

The Scruffy One frowns a little in embarrassment and shrugs. Silence follows. I aim the heel of my boot at a lump of ice in front of me, crushing it flat.

"Does he do it deliberately or is it by mistake?"

He looks confused. "Who?"

"Him," I nod my head towards Gringos. "Act like a total twat all the time."

"Oh," he glances at me slightly regretfully. "It's by mistake I think."

Steam erupts from the door behind us as the bouncer opens it and a tall, narrow figure walks out onto the decking.

"Ahhh...madame!" Skater Boy says grandly, spotting me and sidling over, making a formal little bow and extending a hand towards me. "C'mon. Your presence is required on the dance floor."

"I think I'll pass."

Scruffy-but-Handsome stands abruptly up and puts his

168

hands into his jacket pockets. "I've had enough. I'm gonna go home and watch a film."

"Ahh come on mate, you can't leave now you big Timmy. Things are just getting going in there."

Scruffy-but-Handsome ignores this and looks at me.

"...you can come if you want to."

Skater Boy is undeterred, puffing on his joint.

"Right then Bird. You going home with him? Or staying here with me?" he asks, plainly.

I look from one to the other.

The Chairlift of Lost Hope

Have spent the morning not so much cleaning as poking things ineffectually and getting angry with inanimate objects. The bath soaps wouldn't arrange nicely in the little dish. I couldn't get them to line up properly. In the end, I just chucked them on the floor in a rage and sat down with my head against the bath.

On the marble top was a bottle of perfume belonging to a guest. Safari. The very same my mother used to wear. Without thinking, I reached for it, spritzed a little on my wrist and held it to my nose. In that smell was the shape of her hands, a note of her laughter, and the soft hair on the nape of her neck that I used to stroke when I was a baby. The way she left a magic sparkle on everything she touched. We have to content ourselves with moments like this, as ephemeral as they are - as breath disappearing from your lips on a chilly day. These moments are locked away in little boxes in your mind and can only be stumbled across at random, unlocked by an unforeseen key. And when they are, it's a treat to bask in the sun of a little memory, until it fades again, and the loved one is gone, like a morning's dream.

The truth is, I was expecting a sting in the tail of last year. But the death of my best friend was more unexpected and painful a sting than I could have imagined in my wildest dreams. If only I hadn't let her down so badly. So many chances I missed. The older I become, the less I realise I know. There have been so many jokes and escapades we would have laughed about together in the last few weeks. That sense of emptiness when you snigger to yourself about something only she would appreciate, then reach for the phone, only to recollect there's no one at the other end - that sense never goes away. I could have raved about my new friends, the anarchy of Skater Boy, the beauty all around me. I could have made her laugh with an anecdote about the, frankly, gold plated cunt who's been staying in our chalet avec *(charmante) famille.* Specifically, the giant turd he managed to get wedged in his toilet brush (like a little nugget of gold just waiting for me to find it after breakfast one morning when cleaning the bathroom), and the resulting punishment I administered, by cleaning the toilet with his toothbrush. But somehow all that seems so heartless and bland, knowing Shazzer isn't around to laugh at any of it with her dirty Babs Windsor laugh, or shriek down the phone at me to DUMP THAT ROTTER THIS INSTANT. Or reassure me that it's perfectly reasonable to clean a toilet with a toothbrush, if the person's really a cunt.

Today is a colourless day. We are living in a constant cloud. Often if the weather is bad, tiredness sets in, and with it a deep weariness of routine. On days like this, Skater Boy has no impetus to ski and our time is spent hunkered down in the darkened recesses of the crack den. The days start to slip through my fingers. All too often, I drag my heavy boots up the vertically narrow, concrete stairwell in one corner of the apartment block, to find him having one of his Abominable Snow Bum days, shivering under a duvet on the futon in a swirl of nicotine fumes.

The Scruffy One lost patience with this act long ago and has given up trying.

"The snow's shit – but it's soft. Why don't we go and hire you a snowboard and I'll give you a little lesson," he says this morning, as I sit there on the edge of the bed trying to coax Skater Boy.

"Yeah, come on," I prod the human sack of laundry on the futon. "Wouldn't you like to get out of the flat today? You spent all of yesterday inside…"

"I can't be arsed…it's not like there's powder," it stretches out a weather-beaten hand, a withered, anorexic cigarette trapped in the pincer of the third and forth fingers, and begins tapping the laptop keyboard vaguely. "Gonna watch some porn…"

I pick my way over to the window, trying to touch the filthy floor as little as possible. "Why've you got the curtains drawn – it's like a morgue in here you stinky boy."

"Don't" he explodes, curling in on himself like a petrified vampire as light floods through the gap. "Fucksake Bird – look I've got no green left, I'm skint and I'm fucked off with cleaning up after punters. Either watch a film with me or fuck off. I'm knackered and I'm not going all the way up the mountain just to watch you fall on your arse all afternoon."

I'm silent for a minute, looking out of the window. The stuffy weariness of the room seems to emanate from him and permeate everything. He coughs, loudly. Hackingly. The atmosphere is vile. The Scruffy One pulls on ski pants then sits on the bed to roll a cigarette. I glance down and watch the muscles flex in his forearm as he does it. The hairs on his arm; golden, his worker's fingers teasing out the tobacco gingerly into the delicate paper, as if nervous he might drop it. He rolls the cigarette up, licks the edge in one swift movement, his head going side to side. His thumb and forefinger smooth it down and he pushes it slickly behind his ear. A well-rehearsed gesture. He looks up at me and shrugs apologetically, rolls his eyes.

"Well, look. I'm going," he says snatching up his board and helmet and making for the door. "Give me a shout if you change your mind."

"Why d'you wanna do that shit anyway? You won't like it. Snowboarding sucks," Skater Boy raises a corner of the duvet and indicated the strip of space between him and the edge of the futon, "Snowboarding girls are a double negative. Here…get in…come on, I'm nursing the biggest semi in the world…"

I stare at him, sceptically.

"A *real* friend would…"

I do as he says and lay there in a half-conscious daze all afternoon, ignoring the phone when it rings.

The Great Divide

The road that winds up to Chalet Christina takes me right through the heart of the village. The flood-lit street is lined with immaculate boutiques before it cuts under a bridge beneath the piste and meanders on into the peaceful magnificence of millionaire's row. Wending my way up the quiet road as usual this afternoon, I count the Bentleys, Hummers and Ferraris collecting snow by the wayside. I count the designer billboards - Cavali, Moncler, Cartier, Hermes, Ralph Lauren, Graff, Dolce & Gabbana, and spot the ladies with rabbit fur pompom hats and diamante chains around their pony-skin boots. Then, near the bridge, I pause outside a shop, as I always do. The same one every time. In the window a golden mannequin is swathed in a sapphire-blue, velvet and tulle gown with a peacock-feather head-dress. It is flanked by two vaguely ridiculous gape-mouthed, orange crocodiles sporting black studded collars. Next door to this boutique is an art dealer. You can buy a genuine Warhol or a Dali melting clock sculpture, should it so take your fancy, while getting your skis (inlaid with diamonds, naturally) waxed in the hire shop opposite.

Bling. Oh yes. There's bling. The entire place is an enormous, harlequin theatre. More Michelin stars per head than anywhere in the world, they say. One of the only places the rich can actually make a dent in their wallets and, indeed, nowhere else on earth will you find such a pile of hideously expensive hideous crap. Shops peddling bejeweled goggles, red and white rhinestone headphones, a child's mother-of-pearl snowboard with gold-plated bindings, gleaming pink diamonds the size of your fist, designer handbags, lingerie and more. Everything and everyone is lined with either white fluff from an endangered species or diamonds. There are women with hair like enameled candy floss, who look as if Liza

Minnelli threw up on them. Chihuahuas in pink earmuffs peek from colossal handbags or from elaborate couture coats fashioned from the corpses of a thousand squirrels. These women don't ski...they are chauffeured up the mountain in ridiculously overblown Hummers and totter across the piste to the champagne igloo in snakeskin heels to gorge on caviar and a buffet of puddings and class As. They are the worst kind of, what my mother used to call, with a disdainful curl of her lip, "*snowbunnies.*"

The Russians in particular are a spectacle to be marveled at. Seven-foot, gazelle-limbed, pumped full of collagen and vodka, tottering around on sheet ice in stilettos with their Mafioso husbands (or more accurately, pimps) bringing up the rear, complete with giant cigar and narky, diamante-collared Rottweiler.

The price tags make one gasp and stretch one's eyes. Take a ride in the Hermes horse and carriage up to the Louis Vuitton Moet & Hennecy hotel 'Le Cerf D'Or'. It's the place to be, darling. Twenty thousand Euros a night for the Palace Suite. After all, who wouldn't pay that to stay in a hotel with a golden stag prancing in front of it and a gigantic diamond ring nestled in the branches of a tree outside? You even get an army of minions to put your skis out on the piste for you each morning with a little nametag, if your limbs are too withered with wealth to lift them. Chalet Les Ameriers is the paragon of it all, with its private spa, ice room and pool. Dom P flows from the bath taps, antique furnishings abound and Monets hang from the walls. It has its own restaurant, private ski shop and cinema. The butler and chauffeur come as standard for those with two hundred and five thousand Euros a week going spare for their little ski trip. Hey, you're arriving in a private jet with cocaine-stuffed seats, why not baby?

Once you get past the intense jealousy, the excess makes you feel quite queasy.

And yet, I find myself musing, why do the rich people look so miserable and stressed? I've lost count of the stricken-faced coat-racks I see wondering around the place with their lower lips on their foreheads, towing a Romanian nanny and three small, evil, children, clad head-to-toe in Saber-toothed-tiger hide (dyed pink, obviously). Those pelts must weigh heavy on those knobbly little shoulders.

Still. There is something about the lighting within this particular shop that draws my eye. Deep inside, the walls are lined with heavy, glossy sables, minks and fox furs and I long to run my finger through the cool, deluxe hairs. Tonight, as every night, I am struck simultaneously by a sense of derision for the crassness of it all and a tension that keeps me lingering outside. A sense of my own place in the scheme of things; the disparity between my world out here, and the world of the gold mannequin, in there. It is an unfamiliar feeling, yet I have never ventured inside. I have never had the guts.

As I enter, the bell over the door wobbles into action. It's as if the crystal-vase peace within the shop has been walloped with a jack-hammer. I pass slowly along the rail, stroking the wares. The shop assistant in a corseted grey dress rakes me up and down. She takes in my bashed up Sorrels, shabby ski jacket and messy hair poking out underneath a grimy acid-green bobble hat. Her nose wrinkles, almost imperceptibly.

In my best French (I have been practicing the line for the last five minutes in my head) I ask to try on a divine Hockley number, just for the fuck of it. Not a flicker passes over her face. She merely looks slowly at the coat and then back to me.

"That jacket is over sree sousand Euros," she says, in a husky, patient monotone. She is already steering me towards the door, "I am sorry I 'ave not the time to 'elp you."

Lest I forget! I am nothing here but an unruly *Rosbif* lout. A time waster, and worse still, an *encroacher* on their world.

Not to be taken seriously on any count. Not to be given an iota of respect.

The upshot of this, I decide as I continue up the road (not a little hurt by what has passed), is a strange sort of inverted snobbery which defines the seasonnaire. The mutual act of nose-look-downarie between the baggy-clothed British worker in mud-soaked Primark 'ugg' boots and the gregariously wealthy, propertied punter. My one consolation is that our scorn and contempt is mutual.

But then again, the big two hundred Euro note pressed into my hand at the end of the week sweetens the pill. Then the offender is gone in a whiff of overpowering perfume, presumably never to be seen again.

Needless to say, we don't let the rich spoil our fun.

ou remember someone, what you recall is like smoke on the wind. It changes and moves as you do. When you try to grasp it, get hold of it, it simply vanishes. You are left with impressions and speculations. When there is nothing new to learn, soon your mind begins to fill in the gaps until you don't know what's real anymore, like darning a sock again and again until there is more new thread than old.

Can you ever really know someone? Or is the person you feel you know merely a cipher of 'the real them' that lurks in caves inside your mind? We all dance the dance; hide in shadows and behind masks. You can't internalise people or consume them. You can't know, really, truly what expression they are wearing behind their face. Would you even want to know? It occurs to me how extremely inflammatory (yet oddly liberating) it would be, if everyone whom I secretly thought was a cunt *knew* what I was thinking. Tell the truth... that polite, interested face you put on all the time is exhausting, isn't it? One's inner monologue is often at stark odds to an innocuous exterior persona.

I'd had a dream that Shazzer and I were lying under a tree in a garden, staring up through the lattice-work of fragile leaves, shadows upon shadows. She was silent and when I looked, I saw her lips had been sewn shut. I turned away.

Next morning she rang me.

"How was the discussion? Was it like the Krauts playing football on Christmas Day? Temporary seasonal ceasefire in hostilities? Or permanent peace agreement?"

"We broke up."

"Ah."

"It's exhausting having the same discussions again and again and again," I complained. "How can I think for two when one of the two, me, has no idea what it wants from life? I have all these dreams and goals that are blocked by having a passenger."

"Feminism has achieved nothing," she said, sagely. "It's just made it harder."

"It's just that recently I've been getting an overwhelming feeling that I'd need to be stoned in order to get through my own wedding."

"That can't be good."

"No, I didn't think so."

"Oh…poppet. I really think you've done the right thing."

I had placed the engagement ring, an emerald cut stone with two flanking baguettes in a platinum setting, on the table in front of him, where it shuddered slightly. He didn't look at it. He looked at me and said coldly, "I swore I'd never let anyone do that to me." In that moment, all the joyful memories I had and the castles I'd built in the air melted and swam in a sad muddy pool of disenchantment in my stomach and the widening space between us. First love, you see, feels like the most unique, intoxicating, delicious, just-me-and-him-against-the-world experience when it's good. But now, when I thought of the person I'd always assumed I'd turn into, she seemed to bear no resemblance to me. I was living by another set of priorities and had forgotten my own. In the process I had become cold and unloving. I would thumb through the pages of wedding magazines, full of laughing women eating salad and holding peonies, and wonder which piece of organza origami embodied me.

Later that week, Shazzer hugged me close and said, "Tell me we'll always be strident, boisterous New-Arse-Hole-Rippers extraordinaire!" We had taken a pair of fold-up bikes that day, and cycled along the promenade by the sea, in gorgeous sunshine, she in a baggy woollen cardigan. There was a Labrador lapping up a toddler's Mr Whippy that had plopped off its cone onto the pavement. The child was crying, but its tears turned to giggles as the Labrador began to slurp at its cheeks to finish off the remaining ice cream. We bought a pack of ten donuts at the pier, crisp and abrasive with sugar, and sat on the beach. She ate nothing, preferring to stretch out on her back and smoke. Her eyes were closed. Her legs, exposed, were slender. She'd lost weight and her pale skin looked fragile in the hot sun. It struck me how she looked, all of a sudden, as if life had burned away the puppy fat from her.

It was strange to see so many people at a loose end on a Monday and to be amongst the jobless and the idle. I felt strangely guilty. Yachts slid across the horizon. We walked to the shore where the waves came up over our feet and the wind carried saltiness into our eyes, watching the sea as it constantly changed. I thought of my 18th Birthday and how we had been so drunk in a seafront club, just the two of us, and then run outside and screamed at the breaking waves in high January wind.

We walked back up the beach together. I counted fifteen broken shells on the way and I remember thinking idly that happiness is nothing if not shared.

"So now what?" I asked her.

"Hmm," she put her arm around me as we gazed at the horizon. "Well I think the first thing we should do is get you insanely drunk. And then do something drastic, like dye your hair."

I giggled. "Why is hair dye always the catharsis of relationship trauma?"

"I don't know, my friend," she said, gently, "It's a strange but fundamental feature of the female condition."

After that her mood seemed to change. She fluttered her eyes half shut and seemed listless. Vague, even. After a while she fixed me with her artless brown eyes and said,

"Mate, can I tell you something?"

"Fire away,"

"The other week I ordered some hash off this guy who lives near my house. When I went round there and picked it up he gave me this," she pulled from deep inside her pocket a dusty, black object, wrapped in foil and handed it to me. "I think he might have given it to me by mistake. He did look like a bit of a smack head."

I examined the object suspiciously.

"Isn't this?"

"Yeah I think it is."

I poked it.

"I don't really know."

"I tried melting a bit of it and sniffed the vapours. Nothing really happened."

This news infuriated me. "What the fuck?" I exploded. "Seriously, hun, there's a line and I think you've just crossed it."

"It was purely a scientific experiment," she backtracked, plucking the foil wrap out of my hand.

I held her gaze. "This isn't funny. That is nasty, horrible shit. I want you to promise me you're going to throw it away."

She examined the ground like a scalded child. "Jesus, I know, ok? You're right. I'll get rid of it. I promise I will."

That was the last I heard of it, we never mentioned it again.

I did indeed dye my hair. A few days later, I shed the colour that had defined me for a decade and emerged with a dark, hazelnut-brown bob and fringe which would prove to be a pain in the backside to keep neat. It was around this time that Shazzer had all her hair shorn off too.

"Let's shed the old, embrace the new, forget bad decisions and crap men – none of it counts anymore," she said, enthusiastically, turning up to meet me for a drink wearing dungarees - one of her more idiosyncratic outfits. She pulled off her cycle helmet to reveal a boyish crop, noticed my shocked expression and glanced in the mirror above my head.

"Christ, I look like a nineties lesbian," she plonked down at the table. "Oh well. Now listen, I'm glad it's all decided that you're going on this ski season because I've decided to go on an adventure of my own ..You're never going to believe this...I've signed up to work on a farm in Iceland."

"You're right. That is pretty fucking random."

"I'm going to be an arctic milkmaid for six months!"

I expressed joy and admiration for this bizarre and exciting development, but what I really felt was an unfamiliar bubbling of anger and resentment. Why was she making this about her? Why was she being so inconsistent at a time when I needed her to be my rock? I was annoyed and hurt that she seemed to have secrets from me all of a sudden and felt that a chasm was opening up between us. Just lately, she seemed to have picked up some mannerisms from somewhere or someone that I didn't recognise and couldn't contextualise. This, and the sudden image change, wrong-footed me. We were so close, but sometimes I felt that she existed on a different plane and that her inner world was something I couldn't ever hope to fathom and had no business invading. Sometimes, she would mysteriously disappear for weeks and then resurface, blaming it all on some sort of emotional turmoil that she was unwilling to, or simply couldn't explain.

"...and I think it would be good for both of us to disconnect from each other for a while," she was saying. "It's not good to lean on each other so much. And I think it would be especially good for you to...you know...put yourself out there, without a safety net."

I was stunned and hurt. Was this her way of politely telling me I had become a burden?

I didn't push her for more information. She didn't volunteer it and I was too proud to pry. I know now that I should have. I should have demanded to know everything. Perhaps then, when she had tried to show me the truth – to test my boundaries – I might have responded better. I might have understood.

Rules for the Chalet Bitch:
a general beginner's guide (cont.)

19. Do - smoke like a bonfire but never ever have a lighter. Or cigarettes.

20. Do - Party like a motherfucker, but...

21. Don't miss breakfast. You won't get any sympathy from anyone, least of all your co-Chalet Bitch who *did* manage to make it on time.

22. Do – come from Cornwall, Devon or Manchester. Preferably.

23. Do – carry some form of contraception on you at all times.

Pet Hates

Hidden Treasure

Another lesson learned today. Never forsake your marigolds, under any circumstances, when cleaning bathrooms. Whatever the slightly off-white slimy and difficult to eradicate substance on the shower surround was, it wasn't soap, shampoo or conditioner. When I reached into the bin to empty it and pulled out a full, slimy, used condom my worst fears were confirmed.

At that precise moment, the Foxy Chef called me.

"I may have to now submerge my entire hand in bleach," I said, still absent-mindedly dangling the revolting thing over the sink, "or better still just saw it off completely."

"I cut the end of my thumb off last week and lost it in some caramelised chorizo," she replied, mournfully.

"Are you OK?"

"No..." I could hear a slight tremor in her voice.

"Is it just the tip, or the whole end of your thumb?" "What? No! I mean, the thumb's fine. It's my tits that are the problem mate. They're fucking massive."

"Oh?...Oh..."

"Yeah. It could just be that I've taken the morning after pill like five times this season...but I literally can't go back to that pharmacy again...they'll recognise me"

"You are such a cluster fuck. Do you want me to go and get you a test?" I said, sitting down on the toilet, quietly amused, and also quite impressed with her ability to navigate potential disaster whilst always maintaining such infectious good humour. My offer seemed to be what she was angling for.

"Babe, are you sure you don't mind? This whole situation is making my brain capsize. I've just been offered that cheffing job in Antibes." Cruising around the med on a yacht, cooking food for a multi-squillionaire and his guests. I could see how a baby didn't quite fit into this picture.

"Have you told the Man of Leisure?"

"Non! Pas-du-tout! He'll freak out. He's practically a foetus himself."

Phone Call From La Vache Qui Ski, 8.30pm

"I need you to get down to the bus station right away. There's been a disaster."

"Er…OK…what's happening?" There is a note of panic in her voice that sends a chill into my heart.

"…Head Office has double booked the Edelweiss."

"OK."

"I've got flu. I need you to stand in. I can't possibly go out. If the chalet hosts catch it, we'll be in real trouble," she makes a slightly weird moaning noise and then gives a series of dry coughs. "You're going to have to get down there *pronto* and explain it to the guests…" In the background, I hear a creak of bedsprings and a man's voice mumbling something unintelligible.

"Oh excuse me a sec, I've got the doctor here," she says, sounding not particularly ill. I hear her muffle the mouthpiece and shush someone. Then she's back on "…It's a family of six…called…the Peacheys…" she continues, now sounding a little breathless, her voice cracking slightly on a rising note. "They should be arriving in about half an hour. *Okeydokes?*"

"Fine, but what's the alternative? Where are we putting them?"

"Alternative? Oh, no….there isn't one. You….. need to *find* one…"

Fuck biscuits! At this time on a busy Saturday night, when everything's booked up? Oh Christ this is going to be a complete nightmare.

"Who is responsible for this fuck up?" *Whoever they are they're a gold-plated cunt.*

"Let's not seek to blame. Let's just seek to sort it out," she says, a little more placidly.

"Alright, well where shall I put them while I look for alternative accommodation?"

"I'm afraid you're going to have to figure that one out yourself. I can't traipse round the resort looking for chalets, I'm absolutely sick as a dog. Can you just dig deep and use that initiative a bit, okeydokes? There's no 'I' in team."

No, I think, *but there is a 'U' in Cunt.* That familiar feeling of boiling blood bubbles up through my veins.

"Yes, yes, of course," I say, biting my lip, trying to ignore my own headache and sore throat. Last night I got drunker than I have since about 2005. I threw up in the bubble lift this morning.

I'm suddenly struck by a horrible thought.

"What if they ask for a refund? I expect they will considering they're not getting what they've paid for…"

"Absolutely not!" she bellows abruptly now, suddenly completely on the ball, "Under *no circumstances* agree to give them *any* financial reimbursement. That's absolutely crucial, do you understand? If you do it looks like we're accepting culpability."

"Um…but it's our fault isn't it?"

"That's beside the point. At the end of the day, as long as you do your job, it shouldn't be a problem. Now look I'm really feeling terrible…I've got to go."

Click.

I stand there staring at the phone for a good thirty seconds. How in the course of a two minute conversation has this fuck up become 100% my responsibility?

The Peacheys

Just as expected, the first thing the Peacheys did was demand a refund.

"You'd better tell your superior that I'm expecting serious compensation for this inconvenience," Mr Peachey roared at me, pursuing me stumblingly up the icy road with his bags and family in tow. Having had to bear the brunt of announcing to them that their chalet was double booked, I'd spent two hours scouring the resort while they ate dinner in a nearby restaurant and begging every contact I knew to find somewhere for them to sleep. Eventually I had found two adjacent flats in Les Appartements de Marie. On inspection, my heart sank. They were pokey, badly lit, badly appointed, less than ideal and neither was big enough for the whole family. Left with no other option the Peacheys, (Mr and Mrs, now apoplectic with rage) had to accept them.

The next day Mr Peachey proceeded to phone me almost hourly, demanding to know about his refund.

"I expect at the very least for them to pay for last night's dinner!" he blustered. "And we could do with a bit more snow too..."

Well butter my arse and call me Susan, nothing changes does it? What should I say to that? Do I look like Thor to you? Or Geoff the God of Precipitation? And if I could control the fucking weather, do you think I'd be standing here taking shit from you Mr Peachey? No. I'd be a billionaire. I'd be lying on a bed of rose petals, in a palace made of chocolate full of naked Leonardo DiCaprio doppelgangers feeding me grapes and pleasuring me on demand.

"Call Christa," was La Vache Qui Ski's response when I rang to get her take on things. I did so, and immediately regretted it.

"No, I reaaaally don't think that's necessary," she said expansively, when I eventually got hold of her. I could imagine those chins wobbling in indignation. "What on *earth* should we refund them for? They've got accommodation, it's near the piste, they're being fed aren't they?"

"Well, yes, but they've had to put the children in a separate apartment to the adults and they haven't got enough keys. They have to leave the apartments unlocked at night in case the children need something."

A heavy sigh. "For God's sake! Don't these people have *phones?* Can't you get some more keys cut? It's really not that complicated."

"Appartements de Marie won't let me. They say they're only allowed a certain number of keys per apartment."

Another heavy sigh.

"…and they're complaining about the food too," I added, tentatively. "They say the apartment always smells of cooking because of the portable oven we've had to put in."

"Well tell the chalet host, whoever it is, to clean it!" spluttered Christa. "If she just bloody cleaned it properly it wouldn't smoke. You'd better have a word with her and tell her to pull out all the stops. We need to turn this one around."

I rolled my eyes. Calamity was already having the worst and most demoralising week of her life. On top of dealing with the disgruntled Peacheys, cooking four course meals using a clapped out portable oven and a combi the size of a microwave, she'd broken her thumb falling off a box in the snow park. Her left hand was in a cast that kept the joint at a right angle, forcing her into a perpetual, and rather ironic, thumbs-up sign.

Still, I suppose this experience has given me a new perspective and respect for Resort Managers, if not for La Vache Qui Ski herself. They are the great unloved. Shat on by clients, shovelled up by Head Office and beset from all angles by staff who seem to think that they are a maid, mother, school teacher, psychiatrist and personal assistant all rolled into one. Who seem to think "I was skiing" is an acceptable excuse for never handing their chalet accounts sheets in on time. Who seem to think that it's OK to leave rotting mounds of meat and vegetables in their fridges and sticky sweet wrappers and crumbs un-hoovered under the beds of their guests.

A case in point, just before dinner service I got a call from Skater Boy.

"Eh up Bird, I need your help. I'm all out of shopping and I need to come up with something to make for dinner."

What am I, some kind of Ready Steady Cook emergency hotline? I could hear him rustling something down the line.

"Are you going through the bin?"

"The fridge broke three days ago and all my meat went off."

"Why didn't you buy some more?"

"Didn't fancy shopping on a fresh powder day. I was hiking the needle...fucking banging it was."

"Oh for fuck's sake. Right. What have you got?"

"I've got......a leek....some filo pastry....erm.....and a jar of peanut butter."

"Right." Peanut butter and leek pie it is then...

The Disturbing Tale of the Drunk Ukrainian….

Phone call. 7.30am Wednesday morning (my day off). Calamity at the other end of the line, sounding wobbly.

"Umm. Sorry to call you so early and all. It's just, ahhm. Well. I think you should come down here."

I am so hung over, I can barely speak. "What's the matter?"

"God, you sound awful,"

"I am. What is it?"

"Well, um. There's been a bit of a, sort of, *incident.*"

"Right…"

"The guests are really, *really* upset. They're asking for you."

Oh Christ. I might die.

"What about La Vache?"

"She's gone to Val D'Isere…some sort of issue with a chalet over there. She told me to call you because you'd dealt with them before."

Oh God. Why me?

"They're saying they won't leave the apartment until you come down here."

"What's happened?"

"Right. Well. You're not going to like this…."

Oh. Holy. Fuck.

Calamity proceeds to relate a tale that makes my blood freeze in my veins. The Peacheys were woken in the night by the noise of someone shuffling around in their living room. After half an hour of listening in the dark, Daddy Peachey decides it can't be his eldest son having a midnight snack after all, and pops outside to have a bit of a ganders at what's going on. Opening the door to the double bedroom across the hall, he is greeted by the sight of a six foot three, steaming drunk, naked Ukrainian bloke snoring luxuriantly in the Queen size next to his eight year old son.

He then proceeds to hit the fucking roof.

"Let's just say the gendarmes are currently looking for a confused, hairy, naked, drunk guy with two black eyes, stumbling around the resort stinking of vodka and muttering expletives," I explained to Skater Boy later that evening. Joking aside, I had not been unperturbed by the morning's fireworks. Shaking, sweating and weak with alcohol poisoning, I had managed to drag myself up the hill to the chalet where I had been called every name under the sun by Mr Peachey (who was anything but). He was a physically imposing human and (he took great relish in telling me) a one-time debt collector from Bolton with ruddy, eczema-encrusted cheeks and rabid eyes like two black cherries swimming in a dish of melting butter. The fact that, only hours ago, he had kicked seven shades of shit out of a pissed up six foot three Ukrainian, did nothing to comfort me. His wife, a squat, Mancunian version of Dolly Parton with absurd blonde hair extensions and pink all-in-one ski suit, reminded me in no small measure of Miss Piggy.

"Our child has been sexually assaulted!" she kept shrieking.

In truth (thank fuck), the child had slept through the whole shebang and was none the wiser, pootling off to ski school without a care in the world, just as I arrived on the scene. It was fairly clear to me that the chap wasn't a kiddy fiddler. Just a complete wanker who'd got utterly gazebo'd and let himself into the wrong apartment. Clearly, I didn't say this. I cooed, soothed, apologised, expressed mutual indignation and, at their request, called the gendarmes. But nothing I said would calm them down. They wanted blood. A tirade of fury was shitting down upon me from all directions.

"You might remind them," said La Vache Qui Ski, when I finally got hold of her that afternoon, "that *they* are responsible for locking the door at night, *not* the chalet host. It says so in the Ts and Cs…" After listening to Mr Peachey rant for half an hour about how he was going to sue me personally for damages, I wasn't quite certain how she thought reminding them of this was going to help. "You'll need to write a full report on this and send it to Christa," she continued, "Okey-dokes?"

It didn't occur to her to thank me for handling the situation in her absence.

"Your whole fucking company is a bunch of cunts!" raged Mr Peachey, when I told him the news that my boss saw the escapade as being his fault. I bit back the urge to agree with him wholeheartedly.

The gendarmes, as you might expect, found no trace of the aforementioned Ukrainian paedophile. Quite how a man of that stature with two bright purple shiners managed to give an entire police department the slip in an area the size of an extremely modest Cotswold village *baffles* me, it really does, as La Vache Qui Ski would say. Nevertheless, he disappeared in an eerie whiff of vodka fumes, and was never seen again. In fact, the only evidence of his ever having existed were his clothes (which Mr Peachey had refused to give back to him after nutting him and hurling him out into the street, stark bollock naked) and the bottle of Cristal champagne that Mrs Peachey found outside the door of the apartment the morning after the night before.

Who, in their right mind, would think that is appropriate recompense for sexually compromising someone's offspring?

A whole catalogue of disasters like this one has occurred in the last few weeks. The resort is currently swarming with an assortment of leather-clad Katie Price-alikes. An army of ghastly chavs, who think if it's shiny or made of a dead animal, it's worth having. There they go, hanging off the arms of men with waxwork complexions and giant cigars, only outmatching their bad taste with their horrifically bad attitude. The Russians are in town. They have a reputation all of their own out here. They are the loud-mouthed spivs at the dinner table of life, who hold their knives like a pen and complain the wine's corked when it's not. There should be a chapter in every tour operator's manual on 'what to do in case of Russians'.

"I mean, don't they have wordth like pleathe, thank you and thorry in their language?" I overhead Fenella say to the Irksome-Blonde-19-Year-Old, the day after the arrival of five Russian 'gentlemen' who had requested that she didn't look them directly in the eye whilst serving. They had marched straight past her outstretched, welcoming palm on arrivals day, dumped their luggage in the hallway and barked at her to make tea immediately, before ransacking the place, puking on the sofa cushions and then ordering her to clean up the mess, with the words, "You do it. Is your job, no?"

It would be nice to think the revenge she took (charging them triple the dry cleaning bill and pocketing the difference) made a dent in their enormous wallets, but of course it didn't.

Still, it's an irony to watch guests like this being waited on hand and foot by the cream of British upper-middle class children. Ripped from Daddy's arms, pony-less and forced to slave over the hob while up to the armpits in the cum-stains, poo, pubic hairs and vodka-vomit of some erstwhile serfs who've struck gold.

To add to the hilarity, the mysterious bottle-blonde who has been renting our entire chalet to herself this week has repeatedly asked me to drive her from hotel to hotel from hour to hour, 'visiting friends'.

"You know what is like, darlink" she said to me, sliding fluidly into the back seat trussed up in thigh-high lace-ups, a white fox-fur poncho and pursued by a fog of Chanel No 5, "When you hev dinner invite from four, five different men, but you just rather be home with book…"

I smiled and nodded, thinking "No. No, actually I have no fucking idea what that's like, love. It sounds great."

I spent a very amusing twenty minutes yesterday trying on all her furs and jewels, and prancing around the living room taking pictures.

Pet Hates

Smells

I think this most revolting of phenomena has just over-taken hair and/or the Cupboard of Despair in my top three points of Chalet Bitch loathing. One thing I never expected from this job is that, like a dog, you get to know your clients intimately by scent. Being nostril-raped on a daily basis by complete strangers scores fairly low on my chart of desirable activities. It reminds me of being on the tube. But it's something that I must daily endure. I'm not talking sweat or BO... I'm talking the very individual and personal smell that each of us has. Musky, zesty, sometimes downright fishy. There are those of us who like to mask it with fragrances, expensive perfumes, creams and body sprays, the Lynx effect and so on.

It's true, many ladies and gents have an incredibly sexy personal smell. It's also true that some people fucking stink. They stink so much you wonder how they've got that far through life without it being brought to their attention. Their smells linger in the bathroom and hit you like a cricket bat to the face when you walk in, innocently clutching your window cleaner and bleach. The smells hang, damply in the air and follow you around the chalet.

One French guy this week has this nutty, sweet, dusty scent which wafts around him wherever goes. It is interlaced with something else, which took me several days of relocating his grotty underpants from the floor to the bedside chair to pinpoint, but I finally realised could only be... sweaty ball sack. It literally makes me retch.

I have taken to wearing a Michael Jackson-style cloth over my nose and mouth when I clean his room. This evening, as I was placing a pan of rosemary roast potatoes down on the table, I got a waft of him and had to retire to a safe distance and recompose myself for fear of throwing up. They say smell is linked strongly to memory. Well that smell will follow me to my grave. If he's in the same room as me randomly in ten years time, I'll know it. And probably throw up.

Shudder....

The Green Peril

Skater Boy was in hospital. I knew this because I had bumped into his Resort Manager in the mini supermarket and she had given me the news. She was a youngish girl. Much easier to run rings around than La Vache Qui Ski, a fact which the boys and the rest of her staff took full advantage of. Many was the Friday morning I'd sit nursing a cup of tea in their apartment while they tried to cobble together one complete 500 Euro chalet float out of the remains of each of their portion and whatever coins were lying around on the floor before they saw her for their weekly meeting.

"Shit, I'm a hundred and forty three short," Skater Boy would say.

"Put some of your own cash in to make it up,"

"I don't have any. That's why I've been spending the float..."

The whole thing was a fucking shambles. Luckily Skater Boy was a master of cooking the books.

"Here, I know" he'd say, "Give me a hundred and forty three out of yours, I'll go and see her and say you've, I dunno, gone for a crap or something. Then after, I'll come and get you, give you it back plus – how much are you short?"

Scruffy-but-Handsome totted it up. "Fifty six, eighty."

"Plus fifty six, eighty, and then you can go in, and she'll never know the difference."

The Resort Manager was at the end of her tether. They were a couple of staff down because of an in-resort gastro epidemic already, but somehow Skater Boy had managed to twist her round his little finger and convince her to let him go and ski with his Dad and brother who were visiting for a few days, instead of doing breakfast service. She'd filled in for him herself, out of the kindness of her heart - getting up early and cooking for his guests so he could get in a few runs with his family before they left. Except, rather short-sightedly, she hadn't taken into account the fact that it had recently started dumping with snow. In fact, it had snowed heavily and continuously for the last four days.

Skater Boy had no intention of skiing with his family.

He'd ditched them and taken off on some sort of death ride. This involved hiking up a colossal pointy rock - effectively a cliff face – so he could get fresh tracks and hurl himself across an insane transfer gap where there was, what he referred to, as a '60 foot money booter of a wind lip.' He did this while an audience of disturbed punters watched from the nearby chairlift. The place was known as 'Boucher', a sinister name for a sinister peak. Local legend claimed a cuckolded butcher had once launched himself from there in a parapont with no intention of landing safely. He'd tumbled to his death right in the middle of the main drag.

There was a free ride competition coming to town next month and, without much concern for the consequences, Skater Boy had been keen to hit this particular cliff for weeks. He had been chattering to me about it animatedly at every opportunity. All he had to do was wait for the right snow conditions. This was how he liked to ski. One day, he would pootle around with me at the sides of piste, telling me stories that made me giggle - of places he'd hiked and hucked, pointing out pillow drops inside dense areas of woodland and describing them, watching out for my welfare, insisting on carrying my skis to the lift and going at my pace. The next, he would disappear phoneless and heedless, then come back with a black eye because he'd head butted his own knees doing a five-metre drop.

He carved his own way across the mountain with an unfathomable sort of self-assurance, as if no place was forbidden or too inhospitable to explore; bouncing across rocks and up trees as if they were made of feathers and he was made of rubber. You could hear him shouting and yelling with pleasure as he bobbed in and out of view. It was like skiing with Zebedee. As nimble as a mountain goat; a cat with nine lives.

I loved hearing him chatter about the terrain in his deep, lyrical drawl that always had a vague air of comedy to it to my south coast ears. There was a strange poetry in the way he spoke about the mountain and the words he used to describe things. He knew the names of all the peaks and hidden valleys; *Mario Land* and *Croix de Fougue*, *Boucher* and *Les Avalles*. He knew the texture of the land under the snow and the curvature of couloirs, the location and shape of giant ice balls the size of houses on the glacier, the temperature and movement of the snow, the geological phenomena that had carved out the rocks. He seemed to have an intuitive grasp of it, and could predict the geography before he arrived – every flaw and scar - like an old lover. He could describe places he'd only been once in graphic detail. But it didn't stop him getting himself into scrapes, setting off avalanches and having to hike out of deep bowls all too often. All the wisdom and reverence was peppered by the sense that he had some sort of personal vendetta against himself - a masochistic need to risk his neck and punish his body. He knew everyone's limits but his own.

"You can get some pretty good boosts if you hit the blind bends down there fast enough," he'd comment, joyously, pointing down the piste with his pole. And then he'd warn me that it curved round and then there was a bit of a lip and a dip with some bumps, worried that I might hurt myself. He was both wonderful and impossible to be with.

His Resort Manager told me she was tearing her hair out. No one wanted him to get fired, he was too much fun to have around. Everyone loves the guy who straps himself upside down into a monoski hanging from the bar ceiling and drinks Genepi out of a wellington boot. She had tried incentivising, cajoling, begging, crying. Nothing worked. No job, no friend, no family was more important to him than an untracked face and a spliff. It was near on impossible to get him up in the morning – I knew this. I had witnessed the Scruffy One pour buckets of water over his head and heard the Resort Manager yelling out of the window at him to put his uniform on, instead of shuffling off to his chalet in pyjama bottoms and a Hawaiian shirt. On changeover day, when skiing was banned, one would quite often find him sitting in his under-pants on the chalet sofa, with nothing finished, sheetless beds and a dirty kitchen, smoking a joint at 4pm, just moments before the guests were due to arrive. He was always pushing the boundaries, always pushing his luck and everybody else's patience. There was some vague idea in the back of his brain of becoming a freeride pro, but he lacked the commitment to train. There was no training, no planning. Everything he did rode solely on raw talent, natural god-given sinewy fitness and gigantic balls. Everything he did, he did big, and everything he did, he did baked.

That was why he was in hospital now.

Despite the severity of the injury - he'd almost cleft his palette - a group of punters and a couple of our friends had seen him skiing down the remainder of the face to safety with blood dripping down his front and half of his face hanging off.

One of them tried to call the blood wagon.

"Fuck that...", he said. "Fuckin' daylight robbery."

I hitchhiked down the road to the hospital and found him with fifteen stitches in his lip and an exposed dental root, where the 'invisible' steel support cable holding up a pylon had sheered into his face at 80mph, crushing his goggles and dragging them down over the bridge of his nose, knocking out his tooth and scraping a good portion of flesh from the left side of his cheek. A couple of inches lower and it would have taken his head off, or removed his lower jaw. He was lucky his entire, lovely face hadn't been caved in.

As I stood by his bed, I had the distinct sense that one day soon we'd all be standing around his coffin.

"I knew that cable was there, it was just a couple of feet lower than I remembered..." he said in a croaky lisp as his Dad came in looking tired, with a cup of tea. He made swooping movements with his arms to illustrate the point. "I came off this big, fuckin' curved lip, arced round...you should've seen me, Bird. I literally, absolutely flew. I'm talkin' flew," he indicated how far with a wide, sweeping movement. "It was ridiculous. I was like... I've just gone over a house!"

I couldn't help but giggle.

"I was pointing up at the sky and absolutely crappin' myself. I thought...eh up...fuckin' definitely, I've done it this time..."

"And then you decided to use your face as a brake?"

"Just a little bit."

His Mum rang, and he spoke to her in an uncharacteristically muted voice. Afterwards, he was quiet and looked distracted and not a little bit worse for wear.

"No smoking or drinking or skiing for at least three weeks ," said the nurse who discharged him, but we hadn't even got back to his apartment before he pulled out a tin of Northern Lights from the pocket of his ski pants.

Next day, he was back on the hill by 10am.

Disease

As you may have gathered, seasonnaires have an incredible ability to deny, or ignore illness and injury: It's a matter of pride. To medicate tonsillitis with spirits: To ignore that increasingly painful purple welt developing on the shin: To invoke the practice of 'k-motherapy' (destruction of all cells, both healthy and parasitic in their bodies with the cunning use of booze and fags and other substances): To see how far it's possible to ski on a compound fracture (that's when the bone is actually sticking through the skin).

Disease spreads with the power of an epidemic every season. And it's not surprising. Think about it. You've got a village's worth of randy teenagers suddenly set free from the parental nest, banjaxed to the eyeballs every night on toffee vodka, snogging and shagging their way through the equivalent of six months of Fresher's Weeks. Everyone spends the entire season taking it in turns to lick or fiddle with each other's private parts each night with gay abandon ...yes, and then they go to work and cook your dinner without washing their mitts...

Add to this toxic mixture, a healthy dollop of your basic cynical serial mountain worker on their 15th season, carrying every STD under the sun and up for poking anything with a hole that breathes (Old Man Swiss is like a kid in a sweet shop.) Then there's the network of sex pest French chefs and waiters to contend with, adding a whole new dimension of potential for lurgie to spread like a whore's legs.

Around this time of the season, it all starts to get a little bit incestuous too. This week, pretty much every member of our staff has come down with the same mysterious gastro ailment. Without doubt this is because most of them have locked either lips or genitals, or lips with genitals at some point. The Foxy Chef has been bouncing like a pin-ball between the uncharacteristically love-struck Man of Leisure, who has a harem of desperate little chalet girls queuing up for his attention. Campbell Campbell, who as we know was originally shagging Calamity, then had a knee trembler with The-Irksome-Blonde-19-Year-Old, who in turn had an interesting evening with Calamity's older ski-bum brother, involving a mid-shag swap, with China who was shagging Byron, apparently. Their mothers would be so proud, I'm sure.

When the Irksome-Blonde-19-Year-Old asked for time off this week, because her face was swollen and her throat and lips had become afflicted with a vile blistering condition, I couldn't help but ask, in the middle of our resort meeting, whether she was genuinely ill or had simply been sucking too many cocks. She just snorted and looked sullen while everyone else roared with laughter.

So now, The Foxy Chef has been struck down with some kind of stomach complaint, and pretty much all of us have that lovely deep, hacking cough – the result of months of living off vitamin-free table scraps and turbo drinking while sticking our tongues in every available orifice of every available person in the vicinity. I swear the only reason Skater Boy, Scruffy but Handsome and I have escaped so far is because we spend so much time in that biohazard of a flat. It's an immunity booster.

Unexpected Item in Bagging Area

Text today from the Foxy Chef:

How r u meant to swallow these massive thrush pills? I've got 1 stuck in my throat

I reply: "Suggest you look up word for pessary in French dictionary"

"Oh bother."

I laugh, and then remembered her other problem.

"Are you preggars as well as having thrush?"

"Nop. All clear."

Well that, at least, is some good news.

Half Term

The school holidays are a sad time for the powder-spoiled seasonnaire. The idea of slushy pistes choc full of half-term children careering around out of control and knocking into you in mile-long lift queues is distinctly unappealing. Unfortunately, the remaining activity options are limited. There's only so much you can do in a ski resort without actually skiing. Other options include:

Knitting. Well, Scruffy-but-Handsome's idea actually. To be fair to him, I think it's all part of some hare-brained scheme to get-rich-quick by knitting piles and piles of oddly coloured beanies and scarves and flogging them to seasonnaires for 20 Euros a pop. He wants to start what he calls 'Stitch and Bitch' sessions, where the injured of the Alps (of which, let me tell you, there are by now an alarming number) sit around crocheting and swearing about people who can ski. Fifty quid says the whole thing turns into a complete fiasco, he gets bored and goes back down the pub.

Eating Raclette. You start off enthusiastically tucking into that first scrape of delicious melty goo. Mmmmm it's so morish.... so...so cheesy!

... Ten minutes later, you've lost the will to live. Cheese sweats. The fear. A horrible sense of self loathing starts to creep in. What have I done? I hate myself! Then you make the mistake of drinking a cold glass of water, causing the cheese to solidify in your stomach and sit there for the next three days like a rock, mocking you and your greed. I actually passed out from cheese once. I mean, it could also have been linked to the red wine I was having, but I reckon it was definitely the cheese.

Doing your job. Hand-in-hand with Half Term hideousness is the dreaded mid-season deep clean. Ergo we are all being forced to do some real, actual work in the form of cleaning every last inch of the chalets, every speck of dust. We must defrost the freezer and disinfect the fridge, scrape burnt grime from the inside of the oven, de-scale the kettle, pull hunks of slimy human hair, skin and refuse from plug holes, scrub between bathroom tiles with a toothbrush and polish every surface to a mirror shine, because (threat of terrifying threats) we will have our ski passes confiscated if it ain't done proper. The week where La Vache Qui Ski has been doing her 'product co-ordination analysis', (a posh way of saying her poking her nose into every nook and cranny of every property whilst deconstructing our already incredibly fragile morale with a wrinkle of her hooky nose and a flick of her biro). Deep clean week, for managers Alp-wide, basically entails turning up at various chalets with a clip board, wearing a company jacket and sauntering about looking, cross, harassed and important. Criticising everything your staff do down to the last speck of dust, complaining to all and sundry about how much harder your job is than theirs, and yapping aggressively into a mobile phone.

Today, therefore, in the interests of doing something a bit different with our time, The Man of Leisure and I decided to go snow shoeing. Tiny clouds littered a brilliant blue sky as we set out 'ironically' dressed in neon racing gear into the wilderness, armed with a picnic. He had been rather sulky lately, I assumed because The Foxy Chef had been ignoring him, and I wanted to cheer him up.

"Once you get over the feeling that you look like a total dick head, it's actually quite fun," he said, prancing around good naturedly, legs akimbo so that the snow shoes flapped up and down comically as he walked.

I agreed.

While we were marching down what I, at least, thought

was a very steep incline in a wooded valley, some ancient crone came hobbling cheerfully up the hill towards us in trainers and gave us a jovial 'Bonjour,' before casting a slightly amused glance at our feet.

"Hold on, if she's in trainers, why the fuck are we wearing these stupid things any way?" I asked, staring after her in disbelief. "Not exactly one for thrill seekers is it?"

I sat down on a rock and rummaged in my back pack for a beer. Basking in the sun for a while, we smoked cigarettes and drank, admiring the mountains, intricate, tree-laced and snow capped. A huge Vienetta ice cream.

"By the way," said the Man of Leisure after a while. "What happened with that Ukranian paedo guy?"

I was rather taken aback by the question since I'd been trying very hard to forget the whole unpleasant incident.

"Oh… he disappeared," I said, closing my eyes in the sun. "Hold on…" I looked at him, "how did you know about that?"

He was smirking.

"I never told you about that…"

"I was with your boss when you rang her about it."

"…what was *she* doing with you?"

"In bed," he said, proudly.

"She told me she was in Val D'Isere. Wait. Christ. Ewwwwww. What on earth are you doing shagging *her*? She's vile! She's an evil hell witch!"

"She's not that bad," he looked rueful.

This didn't seem to me to be a particularly healthy way of dealing with the fact The Foxy Chef had rejected him, but I had to concede that bedding an ice queen like La Vache was a testament to his unbelievable pulling power. Anyway, I had a sneaking suspicion this latest affair was more to do with him needing a place to stay than anything else. His parents, a well-known celebrity ex-model and a hedge fund manager, were in town for their yearly ski holiday with his little brother, staying in their apartment and by all accounts making life rather unpleasant for him. His Dad had started to tire of his antics, and in an attempt to push him into getting a 'proper job' in the 'real world', was threatening to change the locks on the apartment when he left.

"Dad wants me to go back to Paris with them at the end of the month" he said sadly.

I didn't know what else to do except pat his arm and look sheepish.

The Massive Wanker's Guide to
Being a Chalet Bitch's Nightmare

It strikes me how incredibly two-faced you can become, without ever realising or intending to, while working in the service industry. Chalets are no different to any other hospitality service in that they operate around what Orwell referred to as '*the boulot*'. That is, an *imitation* of good service. A *façade* of cleanliness and concern for the guest's welfare. One finds oneself saying things like, "Yes, sir, I understand you like your serviettes folded lengthwise and not into a triangle, I'll do it that way next time." While thinking, yes, you demanding self-absorbed cretin, would you like me to ram this snowboard up your arse before or after I drive a snow plough over your balls?

A wise woman once told me that, had she been able to choose an age and simply remain that age for the rest of her days, that age would have been thirty. I've heard it said by others too. Thirty is a great age. A fabled age. A coming of age. An age where you can cast off the shackles of your twenties and just be you. Your twenties are a stressful time when you are hungry to please, earnestly trying to succeed, looking for your place in the world, and concerned about what others think of you. Uncertainty, instability and inexperience all seem to conspire to trip you up. I'm hoping when I hit thirty, I can simply stop giving a toss and start enjoying life, not worry about being able to call a spade a cunt.

After all, I have been fed enough crap advice over the years from enough ill-informed arrogant idiots that I can smell incompetence from two hundred yards and really, I should have no problem saying so. Actually, I've always been fairly good at sniffing out bullshit, it's just that in the past I would have kept my mouth shut, whereas now I'm the first to blow the whistle on a complete wanker. It doesn't always make me popular, but

I do find far fewer people attempt to trifle with me nowadays. How ironic then, with my new-found self confidence and finely tuned 'Crapometer', to find myself in a job where it's actually in my remit to pander to and sympathise with every vulgar halfwit who crosses my path.

Like, for instance, the Brazilian family of clearly delicate sensibility who complained they couldn't sleep because their beds were too 'squeaky'. My gut reaction was to buy them ear plugs and a massive vat of Man-The-Fuck-Up, but what I in fact had to do was apologise and tighten up the bed springs. Then there was the frankly barking mad Dutch woman, quivering with neuroses, who pulled me on one side to complain that Irksome-Blonde-19-Year-Old didn't know how to cook. She was one of those people who stands way to close to you and invades your personal space when they speak to you. Since she hadn't yet actually had the opportunity of eating a meal prepared by us, I enquired as to how she had come to this conclusion.

"Well...she was touching the food with her hands" she replied in a disgusted, hoarse whisper.

Right.

"Erm," I said, "Isn't it quite normal prepare food with your hands?"

"She was mixing something with her *fingers*. I just saw it. I have my grandchildren with me and their parents get very worried about this kind of thing."

Fucksake - I'm pretty sure I've seen Gordon Ramsay touch some food once on telly. Yeah. I'm pretty sure every motherfucking Michelin star chef on the planet touches food with their hands. Unless you're a Jedi it's quite hard to do anything practical without the use of your hands (not that I could entirely blame her for worrying about the Irksome -one's fingers being germy).

I wanted to say: "So am I to understand it that you want

212

to protect your snotty little brood from catching some sort of foul disease from us, by demanding we cook your dinner using exclusively the power of the Force, *you insane old bag?*"

On this note, Scruffy-but-Handsome, the poor lad, is recovering from the worst week of guests so far this season. Here is a potted summary of his experience. Let this be a lesson to all future chalet guests...

..Do Not....

1. On arrival, prove penis is size of dried apricot by shaking host's hand with a finger-crushing grip that could bend titanium and throw a couple of fifties at him with the words: 'You'd better make sure we have a good holiday, son'.

2. Bustle into chalet with shouty voice and social etiquette of a giant black rubber dildo, demanding things the minute you arrive.

3. Insist boorishly on being escorted to a restaurant while snobbishly telling Chalet Bitch he doesn't look like the 'type' who'd know a five star restaurant if he saw one.

4. Complain loudly at Chalet Bitch in accusatory fashion about size, shape, location, colour, smell, aura and planetary alignment of chalet.

5. Introduce bat-shit crazy spouse, who requests that cleaning be done using only washing up liquid throughout. Assure host this is nothing to do with allergies, merely personal preference, thereby confirming that, indeed, you are a prick who likes being a pain in the nuts and not merely someone with sensitive skin.

6. Complain that company does not do enough to protect guests from 'the risk of radioactive clouds' appearing in the atmosphere as a result of unstable nuclear power stations on the continent. (What do you expect them to do? Provide standard issue tin foil hats for all guests? Lead jackets?)

7. Lecture Chalet Bitch who has degree in Biomedical Science on the 'proven scientific fact that cancer is not a disease'.

8. Decide that smell of sewage (which is no one's fault and no one can do anything about despite obvious and repeated efforts) coming from the road outside makes the chalet a bio-hazard. Phone up resort manager and scream down phone at her to: "Get here now and *sort it out!*" Adding that "This place stinks of SHIT. It's pollution and it's already making me ill. I can feel a sore throat coming on!"

9. Fuck with Chalet Bitch's day off by demanding to be transferred into another chalet, thereby sentencing poor bastard to two consecutive 12 hour days of cleaning, bed making and fetching and carrying.

10. Phone the Resort Manager at least once a day every day with a rudely, condescendingly expressed inane complaint because you are bored and want attention.

11. Pompously tell Chalet Bitch off for pouring water from the mop bucket down the sink. Utterly absurd.

12. Lose the plot and scream at Resort Manager to "Fuck off and get over yourself" when she tries to explain it's unreasonable to expect the chalet staff to clean on their

mid-week day off. Fly into a rage and scream at her to "Go fuck yourself."

13. Trash chalet. Steal all light bulbs, pour coffee everywhere, put croissants and orange slices in cupboards, soak towels and throw around rooms, steal door knobs, wine and all the condiments.

"What a ball ache," said the unfortunate victim of all this, Scruffy but Handsome, looking very crestfallen by the end of the week.

"Well," I said, patting him on the back and smiling, "what better way to end the week than with a rigorous cleaning of several chalet toilets using some very handy toothbrushes? Oh, and here's a bottle of Optrex. Use it wisely."

What Next?

A few evenings later, I'm walking down the road with Scruffy-but-Handsome and two large bin bags, feeling weary and thinking about a conversation I had with The Foxy Chef. Just lately, something has been preoccupying me. The something is a question.

"What next?"

It is an unsettling idea.

It had been a text from my Dad that sparked it:

"Poppetto. Hw's life? Missing u. Hv fwdd ur post to chalet as rqsted. DD xx"

Good. This means he hasn't been opening it all himself and reading it like he usually does with my post. Also, in this age of unlimited text characters you have to love my Dad's incredibly unnecessary and inventive attempts at txt spk. I replied:

"Thanks Dad. Xx"

Then a few moments later, another text.

"Jst wndred. R u going 2 pay Southern Water? Only they've snt 3/4 demands now n they're starting 2 get nasty..."

Oh fuck. Bills. Reality. It had been all too easy to sink into the protective cocoon of routine around here, and forget, almost completely, that this life has a sell-by date, and that I have a past. The idea that I'd once had a house and utility bills to pay seemed totally alien, as if it was a life lived by some completely different person in a different dimension. I vaguely recalled having had some notion I'd pay it off after the first chalet paycheque came in, but that idea went out of the window long before I spunked the entire amount on a new pair of ski boots.

I replied:

"How much?"

"£426.82"

Bollocks. "Thanks – will deal with it. Don't worry."

I was with the Foxy Chef at the time, sipping vin chaud in a Creperie. The sky was heaving down great lumps of snow. She had hurt her ankle.

"Yeuch," she said, wrinkling her freckly nose. "Gas and 'lecky bills. Homelife. Council tax. Yeuch!"

"When did you last go home?" I asked, trying to stab the anaemic piece of orange that was floating in my drink with a long spoon. She curled her lip.

"I'm not exactly sure what 'home' is any more. The rentals are divorced. There isn't really a 'family home' as such to go to."

She smiled briefly and looked thoughtful, though not particularly bothered.

"I don't know that I *could* go back any more, and get a stable job and just slot back into life. I've spent so many seasons skidding around here and on the boat. I mean, I love my friends, really I do, and I miss my family like crazy but, you know, going home always seems like a great idea until I get there. And then after about 2 months, I find that nothing has changed. *Nothing.* It's just the same people doing the same shit coke at the same parties, having the same conversations because their lives are no different," she started to toy abstractedly with one of the bosom-length plaits that always hangs from her bobble hat. I looked out of the window at the punters to-ing and fro-ing in the swaggering way only people wearing ski boots can. "They're all just pleasure seeking in dark rooms" she continued, "…or thinking up new ways to avert the boredom, like getting hitched or popping out a sprog or buying a new sofa. I just don't want that for my life."

What she said made me think of a friend, back home. She's elegant, refined, exquisitely beautiful, runs her own business, and, she's a kleptomaniac. She shoplifts for thrills. And steals things from people's houses - small things, you know, like earrings or ornaments. Then she and her husband spend every weekend surfing swinging sites and blowing cocaine up strangers' arses while their kid sleeps upstairs. I have this other friend too, who posts every single fart or brain belch on Facebook as if it's headline news. As if Facebook is Heat magazine and she's a minor celebrity.

Are these methods of dealing with life's mundane drag any more legitimate than doing seasons?

"So you're going back to the boats this summer?" I asked, remembering the job she'd been offered in Antibes.

"I don't know. I'm starting to feel a bit long in the tooth. I'd like to find someone with a bit of sense. Stop shitting on my own doorstep all the time…"

I smiled at this. "Your problem is you're too soft hearted," I said, thinking of us both in ten years time and wondering if we'd still be two hang-dog hags smoking cigarettes around a vin chaud. "You like people too much. You think everyone's got potential. I'm not like that. I think everyone's a wanker until proven otherwise."

She laughed. "Oh, is *that* why I end up shagging rotters all the time? Thank you. I've been trying to figure it out for ages."

Conversations like this one are starting to happen more and more often now, and it is unnerving me. For some reason as we're walking down the road I feel compelled to ask Scruffy-but-Handsome the same question.

"What are you going to do in the summer?"

He doesn't hesitate for a moment. He knows. "Going down to Palma to look for a job on a yacht."

"You won't go back home then?"

"Maybe for a week or two. See the olds. But not for any length of time."

For some reason, this idea makes my heart sink. The thought of him being suddenly so far away from me, and this cosy little intimacy that we have each evening, makes me feel lost in the middle of a huge raging battle. I think of the vast ocean and him afloat on it, somewhere miles away, and feel tiny and insignificant and alone.

And then he says, without warning,

"The first time we met. Why were you crying?"

I hesitate, and then decide to be honest.

"Because I'm afraid of the way people disappear."

He frowns, looks down at the road and nods, but probes no further.

"What will you do?" he asks.

I don't know.

As I say it, I slip on some ice and land painfully on my knee in the middle of the road. I can't tell if it's the shock of the pain or these new revelations that cause me to burst into tears.

"Hey," he squats beside me and holds each of my shoulders. "Chin up."

"I can't help it. I don't know where I'm going."

"You worry too much," he says, with conviction, "Worry less. Do more…"

He starts to guide me down the road again. I wonder at this certainty and at how untarnished by life he is. It strikes momentarily that he is naïve. Or then is it quite the opposite?

We continue down the road. As we walk towards the *poubelle* with our bin bags I look up and see, between two huge shoulders of the mountains in the distance, a fragment of moon shining almost too brightly to look at directly. We stop and watch as the earth visibly revolves under us, until it hangs between the jagged jaws of the rocks; a full, dazzling pendant haloed in gold and bruising the clouds above it maroon and silver.

La Vache Qui Crier

I'm standing in the middle of my flat, half dressed, wearing only my ski thermal top and greyish knickers, wondering what to do next. Only a few minutes ago, I answered a curt knock at the door and, to my surprise, came face to face with La Vache Qui Ski.

She was standing there looking very on edge, clutching in her bony hand a greasy bag of croissants, which made me oddly aware that I had never witnessed her eat. Her clipboard was under the other arm. There was a tense pause.

"I'm doing spot checks," she explained tersely, leaning round the door frame and trying to appraise the room without actually entering it first, like it was some sort of body farm. She made a move as if she meant to step inside, so I turned to let her past, dumbstruck into silence by her rudeness.

"Right," she said, surveying the wreckage of our apartment with disgust. "You know what I'm going to say don't you?"

Yes, I thought, feeling very tired, I probably do.

"It's filthy in here," her voice was hard, "It's never once been cleaned all season has it? You do realise that it's actually in your contract that you have to clean it? It's part of your responsibility as an employee to maintain your accommodation."

Standing there, stupidly, holding my hairbrush, I was temporarily dumb-founded at her complete and utter lack of tact, and the arrogant, patronising manner in which she seemed to feel it necessary to treat everyone, particularly me. I'd had enough. I was on a short fuse with her anyway, now that I knew she'd had her lips wrapped around the Man of Leisure's balls while I'd been desperately dealing with a half crazed, paralytic Ukrainian and a violent Northerner. Rage began to cloud my vision. She had accosted me on my own turf, in a very small space, and the red mist was descending.

"Look, you arrogant cow," I heard myself say. "I've just about had enough of this. You storm in here, unannounced during my precious few hours off and start ordering me around as if I'm some sort of prick. I know you're my manager, but what the fuck makes you think you have the right to be so unpleasant?"

Her mouth drooped open in astonishment, as if she'd spotted a large, juicy fly and wanted to catch it.

I wasn't finished.

"It's not just the fact that you're rude. I wouldn't mind if you were actually good at your job. But you seem to think being Resort Manager is just about bossing people around and shirking your responsibilities. You seem to actually enjoy giving me shit about something as pathetic as the level of tidiness in my bedroom – *which* I might add, was filthy when I moved in anyway due to *you* not checking it. And then when the shit actually hits the fan and you're *needed* to *do* something, you pull a sicky!"

Her mouth opened, again, this time presumably to contradict me.

"Don't think I don't know where you were that time when you said you had flu," I was getting breathless by this point and figured if she was going to sack me, she would have done it by the time I'd got to 'arrogant cow' so I just pressed on. "I'd make a formal complaint to Head Office but you've got your head so far up Christa's arse it would probably be you who answered the phone!"

I was on a roll. I didn't know I had it in me.

But now, something unexpected was happening. Something I would never have bet on in a million years. Instead of the scandalised tirade of defensive manoeuvres I'd banked on, instead of an explosion of wrath and indignation, quite the opposite. La Vache was starting to shrink. She said not a word, but sighed, deeply, and her sharp dark eyes took on a glaze. I saw, with some astonishment, that she was actually starting to well up.

Oh, holy fuck. I'd made my boss cry.

Not now knowing what to say, or where on earth to look, I fell silent and my eyes came to rest on that bag of croissants she was clutching. My focus seemed to remind her of what she was holding, and she glanced down and scrutinised it, as if it was the most tragic object she'd ever clapped eyes on. Then she held it out to me and said, ridiculously:

"Would you like one?"

"Er....No thanks. I've eaten." I said, and sat down heavily on a chair, feeling suddenly awful and also not a little exasperated that no matter the situation, La Vache somehow always managed to get the better of me.

"Ah yes," she drew a sharp intake of breath and looked pathetic. "In the chalet. Yes."

Wishing to God that I could break the tension I pointed at the chair opposite me.

"Are you ok? Would you like to sit down?"

She sniffed, loudly and shook her head, then fixed me with that odd, manic expression as if she was trying desperately to keep control of the huge, black, mascara-infused tear that now bulged mutinously down her cheek. I attempted to look sympathetic and convey compassion through the medium of my eyes while meanwhile my guts were filling up with an acidic mixture of self-loathing, pity and regret for what I'd said.

The next thing she said shocked me so much, I almost laughed out loud.

"Everything's so easy for you, isn't it?"

She uttered it in an uncharacteristically soft tone, staring at me, with what seemed like pure, innocent curiosity.

What an absurd thing to say!

"Um," I genuinely considered the idea for a moment.

"Uh... not really, no." I decided, shaking my head. Her words had made me feel oddly calm. "...But I'm glad it seems that way."

One or two things were suddenly coming into sharp relief. Her aloofness, her dictatorial manner, the immaculate hair and clothes and the proclamations of being so 'busy' all the time. Was it simply a dramatic rouse to hide the fact she was just shy and socially clumsy? Was she really just lonely, friendless and desperate to be liked? After all, why would someone like her – someone who ostensibly hated people – want to work in the tourist industry?

There was a fairly long silence as both of us waited for the other to say more and then, with a loud sniff, she wiped the ball of her thumb across the tear-stain on her cheek and seemed to decide it was time to go.

For a second, feeling contrite, I considered asking her if she'd like to go for a ski tomorrow. I actually opened my mouth to say it. But she got there first.

"You know," she said, more calmly, "I really should confiscate your ski pass and have you clean all this up."

I raised an eyebrow.

"But, I can see you're tired, and I'm willing to give you until Friday to sort it out. Okeydokes?"

I nodded in perplexed compliance. "Alright."

Then, like a spooked mare, pawing at the ground, she tossed her glossy head, sniffed again, and was gone.

Snowflakes

A few days later, feeling rather at peace with the world for once, I'm on the chairlift with Skater Boy, in a ganj-induced torpor, on one side of me, headphones blaring, and Scruffy-but-Handsome on the other. It has begun to snow. Tiny, dusty flakes that are hardly there, drifting onto our faces and clothes as the chairlift rises upwards into light mist. One impossibly tiny mote comes to rest on the dark material of my glove and, seeing it, I let out a little noise of wonder. I hold up my hand so The Scruffy One can see the infinitesimal, remarkable thing, surreal in its perfection.

He looks at it for a moment, silently, then he looks at me and breathes a little laugh, gives me a friendly squeeze on the shoulder and smiles. For a while we watch the mountain fall away beneath us in silence but for the tinny overtones of Skater Boy's music. Scruffy-but-Handsome is never normally this quiet and I wonder for a moment what's going through his mind, until he pipes up, unexpectedly with, "Do you think if I'd met you first, we'd have been the ones that shagged in the toilets?"

He looks genuinely quizzical. I blink at him.

"...possibly."

My arm slips round behind him to offer a consolatory hug. I'm rather grateful for his affable, comforting presence in my life.

"You're too young for me, I'm afraid, Scruffy."

"Too right, Grandma."

"But, then again, I have been subjected to the sight of you eating raw frankfurters in the nude quite a few times."

He looks at me out of the corner of an eye. "Yes that's true."

"That's quite pervy to be honest."

"What are you sayin'?" asks Skater Boy, pushing his headphones to one side and coming round momentarily from his Dubstep reverie.

"I'm stealing your woman,"

"Oh right…." Skater Boy burps and waves a dismissive hand. "She's all yours mate, all yours."

Later that day we find ourselves in Gringo's, heaving with seasonnaires on their worst behaviour. A Disney themed party is set to drag on well into the early hours and thanks to either lack of funds or impressive ingenuity everyone is dressed as some sort of tin-foil and card-board fuck up and/or covered in blue paint. To make matters yet more chaotic, everyone is wearing ski boots since the only way home at night from this place after the lifts shut is by riding. For some reason I can't quite fathom, I am dressed as a Russian prostitute called Svetlana. Head-to-toe leopard print, ski boots, bling jewellery and long black wig. The Disney theme isn't really my bag. Svetlana expresses my inner world more accurately.

The sweaty throng is ten deep at the bar in ski boots and fancy dress, swigging Mutzig straight from the jug. 'Bring Your Sisters' are playing tanked-up, frenetic covers of the Prodigy through distorting speakers and the staff are lining Jager Mega Drives up along the counter in their tens and twenties, then flicking them dominoes style in a line, so they cave in like demolition buildings. "Is that….?" I frown, extending my finger in the direction of The Foxy Chef, who is now sucking the face off a man who looks, from the back, not unlike Sloth from the Goonies. "Yeah, that's Campbell Campbell," nods the Man of Leisure, unimpressed and a little deflated. Campbell Campbell is a full six foot three and built of pure muscle, with a protruding forehead and fists like cannonballs.

"Jesus"

I back away from the snogging pair and find myself arse to arse with the Irksome-Blonde-19 Year-Old, who seems to be dressed as a fat Tinkerbell. She is wearing a tutu and a skin-tight lemon yellow leotard, which looks as if it might be cutting off all the circulation to her tits. Her hair is divided into two frenzied pony tails either side of her head and someone has scrawled 'EYEN-STINE' across her forehead in black marker pen. Shitfaced already, naturally. Over in the corner, sipping a pint quietly by himself, is The Geordie Ninja, looking morose, and quite close to punching someone.

"Eh up," Skater Boy materialises behind us with pint of wine in one hand and a jug of Mutzig in the other. "Which one of you Timmies wants a Jager Bomb? If you're not gonna ski properly, the least you can do is drink properly!" His eyes have taken on a wild gleam which, in combination with the stitches in his face, gives him an appearance that's quite alarming. He leans over to me, looking around the bar shiftily. "This place is full of fucking goblins," rolling around and spilling his wine now. "And that one's looking at me funny…" indicating a short girl in a long bobble hat by the toilets.

"What've you had?"

"Ketamine," he whispers. "only a teaspoon full, or so…"

The Man of Leisure reappears a second later and waves a baggy full of white crystalline powder under my nose. "K… Just say neigh,"

Several hours later and things are getting a bit weird. For a start, I can't feel my face. I am having what fuckheads refer to as an 'out of body experience.' It seemed like an excellent idea at the time, the Ketamine. But now, the world around me looks like a cracked LCD screen, and everyone in it like a hideous oil-slicked zombie. I'm sweating under this ridiculous wig. I have a vague notion that getting home is going to be a major issue, and not just because I don't know the way in the dark. What time is it? I mustn't panic. I must take control of this situation. It's imperative that I get myself home before skiing becomes untenable. Before my arms and legs become wibbly wobbly extensions of my body. I must find Skater Boy immediately and discuss the problem in depth.

"Fucksake bird." The news that I want to go home, and I'm expecting him to take me, does not come as welcome.

"Come on, it's not like I do this often… a *real* friend would…" I try fighting fire with fire. He's not happy about it, wreathed by a halo of tobacco smoke outside Gringos, eyes at half mast, and he makes this patently clear by starting to roll another joint with impressively steady fingers. Remarkable, considering that the rest of him is swaying around like a reed in a hurricane. I suck unsteadily on a roll up which I know is between my fingers, but can't actually feel. The weather seems muggy. A day of rain and sleet was followed by a temperature drop and more snow, but now I can't tell whether it's me that's clammy and warm, or the air around me. The snow that fell heavily has become sticky and thick. Somewhere off to the right of me, from under a section of the overhanging roof that acts as a smoking shelter, I hear a whoosh and a shout of surprise. Then a huddle of people who had moments before been laughing together suddenly scatter.

"Roof slide!" The crowd of people move forward to investigate the deposited pile of snow in the street. Skater Boy shrugs and extends an arm out for me to take refuge under.

"Please," I try again.

"Shit man. Really? Once we leave, that's it, we can't come back. We'll just be sat at home, buzzing"

"I'm feeling a bit weird. We could go to The Drop Inn."

"It'll be shut."

"I need to go home…"

"So go…"

"I don't think I should ski on my own. I don't feel safe."

Now I get the full Abominable Snow Bum performance. He chucks his joint on the floor with a petulant flourish and grinds it under his boot, swearing under his breath. After a lot of huffing, he eventually agrees and we set off, clipping into our skis on a flat section of the piste just below the decking area outside Gringos. I know the piste well enough in the daylight, but at night, with no depth perception and very few of my normal faculties intact, it seems as unfamiliar to me as the surface of an asteroid. There is very little light from the moon and all I can make out of him is a dim strand of moving darkness ahead, distinguishable only from the darkness around by its motion. Incredibly hard to focus on both him and on what's happening to the piste just in front of me. The white expanse seems lit from within, giving everything a weird topsy-turviness, as if the sky has crashed into the earth. As we glide over a ridge into the path of a snow cannon, I'm further disorientated as my vision is suddenly invaded by a fog of ice. I feel a strange sensation because the earth has tilted away from me quicker than anticipated; my stomach pitches around in an attempt to find a source of gravity, I panic slightly, but a moment of clarity tells me the only thing to do is keep skiing.

Hmmm. Something is wrong now. It could be that I have very little control over any of my limbs or it could be that my skis are not functioning normally. Hard to be sure but it feels as if I'm skiing on a duvet full of eels. The skis are sticking and I can't balance. I catch an edge, pitch forward and seem to do a forward roll onto my back and swivel round so that my head is now facing down the slope. I feel the wig, which, for some reason I'm still wearing, ripped from my head and I skid a little way, (I can't be certain how fast), with my skis pointing up hill, finally coming to a halt against something which, mercifully, is soft.

I lie there for a minute, imprisoned in a most undignified position with my knees bent uncomfortably upwards, lying on the backs of my skis, arms splayed, in that split second quite grateful that I'm laced with anaesthetic.

"Ahh shit."

How to get out of this one? Don't struggle. You'll get hot and bothered. Must think clearly.

I wriggle one fast-freezing hand out of the loop of my ski pole and bend my arm, reaching painfully back and under my bottom to try to release my binding. With a lot of heaving, sweating, puffing and mumbling expletives, eventually my boot comes free with a pop and I'm able to move myself round and stand up again, to take in my location. I've landed in a crease of snow at the back of a chalet, piled there by the occupants after months of shovelling fresh falls off the balcony. As my pupils dilate in the darkness just behind it, I can make out a tall tree and the creaking eves of the chalet pointing down at me. Downhill, there is only blindness. I squint into it, hoping to see Skater Boy hiking back up towards me, but no, just black. The darkness seems to actually enter my eyeballs and occupy my brain so I can hardly think. It seems to have density, a physical, spongy presence. Skater Boy is nowhere. I shout for him, suddenly feeling very sober and alone.

"Bollocks."

I shout for him again, and listen, rigidly. Silence. It's as if the darkness is penetrating my ears as well now. I shout again and listen for the promising hint of a distant voice. All I hear is my own, disappearing unnervingly into the Alpine abyss.

And now, whilst being aware of being very alone in an unknown location with no phone (the battery of which went flat hours ago) and no torch, I'm also suddenly very aware of badly needing a piss.

Clipping out of my other ski and abandoning my poles on the ground, I head for the apex of the crease of rather soft, wet snow into which I've crashed. There is a lip and then a slope down to the back of the chalet. The branches of the tree span outwards in a helpful descending pattern for me to cling onto, and as I stumble downwards, I can hear the snow shaking off the branches above me. Some of it scatters onto my jacket and head. At this point, I realise I could have just pissed on the piste since there's no one around. Oh well.

I find a comfortable place to squat, facing the chalet, and fight to get my ski pants far enough down over my thighs so that I don't wee all over them.

The rush comes all at once. The rush of the warm piss on the snow and the swhoosh! whomp! of the roof slide, as it slicks quickly off the chalet eves and hits me in the abdomen, flattening me against the slope and pinning me there by the hips and legs.

It has filled my trousers and compacted around my fanny in the most appalling fashion. The vaginal cavity is a finite space and an awful lot more cold matter has been introduced to it than I'm happy with. The weight of it seemingly paralyzes me from the waist downwards and I shriek, as much in shock from the sensation of receiving an unwelcome shot of something cold, wet and solid to the fanny, as the fear of being trapped. I realise it's also getting colder, fast, and starting to hurt.

"Fuck!"

How has *this* happened? One minute I was being responsible and trying to get home, the next I'm forcibly attempting the word's first uterus-piss-sculpture-snow-angel. I struggle and pull with all my strength to free my lower body, but the weight of the snow is astounding, I can't bend or wriggle an inch. Then as the magnitude of the situation hits me I start to shout; caterwaul. Long, blood-curdling shrieks for help, amidst a rather dramatic montage of thoughts about everyone I love; my Dad, the Big Brother, Shazzer, the Scruffy-One. How will they all feel when the owner of the chalet discovers my frozen, piss-soaked corpse buried up to my ovaries in three days time? And where…where the *fuck* is Skater Boy? My legs are getting stiff and everything below the waist is horrifically cold and numb. The shrieks are turning to sobs, and my body begins to shake, aggressively. I'm hyperventilating. Pins and needles begin to bubble in my hands.

"Oh shit, oh shit, oh shit, oh shit…"

Wait. Deep breath. Slow…slow… breathe. "Get a *fucking* grip,"

And then it's Shazzer's voice in my head, saying something like, "Seriously mate. What sort of dick follows a well known stoner down a piste in the dark…on Ketamine. Massive schoolgirl error."

It begins to dawn on me that nobody is here. Ergo nobody is going to help. The chalet is empty, blinds closed and no lights come from inside; no smoke from the chimney. Skater Boy has spectacularly fucked off. So come on. Don't be feeble. I know I'm not far from civilisation. It isn't a long ski from Gringos to the road and I must have been at least half way down it when I fell.

Sometime later, as I'm side slipping on my skis down the edge of the piste, hugging the tree line where there are markers and I can better judge the incline and pitch of the hill in the dimness, I realise I have no idea how long I have been out here. I have no idea how I managed to dig myself free with my bare hands, but I did. If I tried to dig through a foot and a half of snow with my bare hands again, I am certain I would fail. I'm vaguely aware that my finger tips are sore. I worked them down into the jagged mass of icy crystals and tore it away from myself, lump by lump, wriggling up and down as much as I could with my hips, until my legs started to come free and my hands cramped painfully. Then gasping, actually laughing, giggling and buzzing with relief, I had fought in the dark to empty the rest of the snow from inside my trousers, dripping horribly down against my inner thighs. I pulled them up, piss and frost encrusted as they were, and scrambled back up the ridge to retrieve my skis.

Further down the hill now, I can make out the foot of a chairlift, looming into view, which tells me I'm nearly at the road. Finally, I know where I am, and the fight goes out of me. My limbs turn to jelly. I make it down the final few metres in jolting side slips, and come to a heavy stop, collapsing at the road side.

…Back in my empty apartment I find half a bottle of Scotch at the back of my wardrobe and sink most of it, then fill and get into the tiny bath to warm up.

Bed and sleep (half petrified, un-fidgeting) follow swiftly after.

The Occurrences of the Last Evening

"So…he was just sitting there, asleep with a half rolled joint in his hand and smashed glass everywhere…?"

On the chairlift with Scruffy-but-Handsome. Lunchtime, the next day.

"Yep"

The Scruffy One who, suffering a nasty bout of bronchitis, had chosen to give Gringos a miss and spent the night at a friend's, was relaying to me the scene that had met him when he arrived back at the apartment the next morning. Namely: A pungent stench of burnt rubber, smashed glass everywhere and Skater Boy, prostrate on the futon. He had a half rolled joint in one bloodied hand, a lighter in the other, and on the stove was a red hot, glowing saucepan dancing hysterically, about four minutes away from a nuclear explosion.

"What was the explanation?"

"He wanted a cup of tea."

"The magnitude of his fucktardedness never ceases to amaze…"

Arriving home, after losing me on the piste Skater Boy had put the pan on the hob and sat down to roll his last joint of the evening. Then, promptly, passed out – straight into a K hole I presume. The round knob on the lid had gradually melted during the night, dripped down the sides and formed a seal, turning the saucepan into a scorching, seething pressure cooker.

"Why was the window smashed?"

"Because he forgot that I'd left him a key in the flower pot by the entrance…"

"But then how did he…? Oh my God, no!"

Yes.

In the absence of a key, he had scaled the front of the building, urban dare-devil style, grabbing onto the bars of three sets of balconies and the stalk of a dried up pot plant to get to the top. As a finale, he had smashed the window of his own balcony with his fist, and stumbled inside.

When I, myself, had woken in my still-empty flat, the night's events seemed like nothing more than a mildly perturbing dream. I thought about it hard, but couldn't get a handle on quite what scale of danger I'd been in, if any. Part of me was sceptical about being over-dramatic. The other part was utterly terrified by the whole experience and incredulous that he hadn't even given my whereabouts a second thought before submitting to unconsciousness. "You stupid bastard!" was all I could bring myself to say to him the next time I we met. He looked crestfallen.

"You just disappeared," he protested, "I thought you knew the way!"

I shook my head in disgust.

"I've said I'm sorry. OK?"

Actually, it was pretty fucking far from OK. His excuses could only have been plausible if I didn't already know him to be the selfish, spoilt, child that he was. I said as much but he just shrugged and rolled his eyes at me.

"I don't think I can actually forgive him this one," I say gloomily, as the Scruffy One and I swing towards the top of the lift. Scruffy-but-Handsome seems un-impressed but not particularly surprised by the fiasco. Then suddenly, he clutches my arm and leans over the bar of the chairlift.

"Hold on a minute," he is pointing at something on the ground far below us, near one of the snow cannons. A black, dishevelled object, half obscured by snow, and clearly the worse for having been skied over several times. "…isn't that your wig?"

[just pushed it back up inside"

[R]ight. Now that she came to mention it, I had been [thro]ugh one or two butt-clenching experiences recently to [whi]ch I could attribute this ailment. There was the roof-slide [incid]ent. Then the unsolicited, two metre drop halfway down [the] gully the day before. My ski tips hit the approach-[ing l]ip of snow like a forklift truck driving headlong into a [poly]styrene wall and dug in, resulting in a double-eject face[-plan]t and then lots of scrabbling around trying to relocate [my] skis. And then there was the chilling torch-less trudge [hom]e from the pub at midnight along the windy deserted [road] to our chalet. I'd been alone. The mountains to the north [were] backlit hauntingly by a sunken moon, tinged with red [, as if] from a furnace within, like something out of Mordor. [Ther]e was utter and complete silence of the sort you can find [nowh]ere else but the mountains, where the only sound is [the t]innitus you didn't realise you had. Usually, I would have [appr]eciated the magnificence of it, but four or five gins, four [or fi]ve Jager Bombs and a coffee had given me the fear. All I [coul]d hear, in the silence, was my own heart thudding inside [my] chest, my blood entering my head like a sponge being [squ]eezed from the uphill effort. I'd spent the entire fifteen [min]ute walk glancing suspiciously over my shoulder, in the [hop]e of definitely not seeing a sinister dark figure tailing me [with] murder in mind. Then, ten yards from the safety of the [fron]t door, I had paused to appreciate the view without fear, [slipp]ed on a patch of ice and fell smack, fully onto my back, [wind]ing myself.

[...]I reckon that's when it happened. The hemorrhoid, I [mea]n...

["]I wouldn't worry, you can just push them back in with [your] finger after you've had a shit..." The Foxy Chef was say-[ing,] leaning on the bar. "It's quite soothing actually. Just push [ba]ck up inside and forget about it."

The Wise Lunatics

Technically needless and ill-advised conciliatory purchases to ease the pain of the last 24 hours:

a pair of oversized, uber-trendoid orange headphones

expensive leather gloves designed for hard-core back-country daredevils, light green (when life throws you a clue about the value of good gloves, only a fool doesn't take a hint)

top of range 'next season' free-ride ski boots, orange and black (the least I deserve)

'vintage' 80s canary yellow, green and pillar box red flash all-in-one, with accompanying bum bag (to assuage grief over loss of wig and to be worn ironically to next party)

...I also left a shop this afternoon with a pair of baggy orange Analog ski pants, a set of stripy green and yellow Dragon goggles and a skater hat (why!?). I bought them wearing my chalet uniform, and was observed with clear disdain by the spotty French oik at the till, who was clearly asking himself questions about my ability to pull these items off.

I'll be the judge of that thanks, Sparky.

Walking back from the shop, I saw a woman in a diamante fox fur bobble hat walking up the tarmac road to her hotel lobby *on skis*.
   Yes. Walking up the tarmac road *still clipped into her skis*.
What the fuck are you doing you utter crapweasle?

Conclusion: This place is full of lunatics. Full of them. Myself included. The problem is no one here is old. Not really old in the white haired, frail, bones-of-honey-comb sense. This thought suddenly struck me when I saw a Russian lady being pushed across a car park in a wheelchair a few weeks ago. Her skin seemed the colour and texture of a polished copper frying pan. Burnished and pulled in all directions, as if stretched out to dry in the sun. Her hair stood to attention like soft peaks of whisked eggwhite, stained with iodine. The result wasn't so much anti-aging as the eradication of evidence of age altogether; the denial of it as a fact of human existence. Only the veins on her hands gave her away. No crooked old men walk the streets here, bent double, shuffling up the road. No old ladies hobble for the bus. There is nobody to give up your seat to. I am not certain how I feel about this but I'm pretty sure it can't be a good thing. It makes me realise that there is something very reassuring about the elderly.

What's to become of us in a place where the wise are banished?

What to do on a Slow Day dans le Chalet

A cloud is sitting at the foot of the mounta[...] river flowing through the gorge. It's the exac[...] o'-the-wisp. As I go about my chores, I w[...] window in the chalet sitting room, which [...] view of the valley. It evaporates in the sun, [...] the morning wears on. I stop to rub some [...] the ends of my fingers, paying special atten[...] burns and general chapped dryness. I sit dow[...] table and wince. It appears the chalet hands [...] ailment. No. I'll cut right to the chase. I have [...] only be described as an arse grape.

I was first made aware of it when I tried to[...] side a few evenings ago, after a particularly s[...] The action was met with a shooting pain in on[...] sphincter area, followed by a yelp of pain by [...] shortly thereafter a frenzied, horrified self exa[...] mystified. According to the mirror, everythi[...] looked perfectly normal even though it felt as [...] attacked me with a Swarfega-coated rubber b[...] very least I was expecting it to be an anal fis[...] understand it.

"What the fuck?" I asked The Foxy Chef, n[...] pub later on.

"Sounds like a hemorrhoid to me," she said[...]

"Whaaaat?"

"Yep!"

"Fuck!! Like what old ladies get?"

"Yeah... have you been straining lately?"

"No! ....Well, not that I particularly recall."

"You must've sprung it when you stacked it [...] Muscular spasm. Happened to me once..."

"What did you do?"

236
237

This, really, is not all that surprising, coming from the girl who apparently nicknamed the cyst on her vagina 'Mini-me' last season. Hey. Sometimes it's just best to wear these things as a badge of honour, I guess. So, reeling in shock over this unsolicited foray by my colon into the outside world, I have opted not to ski today. Over the years, I've become quite good at filling idle headspace and time with various pointless yet satisfying activities. Between the hours of 12 and 4 in a chalet, one finds oneself waiting around with bugger all to do. So I've come up with a list of activities to keep things interesting:

1. Fuss about rearranging things - putting candles on the table, tossing about folding towels decoratively in the bathroom. That type of thing.

2. Have a very long poo - steal magazines from people's bedrooms if needed.

3. Get plastered. Drinking wine out of a mug always works, as you can pretend it's coffee.

4. Think up rude nicknames for your clients - over the season we've had 'Princess Haddock Knickers', 'Damian' (that child was possessed by Satan, I swear), and 'Shitstick' (that was the toilet brush turd guy - you remember...)

5. Muse on life, the universe and everything.

6. Scour chalet for objects to toboggan to the pub on. We have tried bin liners, dry cleaning bags and a suitcase. The suitcase was surprisingly ineffectual.

7. My personal favourite...have a wank in the store cupboard - at the risk of being busted or contaminating the fruit and veg, this is a great way to kill ten minutes.

Rules for the Chalet Bitch:
A general beginner's guide (cont.)

Last night, I got severely fucked, and this morning had to deal with a 7am text message from our guest, requesting a lift for his young family from the chalet to the piste.

I was experiencing a bastard behind the eyes. Rolling over in bed, I blearily composed a text message to the Geordie Ninja.

"Alright ya Geordie cunt. Guests need bus at 9. Sorry luv. Wankstain."

And then I sent it.

To the guest.

It was Tourettes-esque in its irony. I was so hanging out of my arse that my brain couldn't cope with two thoughts at once, so it short circuited and fucked me over. The thing that astonished me most was that I was actually thinking to myself, as I scrolled through the numbers in my phone to send it, *imagine how bad it would be if I mistakenly sent this to the guest...*

Which brings me to rule number 24 in my list of Chalet Bitch guidelines:

24. Don't EVER communicate with guests via text. Once it's written down, you cannot take it back.

Russians, Again.

A few weeks ago, we had some Russians staying in our chalet who arrived with a crazed, vibrating Chihuahua for which they had not paid a damage deposit in advance.

"You'll need to get five hundred Euros off them in case that thing wrecks the chalet," La Vache Qui Ski whispered huskily into my ear as we stood in the living room watching them glug down their welcome champagne. I glanced sceptically at the tiny animal. It was hard to imagine it destroying anything. It was pathetic, with its eyes like bowling balls, twitching in terror as its fur-bedecked, maniacal owner strutted around the chalet smoking a long, slender cigar and stuffing banana bread into her gob.

I was wrong.

That very evening, it managed to escape for a few precious minutes and was so beside itself with joy that it crapped all over the next door neighbour's chalet. There was shit in the hallway, shit up the curtains, in the bath and on one of the beds. Needless to say the neighbour was catatonic with rage, and guess who was drafted in to clear up the mess?

On the Wednesday afternoon, I received a phone call while I was out skiing. It was La Vache Qui Ski, back in character as my personal nemesis.

"Where are you?"

"I'm er.... half way down Sauliere somewhere, under the chairlift. Off piste."

"Why isn't your phone switched on?"

"It *is* switched on. How else would you be speaking to me?"

"I've just had a *very* irate phone call from Mrs. Vasiliev in the Christina, made no less irate by the fact you haven't been answering your phone."

"I'm not working at the moment…"

"Look, you need to get down there now. Apparently there's a problem with the toilet or something."

Mrs. Vasiliev greeted me at the door in her bathrobe, despite it being 3.30 in the afternoon, seeming quite furious, shaking hands, red face, shrill voice.

"Is toilet!" she shrieked.

"Oh dear, is it blocked?" I enquired, calmly, coming inside into the warm and taking my helmet off.

"Nono. No is block-ed. Is *toilet* is too *small!*"

"Too small?"

"Yezyez. Too small. Is grazing elbows," she pulled up her dressing gown sleeves and waggled each of her dry, flaking elbows at me to demonstrate.

Was the woman serious? What did she want me to do? Nail cushions to the walls? Knock up a quick extension? Earlier in the week, she had complained that the snow ploughs were waking her up too early and demanded I call the Mayor's office.

"You and I both know this is utterly ridiculous," I said to the Mayor's secretary, who luckily, though reluctantly, spoke very good English. "But my guests have requested that you stop snow ploughing near our chalet in the morning because it wakes them up too early." She listened quietly, then simply laughed down the phone at me, before grunting something rude that sounded an awful lot like 'putain', and then hanging up.

It was not surprising then, as you might think, to receive a random phone call today from these very same Russian guests out of the blue.

"Hjello? Hjello? Is Christina chalet."

"Ahm...*hello?*"

"Is Christina chalet!"

"Is who?"

"No no. YOU is Christina chalet!"

"Ohhh. No... I mean yes, yes, what can I do for you?"

"Is Mr. Vasiliev."

"Yes. How are you Mr Vasiliev?"

"You hev remot control."

"What? Er...*pardon?*"

"You hev remot control."

"I'm so sorry I don't know what you mean. Could you maybe..."

"Remot. Control."

"Er...."

"We be in Christina chalet, we not bring remot control. You bring. You bring. We pay."

"Remot control?"

"Yez yez, remot control. For car."

"*Oh* you mean the TV remote from your car? Yes we found it under the bed."

"YEZ! YEZ!"

"You want me to post it to you? What's the address?"

"No no. You bring in car. We pay."

"Er...er...OK. Where are you?"

"Toorin."

"*Turin?*"

"Toorin."

"You want me to drive your remote control to Turin?"

"Errrrr.......yezyez."

"Wouldn't it be cheaper to post it?"

"No no. You drive."

"I...."

"Ok no. NO! Ansi."

"Ansi?"

"Yez yez. Ansi. You drive Ansi. Bring remot control. We pay taxi come Ansi pick up. OK?"

"Ansi...Ansi? *Ohhhhhh* – you mean *Annecy!*"

"Yez! Ansi! Yezyezyez."

"Well, if you really want but I'm sure it'd be cheaper to post it."

"No."

"OK."

"You leave now?"

"I ah..... I'll have to just check it with my manager and then call you back, OK?"

"Yezyezyez. You come, you come. OK bye."

Click.

"...Fuck my life."

The worst part was, when I got to Annecy the next day, and rendezvoused with the Vasiliev's careworn-looking driver, I realised I'd actually forgotten to put the fucking thing in the car.

The driver, who had travelled all the way from Italy through the night, was deadpan.

"You hev remot control?"

"Ummm...."

Some More Pet Hates

The quickest way to lose all faith in humanity is to serve it food and clear up after it. That is a fact. Never a truer word was spoken, as far as I'm concerned. It astonishes me, some of the rancid living habits one is exposed to on a daily basis in this job. For example, why do some of the daintiest, most demure female guests feel it's perfectly acceptable to leave their dirty, stained underwear in the middle of the floor for you to pick up? Or leave a rank Gillette shaving razor on the sink with crops of (astonishingly long) pubic hairs sprouting out in all directions for you to marvel at when you're cleaning up?

Some other choice grievances to add to my ongoing list:

Porridge oats

Scoffed as a snack and left to crust on the rim of the bowl in the sink. Is there any adhesive more powerful known to mankind? Seriously? You could build car parks out of it. Can't you fuckers put your bowls in the dishwasher? How hard is it?

Reptiles

Those guests with apparently no warm blood in their veins whatsoever, who feel it necessary to turn the heating up on full and then ask you to light the fire, even when it's quite warm outside. The worst have some sort of micro-degree sensor on them too. Even if you're two floors above them and you open the window a crack, because the chalet is like a furnace and you feel you may keel over any second, they yell "Christ it's *freezing* in here, is there a window open somewhere?"

Empty Vessels

Which, as the old adage goes, make the most noise. I remember the house keeper of one family we had staying - a sweet woman but as dense as an ingot of solid iron hewn from the cold heart of a distant comet. She spent the entire week hanging round the kitchen, babbling at me in a hoarse whisper so her boss couldn't hear and asking inane questions like, "Are you going to put the dishwasher on?" "Is this a pomegranate?" (it was an apple) "How much butter have we got?" "Ooh isn't it snowy outside?" and "Oooh isn't it warm inside?" The thing is, she was terribly sweet and helpful - refused to let me clean her room and helped with all the clearing up - and I knew she was just trying to be friendly. She reminded me of a small, cute puppy, unaware that its yapping makes you want to attach kitchen utensils to its head with a nail gun.

Towel thieves

If you're ever staying in a chalet, never, I repeat NEVER, take towels out of the cupboard without asking the chalet host. You must understand that you are interfering with a finely tuned system, here. There are a finite number of towels. You have been given an allocation. There are a finite number of bathrobes. You are allowed *one*. If you fuck with the system the host will run out of towels for the next changeover before the laundry comes back. This will mean she'll have to wash them herself, in house. And this will make her angry, which in turn will result in the defiling of your belongings while you are out skiing.

Bleeders

People that pick themselves in the night - spots, noses, scabs etc - and decorate the freshly laundered, crisp white sheets with specks of claret and puss. Fucking disgusting, can't you just leave yourself alone?

Fingerprinters

Retards who think it's necessary to open French windows by flattening their hand against the glass and pushing. Use the fucking handle, numb nuts. Furthermore, what is it with children and French windows? Do they really need to dip themselves in butter and marmalade and then press themselves up against every available glass surface? Or lick the windows just after they've eaten maple syrup whilst staring at you with defiant glee?

Little Darlings

People who think it's fine to let their children play around your feet in the kitchen during service, under the mistaken presumption that you think they're cute. I don't think they're cute. I'm seconds from cutting off each of their digits with a bread knife and serving them to you as a canapé.

Interferers

Those who take it upon themselves to rearrange things. Cleaning products in the cleaning box, items in the kitchen drawers, the contents of my dry goods cupboard. Be my guest! In fact, perhaps I'll rearrange the set up in your bedroom while we're at it. I could swap the toilet with the wardrobe and take a shit in your knicker drawer.

Best. Day. Ever.

Inspecting the hot tub, after the departure, this morning, of Prince Abdul Somethingorother of Somewhere Sandy, I was repulsed to find a peculiar brownish scum floating on top of the water. The general state of the chalet (stained bed sheets, strange skid marks ....blood?) gave me to assume that he and his entourage had been enjoying the company of numerous local ladies of the night. In fact the inside of the chalet looked as if they'd been filming some sort of scatological porno.

It was fucking rank.

Accompanying the unidentified foam (I'm guessing a mixture of fake tan and cum) was a charming milkshake of condoms, broken champagne flutes and fag butts floating in the water. Hot tubs are revolting things at the best of times. A simmering stew of other people's fluids. Old bathwater, kept at just the perfect temperature to be ripe with thrush and dysentery-inducing bugs. There were no two ways about it. The hot tub would have to be cleaned. The fact that we were actually meant to empty and refill it every week was neither here nor there. A detail we'd managed neatly to skate over for most of the season by chucking in fistfuls of chemicals. However, it was quite clear that all of these delightful accouterments would have to be fished out before the next guests arrived in a few hours. The thing would have to be drained or the filters would block.

The Irksome-Blonde-19-Year-Old and I stared at it for some minutes, in disgust, before either of us spoke.

"I'm not fucking touching it," she said.

I sighed. I was feeling slightly queasy from the night before but I didn't have the energy to argue.

Assembling a make-shift fishing rod out of a coat hanger, I spent the next hour spooning various objects from the fizzy, luke-warm soup. I could almost see the bacteria colonies breeding on the surface, and it was all I could do not to hurl last night's Jager into the cocktail. Tragically, though, things were about to get a lot worse. As I plucked the last condom from the mix and hurled it into the neighboring chalet's front garden, a large piece of broken glass pierced the sole of my in-door shoe and cut the underside of my foot.

"Cunts!" I yelled as I hopped to the other foot.

"Oh Cunty Bollocks!" as I slipped on the three-inch-thick icy surface of the hot-tub's decking.

In horror I saw the mildew-foamy water looming towards me, but it was too late to right myself. There was no foothold and I was in the drink.

Now, this is not somewhere you want to be. Ever. This sort of thing makes you question your very existence. Spluttering, swearing and drenched in weird, slimy, Royal Arabian cum-water from a gang bang you didn't even get to participate in. Launching myself back out into the icy air, I swore again at the top of my lungs and scuttled, shivering to the French windows, screaming for the Irksome One to let me in and knocking on the freshly polished glass, only to find they were locked, and she wasn't there.

She'd gone out.

She'd fucking gone out!

…and just at that moment, I heard the familiar crunch of snow-on-tyres from the drive way, the slam of a car door, and several loud, guffawing male voices, that signaled my greatest fear.

Our guests had arrived.

Rule Number 25: Do bed hop constantly, and without shame or remorse.

A few days later, I am pouring a sparkling stream of champagne into the delicately slim glass of a chiseled slab of manhood. Cross-legged and pensive in front of the fire, his name is Robert. Six foot two, thick, raven-black hair swept neatly back from a high, tanned forehead. Roll-sleeved Lacoste jumper. A touch snooty. He fiddles absently with the black leather strap on his Rolex while the rest of his party chortle and pontificate around him. The leader of this week's group – their boss, Hugo - is the finance director of a prominent European bank, entertaining seven other British chaps of varying ages. Corporates. I duly noted several wedding rings among them when they arrived on Saturday, which have now, by midweek, mysteriously, and somewhat creepily, disappeared. This has coincided nicely with the arrival of three of Hugo's 'daughters', who keep mysteriously turning up to join them in the chalet for dinner.

Oh God. Not more hookers.

As I pour, I muse on the irony that hotties, like Robert, one rarely ever gets pinched on the arse by. Far more likely to be a perspiring, wheezing, mid-fifties estate agent with flaking skin. A nice friendly pat on the back goes a long way, but when the hand slides south and unwelcome fingers work their way into your arse crack, it can be a real mood breaker. That said, a good, deep goosing from Robert would set me up for a week, I'm sure. Not that there's much chance of that. For it was he who first spotted me, dripping with rancid cum-water, and looking as if I was about to enter a wet T-shirt contest, on the day they arrived. Not quite the executive welcome they'd been hoping for, I'll wager. He and Hugo were not particularly impressed by my disheveled appearance, I could tell. Neither were they much amused by my sheepish announcement that, due to a slight accident, we were all locked out of the chalet, and my co-host had gone completely AWOL. I had to send them away to a restaurant while I feverishly tried to locate her, running down the hill to borrow Scruffy-but-Handsome's phone (mine was locked inside). I called her continuously on dial-repeat for an hour, until she finally picked up and admitted sullenly, that she had "popped home to get something and accidentally dozed off." A likely story.

"Get your fucking arse back here with the key right now!" I bellowed.

Whilst Robert clearly has no interest in the low-slung, extra-tight black trousers I wore this evening, exclusively for his benefit, Tim, another member of the group, has made absolutely no secret of the fact that he wants to get in my knickers. It started when he clocked my boobs through the wet T-shirt on Saturday. He couldn't have gawped any more obviously if he'd been a rhesus monkey. Then, when they all clattered in at tea time, discarding jackets, hats, goggles and various other paraphernalia as they went, pissed and red-nosed from a long boozy lunch at the Cerf D'Or, it got worse.

"Organise us, can you!?" boomed Tim, merrily, pressing two crisp fifty Euro notes into my hand.

"Oh, that's sweet, bless you," I said, crinkling them into my pocket.

"No no, not at all," he said turning to his friends, "First on the list, keep the chalet girl happy, then the wife, then everything else is a breeze, hahaha!" They all boomed with sycophantic laughter. "Now, sweetheart, you're in charge. Organise us. We need booze, we need cocaine, champagne... you're in charge, you're in charge..."

"Oh Tim, be careful what you wish for..." I winked, bending over to pick up a jacket that had been hung up on the floor. This produced a raucous round of hoots and jeers.

"Is the hot tub hot?" asked Tim, peering out of the balcony window at it. I eyed it, cautiously. I hadn't, obviously, mentioned to them that the previous occupant had basted it in his royal seed.

"I believe it's fizzing away," I said, hoping to fuck I'd managed to fish out all of the glass.

"Good, go and get your bikini on then...." Another round of hooting laughter.

"Perhaps later, I'm just in the middle of cooking dinner," I said dryly, trying to get a reign on things.

"...And then we'd like to book a taxi and a VIP table at Les Caves – is that place any good?"

"If you like Euro techno trash and strippers, then yes it's great,"

"Brilliant. The wife won't mind, will she?" he asked no one in particular over another cascade of guffaws as if trying to reassure himself.

"What about your wife, Pete? Does she like a party?" said Tim taking a glass of champagne and putting an arm round me as if I was his, "I have to drag Paula out by the scruff of the neck,"

"Oh, Jo loves a party, yeah," sniggered Pete, "In fact, she's terribly difficult to get into bed...." More guffaws.

"What about you sweetheart?" Tim whispered in my ear over the mirth. "Are you difficult to get into bed?"

Christ! I glanced at him. He was hammered. This might have offended another woman, but I figured having a little flirt with him would ensure me a flow of good tips. Hello Ski-Doo rides and posh lunches on the mountain, I thought. He was blonde, not at all my type, and would have been handsome were it not for the Sloane-square manner of dress, and slight lack of definition where the chin becomes the neck. Not a sock face, you understand, just a couple of Mars bars short of a six pack. Impossible not to flirt with, nonetheless.

"I like your trousers," he winks at me as I sway past him now, tray in hand.

"I wore them just for you," I smile, lying.

On Tuesday, the visibility was poor, so they paid me to ski-guide them around the mountain. It was a hoot. I took them to a number of favourite drinking spots and they bought me lunch and poured an inordinate number of shots down my throat. Tim engineered his way into the seat next to me on every lift, fed me a constant stream of cigarettes and the better oiled he became, the more often he would slip his arm comfortably around my shoulders and squeeze me up against him with a good-humoured chuckle. The Chalet Bitch: cook, cleaner, dogsbody, nanny, psychiatrist and now, apparently, rent-a-mistress.

"I think this evening calls for a pre-dinner dip in the hot tub," they said, "but you'll have to abide by our naked-Jacuzzi rule."

The idea of getting back in that goype-infested pool filled me with revulsion, but after weeks of dull, stuck up guests, families and Russians, I enjoyed the banter.

Later, in the kitchen, only half joking, Tim says teasingly: "How much would I have to pay to get you to stay the night with me?" He puts a big, warm, rough hand on mine. I gasp and smack him lightly on the arm; feign what I assess to be the appropriate level of girlish outrage at the suggestion I can be bought. Though the question has certainly been at least half in jest, for a moment I secretly grapple with it, and try to ignore the ugly, female mercenary pragmatist that I bury deep inside. It is rearing its ugly head up.

....*Oh. Fuck it. Why not? I could do with the cash.*

"Well, it's a very kind offer darling. But I think there may be objections from my boss if I start shagging clients in the hot tub." I say. "And anyway, you need your beauty sleep."

253

He leans closer.

"Come on. I've made my intentions to you pretty clear haven't I?"

I glare at him from under my eyelashes.

"Intentions? Is this a Bronte adaptation? Should we consult my father?"

"You're a tease!"

"Oh Timmy. You wouldn't have to pay me dear," I wink, lying. "Dinner's served."

Still. The dilemma stays with me: it snaggles for attention, like a broken nail when one has no emery board to smooth it nicely away.

First Lifts

This evening it came. The bombshell.

"Would we be able to have breakfast an hour earlier?" Robert asked, earnestly, looking up at me from his customary spot by the fire. "I think we'd like to get first lifts tomorrow,"

Fucksake. Here we go. The Curse of 'First Lifts'. My favourite. You get at least one every week.

"Yes absolutely," I beam, offering him a plate of salmon-mousse-stuffed vol au vents. "No problem at all. So breakfast at 7.45 then?"

I swish off to the kitchen, where, grinning manically, I down a shot of vodka straight from the bottle.

"What's the matter?" asks the Irksome one, looking up from the avocado she is massacring with a butter knife.

"They want to get first lifts."

"Well *I'm* not getting up an hour early. I've got a sore throat." She is wearing one of those big, square caps that you associate with ghetto stars and I'm seized by an overwhelming desire to knock it off her head and stuff it up her arse.

"No. Didn't think you would. By the way, are you planning to brush your hair any time this season?" I'm eyeing the massive birds nest of knots and frizz poking out from under the hat. "You'd better sort that out soon, or it'll turn into a massive dreadlock and we'll have to shave you…"

7.45am Ha. First lifts.

The whole thing's laughable.

If you really, genuinely wanted fresh tracks, you'd get off your over-cosseted Gucci arse, hike up a 60 foot rock face at sunrise and scare yourself properly, instead of forcing me to get up at 'extra early' o'clock to cook your sodding breakfast, for no good reason, so that you can go and snow plough corduroy.

I, of course, overslept. The Irksome-Blonde-19-Year-Old simply grunted and pulled the duvet over her head, leaving me no choice but to go it alone, so I decided to hot foot it up the piste, instead of the road. Unfortunately, due to vast amount of snow that just keeps coming at the moment, I sank up to my thighs and had to wade. Panting and swearing, hauling myself up hill, clutching at fir trees to aid my ascent, I arrived looking like Scott of the Antarctic shortly after he wandered out into the frozen abyss.

I entered the sitting room and was immediately hit by the smell; carpet marinating in beer and wine. The entire interior landscape resembled the aftermath of Hiroshima. Oh Christ. Not again. Smashed glasses, stained rug, something brown streaked down one of the walls. Bottles and food everywhere. Tim, lying unconscious in the centre of it all, naked (complete with a lop-sided semi), next to the fireplace, with about thirty wine bottles lined up in a perfect silhouette around him. The boys this week are taking the 'unlimited' wine stipulation in the brochure to its upper limit. My heart sank at the mess. I raked him over for a moment and took in the cock scrawled across his forehead. Lacklustre. There appeared to be candle wax all over his nether regions.

Hmm. A clear cut buckaroo victim.

Moments later, in the kitchen, I heard the tell-tale smash

from the living room, shriek of fear and the thump thump thump up the stairs. Tim had seemingly regained consciousness.

At 10am, the whole lot of them were still fisting around in the sitting room in their pyjamas, hung over. Presumably, they don't even remember asking me about first lifts last night.

And you wonder why I get irate with these characters. Thank fuck tomorrow is my day off.

The Morning After the Night Before

Am feeling decidedly sulky.

I spent yesterday evening at the The Drop Inn, being chatted up by a snowboard bore. You know, the overenthusiastic retarded type who can't talk about anything except with detailed descriptions of all the tricks he did that day…

"…and then I did a heelside turn and just corked all the way down…blah blah blah…"

He was wearing a tall T and had the most intense goggle tan I've ever seen.

My eyes kept flicking over to the corner where Skater Boy and the Scruffy One were entertaining themselves and the in-resort 'new girl' playing drinking games. New Girl is irritatingly pretty, with a kooky, stubby copper-coloured bob and, as Calamity kept reminding me all evening, is a really *amazing* snowboarder. She has been drafted in to replace a ski rep who quit last week and the boys are all over this fresh meat like a fungus. I could hear the Man of Leisure on the other side of me complaining loudly to someone about how sick and tired he was of truffle oil. I didn't feel much like talking to any of them since they had all chosen to disappear off skiing for the day without telling me. It didn't help that I wasn't currently on speaking terms with Skater Boy and had made my feelings about the roof slide incident abundantly clear. Everyone else, annoyingly, seemed to be sitting on the fence. "Where are you guys?" I'd asked The Foxy Chef, when she finally answered her phone.

"We've driven over to Tignes for the day," she said, "We're hitting the park."

"Oh. Thanks for letting me know," I said testily. "Who are you with?"

"Everyone – the boys, Calamity…sorry we didn't know it was your day off."

So it was that I spent a lonely day, skiing on my own with my head phones blaring and feeling rather out on a limb. Then, as if it couldn't get any worse, I realised this morning that I'd left my skis at Petit Pierre's apartment so, after work, I took the bus down the road, paced up the stairs in his building, and rang the bell. There was no answer.

On the off chance it might be open, I turned the handle. The door swung open to reveal, to my very great surprise, Scruffy-but-Handsome standing in the hallway, with all his unruly hair standing on end even more than usual. He was topless, hairy-chested, buttoning his jeans.

Somewhere, deep inside me, my pelvic floor muscle gave an unsolicited heave.

The Scruffy One just looked at me in surprise.

Then New Girl poked her head around the bedroom door.

"Did someone knock?"

"Er…The door bell doesn't work," I said, blankly. There was a pause while they both looked at me. He furrowed his brow, cleared his throat gruffly and tugged his belt into place. She looked confused.

"I just came to get my skis," I said, leaning over and taking them from up against the wall. "Er…and my helmet…" I collected it from the floor somewhere near his feet.

As I dragged my belongings back to the bus stop, I heard the door swing shut behind me. I turned around, but there was no one there.

Too Much of a Good Thing

I had sex with Tim.
It didn't help matters.

I say had sex. It was more like being the object of a complex
and elaborate mating ritual, performed by an exotic, violently
narcissistic bird of paradise with blue Hackett plumage. Much
thrusting of hips and theatrical gesticulating at the point of
orgasm. I faked two or three.

By way of apology for trashing the chalet, Hugo and the
lads had offered to take the Irksome One and I out for dinner.
I wish I could explain why, at about midnight, after a lovely,
civilized dinner at the finest eaterie in town, three bottles of
champagne and a good few vodkas, the words:

'Shall we go back to the chalet
..............and play truth or dare
.................................in the jacuzzi?'

...just, well, fell out of my mouth.

It was like I was possessed or something. I take no responsibility.

Anyway. I have absolutely no idea what happened after
that. I completely blacked out. I can't remember a thing apart
from a swimming picture of the Irksome One being rutted
from behind over the kitchen table by someone...and later,
in the bubbling water, Tim pouring champagne all over my
boobs and in my mouth and clutching at my arse. By 4am
the hot tub was teeming with strange women – hookers
presumably – I'd certainly never seen them before, and there
was, once again, a strange, scummy foam materialising on the

surface of the water. At some point, I offered to do a naked dash to the storeroom to source more booze. Right on cue, as I ran through the chalet leaving a slippery snail trail behind me, a bedroom door opened and I ran headlong into Hugo with one of his 'daughters' in tow. He was on his way to the toilet. I froze, tits to attention and dripping all over the place, and because I didn't know what else to say, said:

"Um. I'm naked."

There was a pause, while Hugo drank me in. Then he stuck out his pelvis and wiggled his willy at me.

"Me too!" he gurgled.

Yuck.

The next day, I woke up with a sore throat. There was no further discussion or even mention of the transaction. Tim did, however, trace the curve of my bottom with one hand and push a sizeable chunk of cash into my sweaty paw this morning as he left. A slightly-too-wet kiss on the corner of my mouth.

I read the accompanying note.

'Can we book you again next year? Best. T.'

I stared at it, suddenly rather underwhelmed by the whole experience, and feeling not a little sick and cheapened.

After work, I went across the road and knocked on the window of the boys' chalet, but both of them had already left. I went to The Drop Inn, on my own, and stood outside for fifteen minutes in a smoky cloud of freezing, beer-soaked seasonnaires. They weren't there either. So I went and sat at the bar, where Old Man Swiss, who seemed to be matching the entire clientele drink-for-drink, was getting steadily more and more annihilated.

"Y'alrigh, missssy?" he enquired, swerving around behind the bar, cloth in one hand, pint in the other. I grimaced at him as he placed a Jager Bomb in front of me. "Sshheer up love. Mi-never 'appen." Staring at him, as he wobbled about, I thought, not for the first time, that perhaps a ski resort is not necessarily the best place to spend almost your entire adult life.

I endeavored to distract my brain by examining the array of ancient ski boots, on the shelf above me, for the thousandth time, charting the evolution of the device from the 1900s to present day. At one end, a decrepit pair of leather and string arrangements, right up to the latest all-singing all-dancing Salomons, which looked as if they might belong to a teenage mutant ninja turtle, or possibly Iron Man. The walls, covered with sepia photographs of craggy shepherds looking slightly narky (presumably in response to all the unwelcome tourists fucking up their peaceful village). Decades of this stuff. Tourists and locals and seasonnaires, young, hopeful and reckless, and thinking this was their world, their adventure, their story.

The next morning, perhaps not surprisingly, I started to feel very ill.

Gastro, Day 1

One has to wonder whether the grot of this apartment is exacerbating my condition. Lying around like a rotting turd, sweating and shivering, wearing every item of clothing in the cupboard, including my ski gloves, does give one plenty of time to contemplate one's navel and the various demons therein. Self-loathing is lying thick upon me. Wish I could call Shazzer for one of our usual raucous and inappropriately detailed conversations concerning size of penis, loudness of grunting and ick factor so I could find the humour in the situation. I am convinced that there *should be* plenty of humour to be had out of it, although I'm unable to find it unassisted just now. The memory of what should have been a salacious special treat, the sort of knickers-to-the-wind, carefree fantasy that tempted me onto this ski season in the first place has turned inexplicably sour in my mouth. The words 'four dollar whore' spring to mind. Shazzer, I know, would have been the first to tell me that men are just a rather easy band-aid solution to more deep-seated ills. Sex works on the opiate reward system, she would say, and exposure breeds need.

I conclude that when a person behaves in this sort of way, when one minute it seems perfectly in character and justifiable, life can wrong-foot them once again. They can suddenly come round and realize, with a nasty jolt, that they seem to have been drunk at the wheel of their life for a very long time. Slaking the un-slakable hunger with chocolate, booze, cigarettes, shopping, adrenaline and sex. Lunging at anything stodgy and cloying that could be used to stop the gap up for a moment, before the bleakness leaks in again; before the hole gapes open. I had been immersed in a swirl of inebriation, trampling over everything and everyone, with only my own gratification in mind for too long. Friends and family had been abandoned, and I was probably starting to look like a bit of a self-pitying drama queen to everyone in the resort. Perhaps it was time to stop and take a breath. Take stock, before I got myself in a really bad pickle.

Text message from the Resort Manager:

"Heard you are ill. You really ought to have notified me yourself and asked permission to miss service."

I reply: "Apologies. Think I have gastro."

"How long do you think you'll be off for? Will need to arrange cover."

"A couple of days at least."

"You'll need note from doctor."

I swear ever since our little heart-to-heart she's been colder to me than ever. I suppose it figures.

The Foxy Chef brought me some soup.

"Ugh, gawd it *stinks* in here," she said as she stumbled in, pulling her sweater up over her nose, tripping over various scattered belongings and nearly spilling boiling liquid from the flask. She opened the stinking bin in the corner to reveal maggots crawling all over the inside of the lid. "Ugh, *Jesus Christ!* Are you alright in here on your own? No wonder you're sick. Shall I open the window?"

"N-n-n-fuck no! I'm freezing," I wailed.

She handed me the flask and I sat up in bed to try a few sips. It hurt to move and the chicken broth made me recoil. "I'm sure it's very nice, but I can't," I grimaced, handing it back to her apologetically. It looked and smelt like day old dishwater to me. I shuffled further down under my duvet, muffled beneath the warmth yet still shivering and pulling it round me in a protective cocoon. It smelt fusty.

"Have you seen the Scruffy One lately?" I had been hoping he'd pop in to see me, but had neither heard from, nor seen him since that morning at Petit Pierre's.

"No. He's been working his arse off I think. Your erstwhile

squeeze got himself fired last week, didn't you know?"

I hadn't spoken to Skater Boy in some time, and this news made me push myself up on my elbow.

"Well," The Foxy Chef was continuing, "*he* claims he quit, but I don't think he would've if he hadn't been pushed. He went AWOL for three days last week and just didn't turn up to work. Their resort manager had to practically pitch a tent outside the apartment and wait for him to show."

"Where was he?"

"Three resorts away... on acid."

So, Skater Boy had finally pushed his manager over the edge. I could hardly feel surprised.

"Then, the Scruffy One is all on his own in that big chalet?"

"Yep. He's not happy."

"Poor thing. He's so sweet," I said absently. "Sometimes, I wish I could just bring him home and put him in the cupboard."

The Foxy Chef raised a knowing eyebrow. "I think it's more a case of bring him home and put him in your bed, dear?"

I considered this statement sceptically for a moment and then said, very sulkily, "No. And anyway, I think he's been shagging that red-head." Only now was I realising how miserable that concept made me.

The Foxy Chef looked rueful and nodded. "Yeah. I've seen them together a few times."

"Ugh. I think I'm going to die." I slid back down under the mound of duvet. "My stomach feels as if it's full of boiling lava."

"You'll be alright mate, sleep is what you need," she said, giving my leg an awkward pat.

"Right, I'm going skiing."

"Cow."

After she left, all I could do was lie still and marinate in sweat and self pity, mulling over what a strange nirvana I was in, so full of joy and friendship and adventure and, at the same time, a pit of vipers slithering over themselves to get at you.

Gastro, Day 6

I'm not a fussy individual. Not really. I'm not one of those people who gets a bulging vein in the centre of their forehead and hurls themselves at the floor in foaming fury at the site of a badly loaded dishwasher.

There is one thing, however, that I am very particular about.

Tea.

If everything else in life has well and truly gone up the shitter – or to put it another way – tits up - in true British form, one can always sit down and have a nice cup of tea, can't one? Man, I have needed tea in the last week. Shut up alone for most of the day, in the grimy, dark recesses of the studio flat. Getting up only to hobble, feebly to the bathroom, sneeze gravy out of my arse, turn round and decorate it with chunks and then hobble back to my sweaty, crumb-filled bed. Each and every bone in my body feels as if it's been placed in an individual clamp and then twisted, slowly in opposing directions.

Being ill all on my own, with no one to check on me, take my temperature or bring me food and Lucozade, in a flat with no fridge and a broken cooker, has been one of the loneliest ordeals of my life. So badly did I want my Mum to appear in the door, with her cure-all Bovril on toast and a nice cuppa, that I cried for nine hours straight on Tuesday.

Then my Dad called:

"Poppetto! Oh dear, poor you, you sound a bit peaky."

The sound of his voice only made me feel sadder.

The only other humanity I've come into contact with for a week has been in the form of The Irksome one and her cronies, flouncing in and out of the flat as loudly and inconsiderately as possible. This is my own personal Guantanamo.

Thank fuck for tea. Although, unfortunately for yours

truly, the French just don't get it. The Lipton Yellow Leaf crap the Frogs try to palm off on you is like drinking stewed gnat's piss and out here, a packet of Tetley's Finest Cigarette Ash Bags costs the princely sum of an arm, a leg and a hand job to the shop assistant who keeps it stashed round the back of the Sherpa for *les desperate Rosbifs*.

Never mess with tea.

This is a personal slogan of mine, and a truism I hold dear. Never rape tea with other substances, such as booze – or as I once tried at 7am after a thirty six hour bender – Ketamine. Bad idea. Drink K-T when you already can't tell your arse from your elbow and you know you've reached the final and most remote outpost of Spangladesh, and now have no compass to get you home. The minute you fuck with tea. Everything is fucked.

Which is upsetting because, as I've just discovered, we've run out.

I turn over in my narrow single bed and survey the empty flat listlessly. No texts. Everyone is out skiing. Another missed call from my Dad.

I put my face in the pillow, turn over and go back to sleep.

Gastro, Day 7

I managed to get up and go outside this morning. I went to the doctor and requested copious amounts of drugs. Apparently, I might have swine flu. I still felt dreadful but I thought the fresh air would do me good, and besides, it was becoming absolutely necessary to get supplies unless I was going to starve to death.

There was a girl walking up the road with what seemed like purpose, heading straight for me, with dark hair, pale skin and broad hips. For a moment I was certain it was Shazzer. Then she turned and walked into a shop. Sometimes, I think I see her like this. Walking somewhere or sitting in a café, and I like to imagine she has simply run away on an adventure somewhere and isn't really gone for good. Like the day she bunked off school for the first time. She came in for roll call with her civilian clothes on under her uniform, then changed in the toilets and walked three miles to the nearest town. She got on a bus to Brighton, free for a day.

My parents knew we met in the local pub, even though we were only fourteen. It was a ten minute stroll from both our houses, but my Dad insisted on driving me there and collecting me.

"I don't want you walking down the road in the dark," he'd say.

Shazzer, on the other hand, would climb out of her bedroom window and sneak off when her parents thought she was doing homework in some crevice of their sprawling home. I think she liked the subterfuge of it. We mollycoddled middle class kids have to create our own drama sometimes.

We would sneak into a dark corner of the pub, drink shandies, guffaw at the locals and smoke Marlboro reds until we felt sick, done up like forty year old transvestites in too much make up and not enough clothes. That evening, she wore a sheer top with pair of faded jeans and when she turned round to show me the large Black Panther she'd had tattooed onto the small of her back I was shocked, disgusted and terribly impressed.

It was hideous.

"I know," she laughed. "I bet I'll hate it when I'm forty!"

She didn't know she wouldn't live long enough to regret that tattoo.

Living with a broken heart is like living with a faulty limb. Every so often it gives out on you - wobbles under you, and you trip.

Gastro, Day 8

I wake up to find a friendly face at the end of the bed.

"Had you considered," says Scruffy-but-Handsome, handing me a bag of left over pain au chocolats, a slice of his own home-made banana bread wrapped in foil, and a second-hand issue of Heat magazine from January, "…thinking twice about getting in that manky hot tub next time? Or maybe cleaning it, once?"

For a second I'm somewhat dumbstruck, fighting the urge to hurl my arms around his neck and cry. But I don't.

"It wasn't the hot tub that made me ill," I say, instead, with dignity, and then stuff almost an entire pastry into my mouth at once. I am grateful for the return of my appetite.

"No doubt it wasn't the only contributing factor," he looks amused, "but when did it last get cleaned?"

"I clean it every week! We have to put those chemical thingies in it," waving a dismissive hand.

"That's not actually cleaning it, you know. That's just neutralising the bugs. It's still full of pubes and bodily fluids."

I then relay the full story of my condom-cum-fag-butt-fishing incident. At which he bellows with laughter.

"Fuck me, I wish I'd seen that!" he giggles, his green eyes twinkling, "I would have paid good money…"

"Yes. Thanks. It was charming."

"Are you better then?" he looks at me kindly. "I'm sorry I haven't been to see you before. I was worried about you. Just didn't fancy catching your wretched lurgie."

"You could have at least popped in and said hi. Or sent me a text, or something,"

His earnest expression is making me feel self-conscious.

"I know, I'm sorry…"

He gives me a sort of half-serious, rabbit-caught-in-headlights grimace which just makes me laugh and disarms me completely. I find I can't really blame him for staying away. Things must have seemed a little bit awkward. It hadn't taken long for the story of my hot tub adventures with Tim to permeate the entire resort. I consider for a moment that, what with being completely irrationally infatuated with his roommate right under his nose and then hurling myself at Tim, the messages I have been sending him haven't been altogether clear. He smiles and for a second I consider telling him the truth, that I'm terrified he, along with everything else good in my life, will suddenly disappear. But the words don't come out. I'm silenced by the thought that he's probably decided I'm half insane in the last few weeks, and besides, before I have time to speak he is clambering onto the bed.

"Move over," he says happily. "It's half past four. I've got at least half an hour for a nap before work."

"What are you doing?" I laugh, as he snuggles down next to me for an impromptu spooning session. "Spooning leads to forking, you know?"

"Not with you Grandma. Jeesus, this bed is fusty. You need a wash..."

Ooops!

Question: Is it ever alright to be shagging someone... and therefore spend some time in his room thereby getting to know his roommate...then decide the roommate is a far superior gent and end up getting intimate with said roommate in the original conquest's bed?

Hmm. Oooops. Well this is what I *may* have done this afternoon with Scruffy-but-Handsome.

To cut a long story short, a few days after I'd recovered from the gastro, I received a text message from him. It said:

"Fancy having a nap-afternoon at mine and watch a film?"

After a long morning's scrubbing and listening to Irksome-Blonde-19-Year-Old whine, how can a girl resist such a delightful invitation?

At some point during the course of the grainy, glitching pirate version of Life of Brian we'd been watching on his bashed up laptop, I began to shiver and the Scruffy One, being a thoughtful lad, put a duvet round me... and then, somewhat to my quiet delight, his arm.

His fingers, it seemed, had accidently found the little area of exposed skin between my jumper and jeans. They rested there without moving. The touch was so light I was almost unaware of it, and for half an hour it remained in place with unnerving assurance. Occasionally his little finger twitched up and down on the skin of my hip. I felt maybe he hadn't noticed. I shifted slightly. After a while, I dared a peek up at his face, and found with not a little alarm that he was staring hard at the top of my head, and now, my face. He turned his head a little and we brushed lips. Then he kissed me as if it was the most normal thing to do in the world.

He hooked his arms under my knees, pulled me onto my back then leaned forward and kissed my cheek; brushing the hair of his beard against the crook of my neck. That hair that had always looked so rough and coarse to me, felt not scratchy, but smooth, and soft as sun-kissed grass. He smelled of warm earth. I felt a sudden urge to sink my teeth into his shoulder. For a second, he stopped and stared at me hard with a concerned expression that I knew meant: "– *should* we?" and at that precise moment, a key turned in the lock, and Skater Boy came striding into the room like a gust of chaotic wind. We both froze, still clamped in each other's embrace and looked at him in terror.

"What are you two looking all shifty about?" he growled, stomping straight past us and onto the balcony. He snatched up the toucan monoski and a packet of Rizlas, marched back towards the door and slammed it assertively behind him. We remained still for a few more moments until I summed up the courage to say:

"I... I don't think he really minds."

The Scruffy-One looked down at me and rolled his eyes.

"I really couldn't give a fuck," he said.

We fell asleep, hot and sticky, as if we'd grown over and into each other. He, an unmoving, silent sleeper with canine hair all ruffled and cast aglow in the flickering light from the film that we weren't even watching.

Resort Life

You can't always get what you want, but, as the song goes, *if you try sometimes, you might find, you get what you need.* If I have learned nothing else in the past few tumultuous months, it has been this. You cannot appreciate the true meaning of an old clichéd sentiment until life teaches you one of its fabled lessons.

I will be the first to admit that, like many a naive young sprig before me, I had a pre-season punter-ignorance of what life up a mountain as a chalet girl would be. I had visions of my fox-fur-hat-clad self sashaying down a mountain in the sun, sipping champagne in hotel bars with mysterious ski instructor types, and being bonked by rich clients in front of log fires in high altitude ski huts. In reality, I have spent the entire time surrounded by a bunch of crackpots, whilst up to my armpits in soap-suds, leftovers and pubic hair. I have been barked at by my boss; abused by rude, demanding guests; goosed by pervy, middle-aged businessmen; chained to the hoover or the kitchen sink and bonked on a Tabasco-soaked mattress by a stoned, smelly, skint ne'er-do-well in a crack-den-esque one-room apartment. When not cleaning, my time has not been spent sashaying, but careering down a mountain at colossal balls-out speed, usually stoned or blind drunk on vin chaud and Mutzig. This, in reality, is what being a chalet 'host' is all about. You're a galley slave. A Chalet Bitch. It's far, far more fun than I could ever possibly have imagined. In fact, I have decided, when I have children one day, a ski season will be compulsory for them. It should be a rite of passage for everyone on earth.

It's true, the world of chalet work gets a lot of false press. There's what society thinks you do (perpetual toilet shagging / projectile vomiting in the street / drinking each others' urine). There's what your boss thinks you do (well-groomed, bright-eyed freshly-baked-cake-wielding hospitality enthusiast). There's what your Mum thinks you do (asymmetric pink onesie and snood-sporting ski bunny). There's what guests think you do (see Jeeves of Jeeves and Wooster). There's what your friends think you do (naked skiing party animal with permanent residence in chalet hot tub). There's what *you* think you do (freestyle back-country daredevil of awesomeness). And then, there's what you *actually* do (toilet cleaner).

The honest answer is that chalet life, and the seasonnaire world, is a fantastical mixture of all of these things. Chalet Bitch-dom is no Cinderella story. It's about sex, drugs, toilet cleaning and skiing. And if you can't even get that right in life, then you're a fucking moron.

Despite all my complaining, I have come to love it; the drudgery, the camaraderie, the lack of culpability, the diet of raw frankfurters, croissants and vodka. Perhaps not the skid marks. I've come to realise, too, that everyone up here in the mountains creates their own drama. Each of us is either running to something or from something and whichever direction you're going in, it's highly likely you'll stumble across something you didn't expect. Nine times out of ten, you'll meet yourself coming back in the other direction, wondering what the fuck just happened. We've all plugged out from reality in the search for something more visceral.

"May sun shine on your snowy slopes of happiness…"

Last night, I had a lot of sex by the fire in a 15 million EURO chalet, which at the very least ticks off one more of the items on my season to-do list.

Things are onto a good rolling boil with Scruffy-but-Handsome, and for the first week ever we have no guests in the chalet, so it would have been, not rude, but absolutely fucking scandalous for me not to invite him round and, in his words, "have more sex than I even know what to do with!"

So we lit the fire, cracked open a bottle from the wine cellar, made up one of the double beds and…

"Hold on a minute…" he said at one point, stopping mid thrust, still inside of me and looking quizzical. "Why does sex have to be all this ooof oooff grunt grunt rhythmic shunt crap?"

"What?!"

He was resting on his elbows and looking genuinely interested in what my response was going to be. I was thrown by the sudden pause.

".. I'm serious," he said, looking mischievous, squidging one of my boobs. "You and me used to just have nice conversations when we're together. Why can't sex be like that…just, like, a nice friendly chat?"

"Shut up…"

"….except with my penis in you?"

"Shut up! Just shag me will you?"

He feigned a hurt expression. "But I have some very important things to say,"

"You have verbal diarrhea. Sex is not a time to chat!"

"Oh alright…"

He gave in and started kissing me. Then pulled away again, looked me in the eyes gravely and said, "I'm just trying to be romantic…"

I pressed his cheeks between my thumb and the flat of my fingers, "Well stop it. Can you just get on with the job in hand, please?"

"OK" he conceded and started shagging me again. And then stopped again and looked at me fondly. "I love being inside you," he said passionately. "It's like being part of a nice, big, warm….sausage roll!"

Now how can you resist a chap like that?

So, winter wonderland hide away, and three orgasms later, who says there are no perks to this job? Well, I say that, but here's the thing. It's all very nice having a ski-resort-lover, in theory, but what to do when the chalet's occupied? We have actually had to plan, engineer and manufacture situations in which we can have a shag. It also doesn't help that neither of us are talking to Skater Boy, or that my next door neighbour is a sour old sexually frustrated prune who clearly doesn't like to be disturbed by our shrieks of passion (and those of the people in the porn film we were watching) at 3pm on a Monday afternoon. When you're being shagged up against a door, the last thing you want to hear is a curt knock and a gruff gendarme's voice, demanding to know what all the racket is about. So failing my apartment, we have now had to devise all sorts of random places to have a tumble. To this end, we've come up with a hitlist - AKA the Fuckit list.

Destinations of choice include:

His chalet (when the owner is out).

Off Piste - needs some research, risk of avalanche.

The Company Minibus - will have to be in the dead of night, or may get caught/fired/both. Uber risky but uber satisfying.

In the bubble - a helpful friend yesterday pointed out as we were going up the bubble lift, skis in hand, that "this particular lift takes 14 minutes"....hmmmn. Interesting.

Chairlift - I'm a bit dubious but Scruffy-but-Handsome reckons it's doable. Risk of body parts sticking to metal a la Dumb and Dumber....

I'll keep you informed on progress.

I think it's safe to say Belle de Neige has found contentment. Oh the joy of finding a regular shag pal who doesn't have any issues. The boy is so laid back he's practically horizontal. Well, he's horizontal quite a lot of the time when I'm around, actually. He has mussy hair, twinkly eyes, laughs at my jokes, is as appreciative of chair-lift mountain views as I am and also knows quite a lot about life, the universe and the laws of physics, (which a man most certainly should do if he possibly can).

His musings are enough to keep any lady entertained for hours...and this is just conversational foreplay. Today he started off on a ten minute rambling stream of consciousness inspired by the question: "Would you lick a bit of sellotape covered in fluff for a tenner?"

"For a tenner I'd lick most things, to be honest," he mused, looking skyward for inspiration. "Apart from maybe depleted Uranium."

"Perhaps you should go and stand on the street right now with a sign saying 'will lick stuff for money'," I suggested.

"What would you lick for a grand?"

"For a grand?! Hell, I'd lick from here to the train station. I'd lick my house. I'd lick the lawn."

There were many other things that he offered to lick.... let's just say I got distracted by him nibbling my ear....

The chance of a good tumble a couple of times a week puts a huge juicy cherry on top of the delectable, creamy chocolate sundae of life out here in the mountains. Yes, you can tell I got laid today, can't you? It's fabulous if for no other reason than being able to say, when asked, (in a French, Audrey Tautou style accent) "Eeeee is not my boyfwend....eeee is my loveur...."

"'What was it I said to you the first time we shagged?" he asked last night as we lay there in the dark, finally, waiting for sleep to come.

"Erm...I think it was 'this isn't going to get serious, is it?'"

He was silent.

"It's not serious though. Is it?"

"No. No. Not serious. Not at all."

"Didn't think so."

I turned my head and, in the dark, I could make out the vague outline of him smiling.

Hitting the Last Run Home

I had been thinking for some time that I really ought to get myself some slightly more credible skis. It was becoming a bit of a sore point. Almost everyone else seemed to be riding fat, floppy lollipop sticks emblazoned with all sorts of modern art and graffiti slogans while I was still plunging into powder on a pair of clapped out piste skis from 1999. I looked like a dork. This is not a good image for a seasonnaire, and certainly not one who professes to love skiing. So it was, one Tuesday afternoon, that I persuaded the Man of Leisure, who has an encyclopedic knowledge of every ski on the market, to go with me to a rental shop and help me choose another pair to try out.

"You need to learn to ski first before you get on a pair like that," he said, as I cooed over a rack of lady's all mountain skis in the advanced section. "I keep telling you you're not getting enough angle with your knees." He was leaning up against the shop counter in his ski instructor's garb, fully aware and enjoying the fact that the eighteen-year-old girl at the cash register was checking out his bum.

"What about these?" he said unhelpfully, holding up a pair of pink blades. "These are more your level."

"Look, can you either be helpful or piss off please?"

He was in jocular mood since his parents had left. I couldn't quite work out whether this was an elaborate act in order to hide the fact that he was dying inside because of his father's constant criticisms, or genuine pleasure that he could now do precisely as he pleased without his parents' interference. I'd quizzed him about it, just once, and had been met with a barrage of flippant comments relating to his mother's mental health which ended with the words, "My Dad's an asshole, what do you want me to say?" The look of mortification behind his lovely eyes was impossible not to see, and plenty enough to tell me that this was a subject he was not particularly willing to be drawn on. He was a skittish, vain beast, the Man of Leisure, with a melancholic overtone of lost boy to him, and I couldn't help but worry about him in a sisterly sort of way. It's not good to be so young and cut loose in the world, with that much money at your disposal, and no one worrying about whether you've got clean pants.

"How about these ones," he relented finally, selecting a powerful-looking pair of K2s and bringing them over to me where he flexed them and held them up against my shoulder to check the length. "You'll have fun on these. They're stable enough not to flap around on the piste but they'll cut through the deeper stuff as well." He took them over to the girl behind the till, and was about to launch into one of his maximum charm offences, when there was a jangle of bells from the shop doorway and La Vache Qui Ski swished in, wearing a pillowy, all black one-piece, and loaded down by an armful of paperwork. Seized with horror, the Man of Leisure leaped behind a rack of sunglasses and squatted down out of sight.

La Vache paused momentarily in the doorway, looking as if she'd just come round from a hallucination, then went over to the girl at the till and started hurriedly going through a list of rental bookings, in a very cross and harassed tone. I continued inspecting the rack of skis I was standing next to. Out of the corner of my eye, I could see the Man of Leisure inching his way towards the door. You could cut the atmosphere with a chainsaw.

"You're such a cock for just ignoring her like that," I said to him, moments later, as we were going up the escalator to get on the bubble lift.

"Why are you suddenly leaping to her defense?" he snapped, flicking a piece of ice off his bindings. "I thought you loathed her?"

"There's no doubt about it, she's not a massively likeable individual," I said, aware of my own double standards, "but I'm sure she has feelings under all that bravado."

"Did you check the dins on those things?" he said, nodding at my skis. He had the slick ability of avoiding the issue that any politician would be proud of.

"Sorry?"

"The...the *din settings*...come on, seriously? That blondie in the shop didn't look like she knew what she was doing."

"Ooooh, the *dins*. Yes. Obviously," I said, squinting at the bindings, trying to locate these wretched din things. "Yes, it's fine. They're fine."

The snow was chopped up, but still fluffy in places, and thanks to some helpful (and not so helpful) tips from my companion, I was soon careering down the hill on the new skis having a splendid time.

"Stop sticking your ass out, stand up more!" he kept yelling.

"You know, you're really fucking annoying when you start ski instructing," I yelled back.

"Tuck your bum in and bend your knees!"

Although the skis were a lot softer than my own, I was beginning to embrace their pop rather than fear it. As the steepness of the piste increased, I took a hop off a lip into deeper snow, landing only with a slight wobble in a tracked out field. Where my old skis would have dug in brutally, the new ones simply bulldozed through it with no problem, giving me confidence. I gathered momentum and swung myself up, back over the cornice and onto the harder, icier snow. I was going really quite fast now and squealing with glee as I knew at the foot of the next slope was a roller that I'd been too scared to get air off all season. Bubbling with endorphins, confidence and the joy of contentment that had recently started to pervade my very being, I decided to go for it.

Contrary to what you might expect, my overriding memory of that day was not of the accident.

Neither was it the pain, the fear and the cold hard disappointment of reality.

No.

It was of my last ever ride on the chairlift.

…of floating up through the misty cloudbanks into a pale blue sunlit sky, as snowflakes powdered my face. Travelling through the air, slowly breaking through the daylight on a new day, feeling fresh and healthier than I had in weeks; a little excitement in my heart, a little flutter of hope in my belly. For the first time in a very long while, feeling truly content and that life was just goddamn peachy.

The problem is that in the mountains you put yourself in an extreme situation on a daily basis; cold, speed, lack of oxygen, cornices, unstable footing. You forget. Extremity is normalized. One minute you're standing on terra firma, the next the snow has shifted underneath you, purging everything in its path and leaving you perched on a precarious ledge with nowhere to turn and no way back. It's a sticky mountain path and a lack of barriers is part of the freedom. If you desire to kill yourself doing something stupid, on your own head be it. If you don't know your own equipment, who are you going to blame?

A simple short radius turn that was going quite nicely to begin with sent me over that roller into the air and then suddenly turned sour. As I flew forwards over the tips of my skis and saw the ground looming towards my face, bizarrely, I felt myself relax. I hit the ground face first and my legs bounced upwards. The left ski impacted with the hard pack and flew off, but the right ski didn't. Instead I felt the length of it helicopter round behind me, so that my knee crunched inwards like a pestle turning in a mortar. There was no pain exactly, merely a razor sharp, bright white awareness of having done something very grave to myself that would take more than a couple of Neurofen and a plaster to fix.

Fortunately (or unfortunately depending on your point of view) a snow cannon broke my fall and prevented me from rocketing off a cliff of doom into some trees.

And now, there I am, laid out spread eagled, face down. Goggles, poles and dignity scattered to the wind, screaming blue murder and hyperventilating so much, my entire body starts to melt into pins and needles.

Isn't it funny how falling feels like flying for the longest time?

Death by Miss Adventure

Is it better to go through the unthinkable pain of losing someone while they are beautiful and young and hopeful, than to have them live, but be forced to watch them turn into something unrecognisable; a monster. To have a few precious moments with them preserved in you eternally, or a lifetime with them that ultimately destroys your love?

I pace the secret corridors of Shazzer's childhood home. I know it well - yet still, even now, it's obscure to me, full of mysteries and secret, intricate corners. The garden, an Inca trail of memories; a Japanese Maple, a rusty, lean-to green-house where we once put hot, red tomatoes in our mouths straight from the vine, a sun dial and a pathway rippled by time and clothed in moss. Her bedroom is a museum of the incidental, with collage-covered walls where she chronicled her life - pictures, objects, words. The diffusion of colours on a porcupine quill set on a yellowing piece of cardboard. A chunk of salt from the flats where the sky meets the earth. A hand-drawn map with tattered edges and doodled annotations, and a collection of strange items – debris – the smooth, white adhesive from the back of a plaster, a transparent plastic ice-cream spoon, three bottle tops, a Peruvian coin and a bus ticket to Glastonbury. The crime-scene of her life; individually, pieces of junk or meaningless abstract colours. There is no significance to any solitary item. The significance is in the composition of it all. The shadow of the hands that assembled it with pins and sticky tape. A fragment of the mind of the person who collected each item, tenderly, carefully, and kept it for this purpose. A fragment of that mind is preserved there as sharp as a finger of light through a crack in the wall of time. A mind lost in the detail of life, enraptured by the beauty of it all and also painfully overwhelmed.

Death is strange and fascinating in its finality. I know why they call it a veil, because it is as if some strange elusive divide has been drawn across the person that alters them irrevocably. Something has been done that cannot be undone, no matter how much you will it, no matter your tenacity or stubbornness, you cannot undo it. Nothing else in life is certain.

The spot where she fell is behind her bedroom door. Many times I've tried to imagine what it must have looked like, you know, *the act* of it. It's hard to summon the image of her and the spoon, and the flame, and the needle. It seems ridiculous.

I finger a page in her diary.

The deed is done. The horizon constricts. I have opened Pandora's Box and it cannot be resealed.

What if you go in search of yourself, and find something you don't like? What then? It is too late. Innocence lost is lost forever. It must have been frightening. Drug addiction, separateness, anger, despair. What other pathways could her life have taken? Many times, I have asked myself how I didn't see. So many chances I missed. Were her eyes a little sunken in that photo? Did she look pale? The shorn hair - was it a purging act? Those scaly, dark half-moons under the eyes, when did they appear? The uncharacteristic flakiness, the days she was quiet and withdrawn or simply disappeared for weeks without contact. Was she with strange people who knew her by another name, struggling with something dark and unseen that I would never understand? In hindsight, it's easy to find the clues that fit the picture to the puzzle.

For a while, I was angry at her for lying. For wearing the mask she thought I'd like the best. Then I realised it was an act of self-preservation. Just as she knew reality was no longer good enough for her, she knew the truth – that she had opened the box and couldn't handle the contents – wouldn't be good enough for me. I have realised she was always protecting me; all our lives and even then. Even from herself. Our closeness was a splinter of her past, un-sullied by the present. If she could preserve it perfectly, then maybe one day she could find her way back. Her acts of great friendship were as much a refuge for her as they were for me. Something of value to cling to in the tempest.

I take the items I have decided I will remember her by, only three. A hat, a photo, an LP. I close the door on her room for the final time.

May 20th

It had been two months since the Man of Leisure had driven me, sniveling, with my leg trussed up in a very uncomfortable splint, to the airport in the back of his Land Rover. Two months since I'd watched Scruffy-but-Handsome's figure receding in the back windscreen. Two months since my bubble had burst. And now, at this train station, here he was. Standing with his back to me, wearing a blue corduroy jacket and a pair of headphones, carrying a satchel. He looked so unfamiliar and neat, without the grey checkered jacket and frayed snowboard pants I was used to seeing him in. I was poised behind him, frozen to the spot, too terrified to tap him on the shoulder. Too afraid to take the next step.

No one can explain to you the pain, frustration and inconvenience of a really bad injury. You just really have to experience that delight for yourself. Life, the universe and everything turns on a sixpence. It's all governed by the caprice of a second. And then suddenly, you're incapacitated and back home. You're transformed instantly back into your four-year-old self. Crying because you've got a sore knee. Having your shoes put on for you. Being brought your dinner on a tray in front of the TV with a bib because you can't lean forward enough not to streak gravy down your top. Oh the indignity.

I crash landed back at my Dad's house and descended into a misery of sitting around, smoking prolifically and drinking whiskey. Every muscle in my body tingled and twitched with expendable energy that had nowhere to go. Add to this my fairly advanced caffeine addiction and ....jumpy? I was like a freaking jack in the box. I'd wake up fifteen times every night buzzing with energy and pain. Luckily for me, my Dad is a juvenile delinquent in the body of a seventy one year old and thinks the cure for everything is a well-iced Gin and Tonic, setting fire to things, or a bacon sandwich. He also drinks, without fail, a large glass of freshly squeezed orange juice from his (much beloved) industrial juicer each morning. Having smoked about seventy fags a day for most of his adult life and survived a triple heart bypass whilst still putting away a bottle of vino every night, I have come to the conclusion that he has actually discovered the elixir of life. It's Orange Pressées. So don't say I never tell you anything useful.

By the time I got home, the leg was a sort of purplish colour, the central features being a cankle and a hideous swollen-out-of-shape knee with a mottled effect. Dad took me to the hospital for a checkup and to have an ultra-sound scan to look for blood clots - where they put goo on your leg and roller it with this object that looks like an epilator. We had to sit in a waiting room the size of a broom cupboard for about two hours, dying of boredom. There was a magazine in there which was so dull it made me more bored than if I had simply stared at the wall - which was that horrific pebbledash you only see in hospitals. In the end, I got so excruciatingly fed up that I starting pacing up and down, counting my steps. By the time the nurse came to get me, I was trying to balance one of my crutches on my forehead and Dad had mischievously removed one of the ceiling tiles with the other one.

Even with the best intentions, no amount of Gin, tonic, burnt stuff, bacon or orange juice can relieve the acute boredom of sitting on your arse, particularly after being so incredibly active for so long. The scope of my world was condensed from the freedom of a colossal mountain landscape to the gap between the bed and the couch. In actual fact, achieving this movement was a sizeable accomplishment in itself, since after all the anesthetic, my brain felt like it had been pushed through a tea strainer.

Hobbling around the ski resort on crutches had been no joke, let me tell you. I considered putting one of Scruffy-but-Handsome's invention's into fruition by rigging myself up with a sled pulled by 100 Chihuahuas, so I could cruise around tucked up in a fur coat and diamonds, smoking and swearing loudly at people on skis.

I'd had to be rescued; carted off the mountain strapped into a blood wagon. This is not an experience I can recommend. It's incredibly humiliating, disorientating and perturbing. They sort of vacuum pack you in and then whizz you down with an escort skiing behind. All I could see was a slit of blue sky, fairy dust still dancing around me and the Man of Leisure's concerned face gazing in from above at intervals.

"'Ow are you going to pay for ze treatment?" a nurse was asking, short tempered and fussing over me with large bosoms.

"Credit card!" I yelped, wondering bleakly through the fog of pain if I had any money in the account, and also wondering if and when the fuck they were going to give me any pain killers.

"Is there anything I can do?" Calamity was leaning over me now.

"Call my Dad please. Get the Scruffy One…and get me a fucking gin!"

"Your knee – it's *exploded*!" was the diagnosis explained to me by the moustachio'd and ostentatiously French Dr Pepin (if you call explaining flailing your arms around and hopping up and down while shrugging a lot in an 'I honestly couldn't give a monkey's left testicle stop wasting my time' kind of way). Not famed for his bed-side manner, Dr Pepin. Indeed, I had done something rather nasty to all the ligaments, which would have to be fixed. No two ways about it.

The French hospital room was minimalist. For three hours, I had no choice but to lie on my back staring at the pebbledash ceiling while nurses and doctors hobbled to and fro taking my blood pressure. I couldn't bear to even look at my knee, which had inflated to the size of a watermelon and was all throbby and wibbly. The reality of it was too hideous. A depressed punter with a very nasty broken humerus and a fractured collar bone dribbled in the bed next to me. I wished they'd give me his sedatives.

The operation came soon afterwards, along with a colossal dent in my bank account. The nurse practically came to my bedside with a credit card machine. I was strung back together with some bits of sinew, packed in with sawdust and glue, and all taped up. The result was very pretty indeed, if you like the film 'Crash'.

Scruffy-but-Handsome was there when I woke up. I beamed at him and lay scratching myself luxuriantly through the retreating malaise of this most enjoyable morphine and anesthetic experience. I was momentarily at peace with the idea that, for the foreseeable future, I was buggered, wouldn't be back on skis for at least a year and was probably bankrupt to boot.

"This is nice," he said, smiling widely and coming to sit on the edge of the bed. He was scoffing a sandwich and guzzling a can of orange drink under my nose.

"How can you eat at a time like this?" I croaked.

"I can always eat. It's a dominant feature of my personality. It's what makes me so adorable."

"Oh."

"That, and stress makes me hungry."

"I'm afraid the reverse cowgirl is off the menu," I gave him a watery smile.

"Oh, what have you done to yourself, you clutz?" Tenderly, he pulled back the covers, looked at the bandages, stitches and streaks of antiseptic and gave a heavy sigh. He leant forward and kissed the shapeless mound that had used to be my kneecap.

"I wish I could fix you," he said.

I burst into tears.

The next afternoon, they strapped me up in a splint and discharged me, or rather, dumped me shivering outside in my socks, on crutches, to hail a cab. Sucking brutally on a cigarette, I demanded immediately to be taken to the pub where, on top of the unidentified liquid painkillers they'd given me, I consumed several neat whiskeys and a couple of pints before being escorted to the Man of Leisure's apartment to pass out in the spare room. So, what to do now? As I said to La Vache Qui Ski, who nodded with a look of slight embarrassment tinged with smugness, "I am now about as much use around here as a chocolate teapot, aren't I?"

As the days crept past, it became clearer and clearer that I would soon have to face the lonely road home. I spent a jobless, lonely week hibernating in Scruffy-but-Handsome and Skater Boy's apartment, unable to do anything or go anywhere, except occasionally The Drop Inn, for fear of falling over on crutches and fucking up my other leg as well. Then finally one morning I realised, as I lay on my back listening to Skater Boy snore in the bunk bed above us; Game Over. I had turned into a pumpkin. I felt my heart, which had just started to heal, had been broken all over again. There were so many things it would break me to leave. I wasn't sure what was causing the most pain; the leg was excruciating but nothing on the heart.

Back home, I spent the next weeks sitting around in various friends' houses feeling sheepish, with a wide variety of packets of frozen vegetables on my knee. Frozen sweetcorn, I decided, is the most comfy owing to the size and shape of the bits. It's amazing how annoyed people get when you raid their freezers and defrost their vegetables without permission. Next, I began to swing like an almighty pendulum between chipperness and despair. How long, I wondered, can you get away with sitting around in your underwear, heckling crap daytime telly and throwing things at people before you get sectioned? My grand plan for escapism; dream-living and freedom seemed to have backfired in spectacular fashion. How had I got myself into such a pickle? I had no independence. I couldn't leave the house without cadging a lift from my Dad, as I couldn't depress pedals in the car. Besides, I had no money as I'd spent it all on treatment and getting back to the UK and - oh yes – I was also now unemployed. Cream on top, *n'est-ce pas?*

For a few weeks, I attempted to amuse myself by sending rude pictures of various parts of my anatomy to Scruffy-but-Handsome. I missed him far more than I wanted to. It was most inconvenient. The Foxy Chef, Calamity and the Man of Leisure called me from time to time. But soon, as resort life rolled on, the intervals between contact became longer and longer. Part of me understood, that's just the way life is. But I also felt hurt. I had begun to like the person I was becoming in the mountains. She was gutsy and active and strong; independent and daring. She spoke her mind. She was so much more like the person I had always wanted to be. She didn't care about having chipped nails, or reading fashion magazines, buying a new sofa or making mortgage repayments. She just wanted to live and breathe fresh air and meet new, exciting people with shared passions and desires. Shazzer would have been proud of her. I didn't care about the past, any more. But now, with great sadness, I felt that if I didn't hold on to my present, all I had learned would start to drift away from me like clouds. Everything I had gained – this new universe and all the people in it, might disappear from me. I couldn't stomach the idea of losing so much all over again.

It's why I now find myself here, standing behind him at the station, wondering whether I should tap him on the shoulder and invite him into my future, or whether it might be better to just turn and leave him in the past.

Summertime

As many a seasonal worker will tell you, living back at home is much like teetering on a knife's edge. Question: How did I suddenly become the black sheep of the family? I used to be an A student. I used to do constructive things like playing the cello, taking brisk walks and handing in my prep in on time. Now I am the family member everyone rolls their eyes about at the dinner table. Two weeks ago, I got food poisoning. Do you know what my 90-year-old grandmother said to me as I was shivering under a mountain of duvets?

"This *is* food poisoning, isn't it darling? You're not going cold turkey?"

My Dad is a bit of a grumble fairy where I'm concerned these days too. Recently I haven't exactly been the model daughter I used to be. In general, you see, people don't like it when you decide to stray from 'the path'. It scares them. Coiled within the evolutionary drive to take care of our loved ones and the need to keep them safe is a propensity to encourage the path of least resistance. Our biological instincts are all snarled up in modern economics, so the knee jerk reaction is to encourage friends and family members to stay in a good job, think of their long term future and financial stability. It's only rational, after all. But how do we know when these rules must be forsaken? What if these very defences are, in themselves, the source of an unreasonable level of misery for the very loved one you wish to protect? It's not that I think I'm different, or better or cleverer. If anything, I'm weak; unable to get on with it and put up with the 'daily grind' like everyone else and just be happy with what I've got – an Aga, a fuel-efficient car and a career. I'm sure my perspective will suddenly landslide when nature hits the 'critical emergency rationality override' on my ovaries in about five years' time, but until then I must ask myself: what do I want on my gravestone? 'She paid off her mortgage every month?' 'She got good grades at school?' or 'She had her cake and gave a good stab at eating it too?'

I must admit this wasn't exactly where I saw myself a year ago – that is, housebound through poverty, with nothing but a partially mangled limb and a layabout studenty shag pal to my name. I have moved into a secondary phase of teenaged petulance. Since I was actually a delightful, studious teenager who rarely slammed doors, I think I'm owed it.

Unfortunately, when you're killing time between seasons, the devil makes work for idle thumbs. Living at home with a parent at my age is a dangerous game…and I think I am now qualified to write the book on how *not* to do it.

…here's the basic guide:

How to really piss your family off:

Don't break up with (from your Dad's point of view) a perfectly respectable young man, abandon your responsibilities, quit your job, do a ski season and cripple yourself.

Don't then insist you want to do *another* ski season, despite the fact that the doctor says you can't ski until next March at the earliest and against Daddy's express advice.

Don't invite your new layabout studenty shag pal round to the house for protracted periods of time and lie on the couch eating crisps, snogging and watching Top Gear in your knickers while the rest of the world is at work. It riles them up, it really does.

Don't leave your dishes piled up next to the sink as you would do at your own gaff or in the layabout studenty

296

style accommodation you've been squatting in all year, with a view to tackling them later. When you live with your parents, this sends a signal. The signal is this: "I can't be arsed. The punkawalla will do it."

Don't turn your childhood bedroom into a soup of unwashed clothes, cigarette butts, wet towels, papers, odds and sods and bottles of whiskey. Open the window when you smoke the weed.

In fact, if you are over 24 and live at home, *don't do drugs*…well, *don't get caught*…and *don't* invite Scruffy-but-Handsome the Man of Leisure and Calamity round for dinner and then, when the evening goes slightly the way of the Winehouse, crush up some old Codeine pills you found in a drawer (in the absence of anything stronger) and snort it off the kitchen table through an old biro pen for old times' sake, then pass out in a heap without doing the clearing up. Why? Well, *we* know there was an unidentified pile of white powder on the table when we went to bed. *Dad* knows there was an unidentified pile of white powder on the table when he got up in the morning. But it wasn't there when we crawled back into the sunlight at midday. The irony is it wasn't even prescription, let alone illegal.

Don't forget to feed the cat occasionally. Even if it is the fluffy spawn of Satan.

Oh yes. And finally, d*on't* get caught shagging said layabout studenty shag pal in the house in the broad light of day by Big Brother 2.1 on a bog-standard Thursday afternoon when the rest of the world is at work. Today I came scurrying down to the kitchen from a particularly noisy encounter, charged with fetching some ice. I arrived, butt naked, in the kitchen to find BB2.1 calmly reading the paper with a cup of coffee.

"Alright?" he said dangerously, glancing up from Dad's Daily Mail. He was wearing a blue striped work shirt, very neat and professional, his dark brows knitted in sardonic disapproval.

"Ummm...*hi!* Yes. Er…. Sorry…um…what are you doing here?" I spluttered, unsure whether to hide my boobs or fanny first, groping for some clothes I'd left on the floor behind the easy chair.

"I popped round to borrow Dad's clubs. I'm playing golf with a client this afternoon…"

"Well, I don't know where they are and Dad's not here. He's gone out… so bugger off! Go away!"

"No. No I don't think I will," he said, looking evil. "I think I'm going to have a bacon sandwich." He turned a page of the Mail without breaking my gaze.

It was a good ten minutes before Scruffy-but-Handsome got bored of waiting for me, and the ice, and decided to come down to the kitchen to investigate.

"It's a good thing you've such a cool brother," he said, merrily wrapping a towel round himself and climbing onto one of the kitchen stools. "Most other brothers would be chasing me across the field with a shot gun by now."

I looked over at Big Brother 2.1 who, without tearing his eyes from an in depth article about the credit crunch, had raised an eyebrow. He licked a finger and turned another page of the paper. "I *am* going to chase you over the field with a shotgun," he said mildly. "I've been giving you a head start for the last two minutes, you're just too stupid to realise."

These days are strange. The Scruffy One and I exist in that empty space between the end of an adventure and the start of a new one. It's a place where real life lingers and asks lots of awkward questions, like an irritating Aunt who's come to visit. This morning, for example, Dad came down into the kitchen, where we were sitting, and started making himself a fresh orange juice and a bacon sandwich.

"What have you two achieved today?" he growled from the cooker, observing The Scruffy One, who was sitting topless at the breakfast table, poring over a collection of newspapers and scoffing a KitKat.

"…Fuck all, I s'pose?"

Thinking about it, I guess it could be described as a bit of a liberty. My behaviour, I mean. Unemployed, directionless, skint, living at home for free and spending all my swiftly dwindling savings on train journeys to go and see my equally skint, directionless boyfriend. Flouncing in and out of our respective parental homes like overgrown adolescents, leaving him covered in scratches and bites, with clumps of hair missing and a toy up his arse. Meanwhile, everyone else on earth just keeps buggering on in a hurricane of grown-up efficiency.

In my defense, they do say life is what happens to you while you're busy making other plans. We spend our whole time on a hamster wheel, constantly striking out for the horizon and never stopping to enjoy what's around us. So, I have sworn to appreciate this rare and unusual time at the crossroads of life. I suspect that one day, in twenty five years, when I have a grown up daughter and am feeling wistful for simpler days, I will squint back over my dim memories at these sweet summer days, melting into autumn, when I spent so many luscious and lazy hours with a boy, and wonder …whatever happened to him… and us? If I could, I would bottle this time, put it on the shelf, and one day when I'm close to vanishing, take little sips to remind me how warm and delicious and naughty life can be.

Achievements for the Season

1. Learned how to use snow shoes.

2. Collated many sickening pictures of idyllic seasonnaire lifestyle...but also quite a few shameful ones of self sucking face off randoms and chundering in ditches. Not so good.

3. Shagged 1 x European ski instructor with sexy accent – success!

4. Shagged 0 x Russian oligarchs, but it's all for the best really as Russians are really quite terrifying and besides have decided I prefer my men short and shaggy with a propensity to rant

5. Shagged: two ne'er-do-well studenty-ski-bum-types with no prospects and personal hygiene issues. Also, one is now my boyfriend. Massive, huge fail.

6. Learned how to make a Seasonnaire Nightmare cocktail and down it without puking – very important skill for any respectable girl about mountain.

7. Tried Heli skiing – er didn't quite manage this. But I did learn how to toboggan using only a bin bag, which is actually, as it turns out, far more dangerous.

8. Aerobatic spins (or as the kids call them: '360s'). Didn't quite manage to accomplish the whole 'being airborne' thing – see my earlier comments on problems associated with coming into land. Only real

attempt resulted in 1 x mangled knee ligament...but no actual breaks, so on balance...success!

9. Can now ski powder (or at least I could until the accident) and can confirm it is the best feeling in the world that doesn't involve your genitals.

10. Fabulous levels achieved: Anyone who's had a shag in front of the fire on a zebra print rug in a luxury chalet while wearing nothing but a pair of ear muffs, ski boots and a garter deserves some fabulous points, surely?

Epilogue

This afternoon, a large blackbird with an orange beak flew in through my window. It alighted nonchalantly on the armchair and peered calmly at me through one of its spry little eyes. It winked at me.

"Cheeky fucker!" I thought.

Then it hopped twice and ruffled some rather glossy feathers. A fine looking specimen, and unusually for a bird, it seemed completely calm about its presence in the house. Usually birds go ballistic and hurl themselves at the walls, braining themselves in desperation for escape. My next reaction was to roll my eyes and mutter, "*fucksake*" under my breath, before stalking off to the kitchen to retrieve a tea-towel. A tea-towel is the time-honoured tool in my Dad's household for ushering spooked, confused wildlife that has strayed over the threshold, back to the wilderness. One can either flap it around extravagantly, matador-style or discombobulate whichever rodent or feathered friend one is dealing with by shouting 'FREEZE!' and chucking the tea-towel over its head. Anyway, before I had time to plan my tea-towel strategy, it had relocated to the top of the kitchen door and then the laundry pile. I cornered it near the coat rack and made a shushing sound at it.

"Bugger off!" I said firmly, indicating the door.

And it did. Just as calmly as it had arrived, it flew out of the door. I stood for a minute and stared after it, slightly moved, in spite of myself.

It is said, by superstitious housewives the world over, that a bird in the house can mean two things. It is both a portender of death, and a visitation of comfort from a loved one. Now, don't get me wrong. I have no time for superstition. Superstition is the reason the Scruffy One spends his entire time scampering around looking alarmed and saluting thin air whenever he comes to visit.

"There's a shit load of magpies round here," I always tell him, "you're never gonna get them all!"

He eventually, and very grumpily, conceded that saluting all of them was impractical, and now (demonstrating a note of stubbornness which is both endearing and infuriating) just does one massive comprehensive salute when he arrives, a general big up to all the magpies in the locale.

Yes, I dislike superstition, but I must nevertheless concede to finding pleasure in the fleeting notion that Shazzer popped in today to see if I was OK.

Maybe it was her making a little visit.

Maybe it was nothing.

Fin

Glossary

Essential terminology for the savvy seasonnaire:

Punter – A paying ski customer/ anyone sporting an all-black ski outfit or gear made by Spyder with some sort of silly hat and / or wankers who wear sunglasses with a helmet.

Riding switch – The art of skiing backwards. Usually the practice of show-offs, lunatics, park rats, and beginners who have lost control.

Park Rat – Casual, Alpine-ghetto-garbed hoodlums who are not happy unless sailing through the air upside-down all day. Often to be heard boasting about various shattered limbs.

Onesie – All-in-one ski suit. Your common-or-garden variety usually comes with a bum bag, big poufy shoulder pads and is often worn by awesome ski veterans or 19-year-olds who think they are being 'ironic'. Camel toe is a given.

Fresh Tracks - The golden fleece. When achieved is arguably superior to any other feeling on earth. A single line, cut through a field of pristine, untouched virgin snow.

Beeps – Avalanche equipment. Only twats attempt fresh powder without it.

Pow – an abbreviation of 'powder' used by individuals

who are either too lazy or too important to say the whole word. You should not attempt to use this terminology unless you are 100% certain you have achieved the necessary level of mountain credibility or you will look like a dick. i.e. Imagine this phrase from the lips of Piers Morgan: "Right, let's go and shred the pow guys. Yah." Icky.

First Lifts – The first round of chairs before the lift completes its first rotation in the morning. Often intended, rarely achieved, by boozing punters the Alps over.

Dins – DIN settings. A German standard for the release settings on your ski bindings determined by a combination of your height, weight and boot...Fairly important to know about if you want to avoid rearranging your joints.

Bluebird – It has snowed all night and then you awake to wall-to-wall blue sky and fresh, untouched powder. A feeling akin to Christmas morning when you're six years old. Possibly better than sex. Well, oral sex at least.

Corduroy – The corrugated trails left on the piste first thing in the morning after they've been groomed. Very satisfying to ski on. Punters often mistakenly think that being the first one to hit this stuff is the same as getting first tracks. It's not.

Gold Rush – The last two weeks of the season when everyone panic shags.

Jager Bomb – Foul, repulsive drink invented by Satan. A shot glass of Jager dropped inside a one third full tumbler of Red Bull. Toxic. Starts your engine like a mother fucker though.

Jager Mega drive – A Jager Bomb with an added shot of blue

Curacao and Cassis. What to drink if Jager Bombs aren't working.

Jager Hand Grenade – A Jager Mega Drive with an added shot of Sambuca. Prop the Sambuca and Jager shots up against each other on top of the glass. Pull the pin and down it. What to drink if Jager Mega Drives aren't working.

Seasonnaire Nightmare – A concoction designed specifically to hospitalise the drinker, usually bought for you on your birthday. A pint glass filled with a measure of pretty much every drink in the bar, plus bodily fluids if your friends are real cunts. If you're unlucky enough ever to be bought one, down it. There's no point prolonging the agony. Your fate is already sealed.

Gnar – An abbreviation of the word 'gnarly', which is in turn a bastardisation of the word 'gnarled.' Meaning: Extreme balls-out danger. For more detailed explanation see the film, G.N.A.R. (A must-see for any self-respecting seasonnaire.)

Steezy – The art of doing something remarkable, breathtaking and astonishing while looking nonchalant, casual, blasé, laid back and cool. Stylish, yet easy. This concept has spawned a whole fashion trend.

Huck – To hurl oneself off something without much thought for the consequences or landing protocol.

Shred – To tear the whole mountain to pieces with your skis or board.

Core shot – When you ride over a rock and it scrapes to the core of your ski or board. Result: a write-off.

Hoon – To straight-line down the piste, without turning

or swerving to avoid other skiers, children or animals, at a ridiculous, unreasonable and gut-emptying speed. Every run is a race.

Kicker – A large, terrifying man-made launch-pad designed to 'kick' you into the air. The landing is your problem.

Timmy – You will find large numbers of these on the slopes. For a clear explanation, please refer to the TV phenomenon 'South Park'.

Base grind, edge wax and tune – What your average ski rental shop will do to your skis or board if you're not careful. Learn how to service your own.

Jib – Fart around doing tricks on the piste and getting in people's way.

Jellyfish – A high-speed crash where the victim is knocked unconscious and therefore flops down the rest of the incline like a wet invertebrate tossed down a child's slide. Not ideal.

Yard sale – A high-speed crash where the victim is forcibly relieved of all their accessories. Under usual circumstances, this will include skis, goggles, hat, gloves, poles, and dignity being scattered to the wind in the manner of a front yard auction. Most unfortunate if it happens in deep snow. A full yard sale for a snowboarder would probably result in missing limbs too since snowboard bindings have a pretty serious DIN setting.

Tomahawk – A high-speed crash where the victim is catapulted into a down-hill cartwheel. Can be exceedingly difficult to stop if you're going fast enough. Extremely amusing to watch.

Acknowledgements

Four years ago, I was sitting in a pub in London, during the hiatus between the marriage and the wedding breakfast of some friends of mine. I wasn't feeling too good about myself, and I was about to go on a ski season.

A friend of mine leaned over and said, "Your Facebook updates make me laugh. You should start a blog about being a chalet girl. You could call it 'Belle de Neige.'"

And lo, she was born.

It took four years. Four years since Belle ranted her first rant. Three years since someone suggested it would make a good book. And throughout those years, I fantasised about writing just one, particular page.

This page.

Because, without this page, Belle de Neige would not exist.

So, finally, I get to say thank you…

…for more than I think you realise: V & Big Dog

…for sewing a seed: Araminta

…for boundless generous advice and patience: Maeve, Blue & Polly

…for constructive criticism and much encouragement: Nim

…for inspiring me and encouraging me to write by being funny, fascinating, inspirational, unhinged, intolerable and wonderful: The Bens, Ed, Louise, Katy, Raquelle, Frank, Elsa, Charlie, Raab, Louis, Amber, Hannah, Lizzie, Big Gilly and minions, Phil and Jimbo, Lucy, Scottish Jen, Alex, and every seasonnaire I've ever met

...for you know what: Beth and Ru

...for humouring me: my family

And finally, though perhaps most importantly...

...for reading and re-reading, laughing at the bits you're meant to laugh at (and some that you're not), encouraging, enhancing, scalding, understanding, legitimising and simply believing I could do it: Oscar.

Thank you.